P9-DDC-849

DISCARDED

B47 8-04

DISCARDED

THE Truth
ABOUT
Children
AND Divorce

Robert E. Emery, Ph.D.

THE Truth
ABOUT
Children
AND Divorce

*Dealing with the Emotions So You
and Your Children Can Thrive*

VIKING

VIKING
Published by the Penguin Group
Penguin Group (USA) Inc., 375 Hudson Street,
New York, New York 10014, U.S.A.
Penguin Group (Canada), 10 Alcorn Avenue,
Toronto, Ontario, Canada M4V 3B2 (a division of Pearson Penguin Canada Inc.)
Penguin Books Ltd, 80 Strand, London WC2R 0RL, England
Penguin Ireland, 25 St Stephen's Green,
Dublin 2, Ireland (a division of Penguin Books Ltd)
Penguin Group (Australia), 250 Camberwell Road,
Camberwell, Victoria 3124, Australia (a division of Pearson Australia Group Pty Ltd)
Penguin Books India (Pvt) Ltd, 11 Community Centre,
Panchsheel Park, New Delhi - 110 017, India
Penguin Group (NZ), Cnr Rosedale and Airborne Roads,
Albany, Auckland, New Zealand (a division of Pearson New Zealand Ltd)
Penguin Books (South Africa) (Pty) Ltd, 24 Sturdee Avenue,
Rosebank, Johannesburg 2196, South Africa

Penguin Books Ltd, Registered Offices:
80 Strand, London WC2R 0RL, England

First published in 2004 by Viking Penguin,
a member of Penguin Group (USA) Inc.

10 9 8 7 6 5 4 3 2 1

Copyright © Robert E. Emery, 2004
All rights reserved

CIP data available

ISBN 0-670-03287-5

306.89
EME

This book is printed on acid-free paper. ∞

Printed in the United States of America
Set in Adobe Garamond
Designed by Francesca Belanger

Without limiting the rights under copyright reserved above,
no part of this publication may be reproduced, stored in or
introduced into a retrieval system, or transmitted, in any form
or by any means (electronic, mechanical, photocopying, record-
ing or otherwise), without the prior written permission of both
the copyright owner and the above publisher of this book.

The scanning, uploading, and distribution of this book via the
Internet or via any other means without the permission of the
publisher is illegal and punishable by law. Please purchase only
authorized electronic editions and do not participate in or
encourage electronic piracy of copyrighted materials. Your
support of the author's rights is appreciated.

This book is dedicated to all of the parents and children who have opened their hearts to me, shared their pain, and shown their strength.

Acknowledgments

My overriding goal in writing this book has been to reach parents and children lost in the hurt, pain, sadness, uncertainty, and grief of divorce. I hope that the insights and the stories of others who have shared your struggles can help you through this crisis and guide you to a better place as a person and as a member of a family, albeit a family apart. If this book touches you, you can thank, as I do here, the many people who have shared their stories and, most important, their emotions with me as clients, as participants in various research studies, and as friends. I have learned so much from you.

I also especially want to thank Beth Vesel, my agent, who was instrumental in assisting me in turning my desire to help into this book and who along the way was an advocate, a confidante, and a gentle but incisive critic. I extend equally warm feelings of gratitude to Patty Romanowski Bashe, who acted as editor/writer and with great humor and perseverance taught me how to relax my academic style and encouraged me to write more like I think, talk, and feel. I also offer my warm gratitude to my editor, Janet Goldstein, who from the outset believed in my work and what I wanted to share and who at times had a better sense than I did of where this book needed to go. Associate editor Lucia Watson effectively managed innumerable details in writing style and organization in bringing this book to fruition, and I thank her too for her thoughtfulness and efficiency.

I have been extremely lucky over the course of nearly twenty-five years to have terrific graduate students who worked extremely hard, helped me to refine my ideas, and shared their original thinking and experiences with me. Lisa Laumann-Billings, Dave Sbarra, Mary Waldron, and Pete Dillon played central roles in recent studies, many of which are discussed in this book. The mediation study began almost two decades ago, however, and I want to acknowledge and thank past students Susan Peterman, Dan Shaw, Melissa Wyer, Susan Joyce, Jeff Haugaard, Sheila Matthews, Shelly Tuer Martin, Katherine Kitzmann, and Mary Jo Coiro. I also want to thank Joanne Jackson, the principal mediator in the early days of the mediation study, and Catherine McLamb, a student whom I took a special interest in and who, in turn, has taken a special interest in this book.

The William T. Grant Foundation has been like a generous relative over the years, supporting not only my research but also my ideas. The distinguished members of the W. T. Grant Foundation's Divorce Consortium especially helped to shape my thinking in our unique and lively gatherings, as have my friends and colleagues at the University of Virginia. I especially want to single out Mavis Hetherington, with whom I probably talked more while traveling away from Charlottesville than during our twenty years in the same department.

I also want to give special thanks to two friends/colleagues who provided very helpful comments on drafts of this manuscript, Alice Licata and Jan Pryor.

Growing up, my sisters, Susan and Kristan, said that we spelled family with a capital "F," and we did. I grew up in an extended Italian American family where everyone worked in the same business and everyone got into one another's business. My parents were married for fifty-seven years. I miss my father, who died in 2001, and want my sometimes-overinvolved but always loving mother, Mickey, to know how much I love her too. My deepest love and gratitude go to my wife, Kimberly, for pushing me, keeping up with me, and keeping things more than interesting, and, of course, to my five children. I have learned far more from Maggie, Julia, Bobby, Lucy, and John than from any textbook, especially the hard work, the joys, and ultimately the limits of parenting. For this book, special praise goes to Maggie, who went through my divorce and came out stronger on the other side.

Author's Note

All of the cases described in this book are composites. Extensive details have been changed to protect the confidentiality and privacy of my clients and research participants. The cases in the book are emotionally real, but no case corresponds to any actual person, living or dead.

Contents

THE Truth
ABOUT
Children
AND Divorce

Putting Children First When a Marriage Comes Apart

The telephone call was typical of many that I receive as a marriage therapist and mediator. After fourteen years of marriage, Danielle and Frank were separating. Normally, only one partner calls to make the first appointment. It's usually the one who wants out of the marriage. I know to listen carefully to the caller's version of events while bearing in mind that in marriage there are at least two, and sometimes even more, sides to the story. What was different here was the timing—just a week before Christmas, an understandably unpopular time for separations—and the timetable Danielle had set for the split: now.

As a psychologist and a dad myself, I found this especially distressing since the couple had a six-year-old child, Sam. Danielle and Frank had each met with lawyers, but Danielle told me that she—and, she hoped, Frank—didn't want to go that route. They both made the same amount of money, so they weren't going to be fighting over finances. Even though Frank wanted to work things out, Danielle said, there was little chance of saving the marriage now.

"Could you please meet with us before Christmas?" she asked urgently.

After we agreed on a date, Danielle offered some additional, crucial background: She had only recently confessed to Frank that she was having an affair. She was worried about what Frank might do. Whenever she tried to talk seriously about separation, he made it very clear that he wanted to have Sam with him all the time. Danielle said this was a ridiculous suggestion. After all, she had spent more time raising Sam, and she loved him so much. She couldn't stand being apart from him. But Danielle also felt guilty and uncertain about what was right and what might happen legally. After all, she *was* having an affair. As I penciled in the appointment, I wondered how much Christmas spirit any of us would be feeling by the time they left.

Later, as I read through my notes from the conversation, I saw that Danielle and Frank had all the ingredients for a volatile and ugly divorce: a one-sided separation, the surprise and betrayal that comes with a partner's affair, a rush to accomplish in a matter of days the tasks of separation that typically take months or even years, potentially adversarial lawyers, and terrible timing. What could be worse for young Sam than his parents' separating over Christmas break? There was no question that as former partners and future exes, Danielle and Frank were in for a rough time. Despite all this, though, I hoped that one thing Danielle had told me on the telephone would hold true: that she and Frank shared an abiding love and concern for Sam.

Really Putting Kids First

Sometimes I wonder why I put myself in the middle of the agony— and the anger—of couples like Danielle and Frank. As a psychologist, mediator, researcher, and college professor known for my twenty-five years of scientific studies and work on families and divorce, I could choose to remain in the academic realm rather than jump into the fray and fury of divorcing couples.

But children like Sam don't have a choice. In the United States today over one million children every year find themselves in Sam's shoes. So I put myself *in* the middle in the hope of getting children like Sam *out* of the middle. For I know with absolute certainty how important it is to get kids out of conflict and put them first in a divorce. All of my research and all of my work with couples and families demonstrates that what parents do after divorce—how they parent, how they handle their emotions, how they relate to each other and work together—is the key to children's resilience in coping with divorce.

Believe me. I know just how real (and just how *un*real) the world gets in divorce. I know the helpless, sinking feeling you get facing the end of your marriage and grappling with what you are supposed to do *now*. I know this from those twenty-five years of professional work. And let me be frank up front: I also know the pain of divorce from personal experience.

As I write this, my daughter from my first marriage, Maggie, is a happy, energetic, and independent twenty-one-year-old woman who is soon to graduate from college and chart her own course in life. (I have since remarried and have four more lovely and lively children.) Maggie's mother and I certainly have our share of regrets, but we also are incredibly proud of Maggie and the job we've done in raising her.

Sure, with divorce or the separation of their unmarried parents a part of the lives of close to half of children today, parents and experts alike *want* to put children first, at least in theory. But one of the things I have learned from the real world, and especially from my personal experience, is how *hard* it can be to keep our children's best interests first in the middle of all of the emotional complications of divorce. What isn't obvious, but what research and clinical experience can explain, is *why* it's so hard and what steps can be taken to overcome the difficulties— no matter what kind of divorce you might be experiencing.

The insights in this book apply to all couples—whether they are facing angry, distant, or cooperative relationships with their exes. In the case of Danielle, she was ready to focus on Sam, but Danielle *wanted* the divorce. She had a new life all planned for herself. But could Frank put Sam ahead of his own emotional devastation? Could you? Or maybe the question is, *can* you?

My goal in writing this book is to give parents the understanding, practical advice, and, I hope, some compelling arguments for putting children first—and keeping children out of the middle—during the crisis of separation. Ideally, this means devoting a few months before your separation and two to three years afterward to working through the legal, social, practical, and especially the *emotional* process of divorce.

My goal is to help you do with your heart and your actions the things you might know in your head you should be doing. And if you didn't do it right from the beginning, the time to start doing it right is now. This book offers you a new understanding of this crucial time and shows you how to take steps toward building a new life and how to lay the foundation for a respectful (if, in some cases, a distant), low-conflict relationship with your ex and continuous involvement with your kids. It will help you understand the emotional realities so you can make better choices in dealing with the practical realities. Some of the key points you will learn are:

- Why anger and fighting can keep you from really separating
- The unique and complicated grief cycle associated with divorce and how it affects the way you deal with your ex
- The truth behind "his" and "her" divorce
- The difference between power struggles and intimacy struggles and how they complicate things even more when it comes to day-to-day parenting plans
- Why legal matters are one of the last tasks of divorce
- Why parental love and parental authority can be the best "therapy" for kids

Finding Truth—and Hope—in a Time of Crisis

When we think of divorce (and here the term refers to separation, legal divorce, and never-married partners who end their relationship), we typically see it in terms of ending a marriage. Legally, people can get divorced on demand in a number of states. Emotionally, however, a divorce can take forever.

Public discussions of divorce often center on the legal, financial, and social aspects of divorce, not the emotional ones. It is all too easy to forget that the primary responsibility of parents at all times, but especially in a time of crisis like divorce, is to be parents, and the primary right of kids is to be kids. Children are at risk when parents fail to contain their own emotional issues (which then, in turn, often complicate and exacerbate their legal issues). When parents abandon their parental responsibilities in divorce, children lose one of their greatest gifts and rights: the opportunity to be children.

Reading this, you might have thought to yourself, "This is so obvious and so simple." And in some ways it is. Yet I know from the statistics, my studies, and hundreds of personal stories, including my own, that for many people there is no harder time to be a parent or a child than in the wake of divorce.

I am convinced that professionals like me now have a more realistic, more nuanced, and in many ways a more hopeful picture of the prospects for children in divorce. This is not to diminish the real challenges and risks children face. For virtually all children, divorce is a deeply painful, difficult transition—but it does not remain so forever. Children whose parents have divorced are not "doomed" or "damned." The vast majority of children are resilient. Yes, they are, to varying degrees, shaped by their parents' divorce. Yes, in their eyes, divorce is a life-changing event. Yes, most wish the divorce had never occurred. Despite all of that, most children carry the marks of their parents' divorce, but they are not permanently wounded by the experience.

The fact is, even if you have failed at your marriage, you can succeed at divorce. While some may feel that all divorces are bad, the fact is there are better divorces and there are worse divorces. Children fare better in a divorce when parents work together cooperatively and limit their children's exposure to conflict. Dozens of studies, including my own, have found this to be true.

Children can emerge from divorce emotionally healthy and resilient, but it takes a conscientious effort—sometimes a heroic one—on the part of parents to manage the personal and legal business of divorce in a responsible, adult manner. Protecting their children demands that parents deal with their own anger, hurt, grief, fear, and longing on a schedule dictated by their children's needs, not their own.

Parenting Through Divorce

Parents have many specific tasks to accomplish in divorce: working through grief, reducing conflict, renegotiating their relationship, establishing a working coparenting relationship, resolving all legal issues, learning how to parent effectively on their own—to name only a few. In the best of worlds, they would do so quickly and easily so that they could be available to their children every step of the way. In that ideal divorce (an oxymoron), events would proceed in a clear, logical order. You would, for example, discuss your separation with your children when you were both ready—or at least before one of you moved out in a rage, had the other served with divorce papers, or your child heard the news from a well-meaning relative or friend.

In real life, however, people make mistakes. Things happen that are sometimes unpredictable, unexpected, and unintended. One of the most challenging aspects of divorce is not that parents have so many things to do, but that they often must do them all simultaneously when they may be feeling depressed, angry, sad, confused, anxious, and perhaps not able to be the parents they would like to be. And we can add the fears, guilt, and conflict parents have about their children to this bubbling emotional stew.

Controlling Emotions Before They Control You

The message of this book is very simple: Children whose parents put them first from the start have a tremendous advantage over those whose parents cannot separate their feelings about their failed marriage from their feelings about the coparenting partnership that will last the rest of their lives. Most of the couples I see for the first time walk into my office thinking about the relationship they are ending. My first priority, if the marriage cannot be saved, is to convince parents to focus at the same time on the *new* relationship they are about to begin.

Rather than ruining my Christmas, Danielle and Frank made my holiday. At the beginning of our first session, Danielle, a confident, assertive corporate accountant, took charge. A redhead in her midthirties, Danielle was conservatively dressed, radiated a healthy glow, and had a sense of ease about who she was. For the first twenty minutes or so, she did most of the talking. As she did, I closely watched Frank, her husband of nearly fifteen years, out of the corner of my eye. Frank had the weatherworn permanent tan and lean build of a man who obviously loved working outdoors. A top landscape architect, he had a national reputation for several major corporate projects and the newly renovated local park. Sitting in my office, however, he looked deflated. He was clearly distraught as Danielle repeated in greater detail what she had told me on the telephone. She admitted to her yearlong affair with a co-worker and confessed the guilt she felt over her indiscretion and the pain it caused Frank.

Looking at me, Frank said quietly, "I've loved Danielle since high school. I never thought this would ever happen to us." He reminisced about how long it had taken them to conceive Sam and how he had always believed that no one could ever have had a better family than he did. "Why?" he seemed to be asking no one in particular. "Why?"

"Because . . . ," Danielle began, as tears ran down her cheeks. "I'm sorry, Frank. I'm really sorry. What can I say? I feel so guilty."

"Right," Frank snapped sarcastically. "Sorry if *I* make you feel guilty. It must be my fault."

Frank was hurt, and he wanted to hurt back; that's human nature. And Danielle felt guilty and defensive; that's normal, too. What does not come naturally at a time like this is an ability to put aside these powerful emotions. I could see that Frank was at war with himself. He wanted to rage and to attack Danielle, but he knew that Sam would be devastated if he did. Frank desperately wanted Danielle back despite her affair, and he wasn't ashamed to admit it. At the same time, he wasn't blind to her actions and desires. He knew that he couldn't force her to stay with him and that trying to do so would only drive her further away.

The only time Frank raised his voice was when the custody issue came up. Frank wanted sole custody of his son. His arguments about sole custody caused Danielle to lose her composure and she angrily blurted out, "If anyone should have sole custody, I should!" But when she calmed herself, Danielle made it clear that she wanted to share custody equally. Frank wanted Danielle to lose some of her time with Sam the same way he was losing her. After all, he reasoned with an edge to his voice, "Why should I lose my son for even one day a week just because she decided to cheat on me?"

Danielle looked away; I held my breath. "You're right, Frank," she said softly. "You shouldn't lose. But neither should Sam."

Frank nodded, then said sadly, "You're right. I'm so angry with you, but this isn't Sam's fault, either." Then looking at me to avoid Danielle's gaze, he added, "He loves his mother, and she loves him. I could never stand between them."

"We're not here about our marriage, or even the terms of our divorce," Danielle said, as Frank nodded silently. "I think we agree that we're here about Sam. He doesn't even know that we're about to separate—"

"He doesn't even know that Mommy and Daddy ever fight," Frank quickly added, completing Danielle's thought the way even parting couples sometimes do. "I know this is going to break his heart, and we worry how it may affect him."

"We love Sam," Danielle said. "And we want to have a plan for him. Despite the mess I've made of our marriage, and the horrible way it's going to end for us, we want to do what's best for him."

Frank won my respect with his ability to separate his feelings from Sam's needs, and Danielle did, too. Rather than going on the defensive, she admitted her mistakes and absorbed Frank's anger, painful as that was. She listened, reflected, apologized, and compromised. They touched hands, and both admitted to their ambivalence about splitting up. Danielle repeatedly made it clear that she wanted a separation despite her caring for Frank. Yet she and Frank confessed to fighting one minute, crying the next, and, soon thereafter, comforting each other with a hug.

Their mixed emotions confused them. It would have been much

easier to just stomp off angrily and never speak to each other again, never admit to the sadness and tenderness that accompany the anger and hurt of divorce. Fortunately for them—and especially for Sam— Danielle and Frank were mature enough to contain their own emotions and work together for their son.

In the two years since I first met them, Danielle and Frank have lived up to the promises they made for Sam's sake. They found a way to cooperate as parents even as their marriage unraveled. Was it easy? No. Perfect? No way. Danielle and Frank took several missteps along the way. But overall they have done a remarkable job, and the first years bode well for the rest of their relationship and for Sam's future, too.

My Professional Journey Through Divorce

You may be surprised to learn that almost everything I have said so far about divorce runs counter to what was considered the common professional wisdom just twenty-five years ago. In 1977, I was a graduate student in clinical psychology at the State University of New York at Stony Brook on Long Island. As part of my graduate work, I treated a family I will never forget—a family that did not have the knowledge, support, or professional guidance to help them make the kind of decisions Danielle and Frank could make today. I have thought of them often in the years since.

My client was Beverly—attractive, thirtysomething, and recently divorced, with a seven-year-old boy, Adam, and a five-year-old girl, Hannah. Like most parents living through divorce, Beverly was struggling. She had not asked for this divorce, nor did she expect it. One day she was a happy suburban homemaker, and the next she was a divorced mom struggling with her emotions and sense of identity, her children's emotions, her drastically reduced financial resources, and ongoing conflicts with her ex-husband, Jake. One afternoon, Beverly arrived at our session panic stricken. "I can't believe this," she said between tears. "The divorce was final just two months ago, Jake has already remarried, and now he's threatening to seek full custody of Adam and Hannah." As Beverly explained, Jake argued that he could give the children a home with two parents. And wasn't that "better" for the children than living with only one—even if she was their mother who had provided most of the caregiving throughout their lives?

Though Jake's argument might sound far-fetched today, it didn't to Beverly. Her ex spoke with authority; she was full of self-doubt. He had money for a court battle; she didn't. He spoke with a lawyer often; she spoke with a lawyer briefly, one who told her—honestly and accurately—that, technically, she *should* win a custody battle, but nothing was certain once one went to court.

What strikes me when I look back on this case is that although Beverly and Jake were positioning to fight *over* the kids, it had not occurred to anyone to fight *for* the kids, for something *better*. At that time, most child psychologists and other experts on divorce believed that the chief threat to the emotional well-being of children was the lack of having both parents, or at least two married adults, in the household.

The emotional problems of children whose parents were divorced were understood in terms of the psychological theory of the time, particularly Freudian theory, which viewed children's emotional problems as all in their heads, seemingly ignoring the upheaval in children's lives. At the time, almost no one focused, much less did research, on the actual turmoil caused by divorce and the toll parental conflict exacted on children. Like too many divorcing parents then—and today—Beverly and Jake naïvely assumed that the professionals and the system knew more about the consequences of divorce and could make better decisions for their children than they could. After twenty-five years of work on this topic, I am absolutely convinced that while professionals certainly can help, in the final analysis parents are by far the best experts for helping their own children through divorce. The task for parents is not to master Freudian theory (or, really, any theory), but to begin to master their own emotions so they can really put their children first.

When Beverly, who had little confidence left (much less the re-solve to take on Jake in another legal fight), asked me what I thought she should do, I wondered about the very real and immedi-ate problems for Adam and Hannah in dealing with two parents who were at war—over them. I urged Beverly to trust her feelings. She knew that her children loved and needed her. She also believed in her heart that her children needed their father, too, but she didn't think it was possible for them to have both. Everyone—including Jake and even her own attorney—told her that it had to be one way, one parent, or the other. Was fighting this out with Jake the only way to go?

Beverly could see what a battle between her and her ex was going to do to the kids. She had told me how Adam got mad at his dad when they fought and how he screamed at him to "leave Mom alone." Han-nah withdrew into her shell during fights, and when pressed, she said in a plaintive voice, "Please don't fight. It makes me scared!" Beverly's observations of her children coupled with her own self-doubt left her torn with indecision.

I decided to trust my intuition and asked Beverly, "What do you think about getting the children's father in here to talk about these things?" Today this seems so simple and so obvious. At that time, however, it was anything but. There were no textbooks or studies or experts I could cite for this approach. Still, it felt right. What I didn't know then was that not only were most divorce professionals reluctant to encourage parents to get together to work out their problems, but they were actually reluctant to have them get together at all. There was too much fighting, too much conflict and recrimination. I now find it rather ironic that adult professionals with no emotional stake or in-volvement in a couple's conflict were afraid (and I do mean afraid) to share an office for an hour or two with a divorcing couple. What about the kids who were exposed to that conflict for days, weeks, even years?

Within a few moments of Jake's arrival at our joint meeting, I won't say that I had second thoughts, but it was clear that this was not going to be easy. "Let me just tell you something," Jake said in a no-nonsense voice. "My attorney is not happy that I'm here. Not happy at all. He says I've got a good case for getting my kids, and that's what I think is best." With that, he folded his arms across his chest and glared at Beverly.

She glanced at Jake, then at me, then looked down at the floor. No wonder she's as nervous as she is, I thought. Jake was an intimidating presence. After talking a bit to Beverly and Jake, I convinced them that I wasn't there to be on anyone's side, only to help the two of them try to reach a decision about their children that neither of them felt co-erced into. For all of his bluster, Jake was a loving dad; he would tear up at the mention of either child's name, and he gave both kids a big, long hug when he met them in the waiting room.

Once we got through some tense moments, Jake began to relax and Beverly could see that she actually had more power in the situation than she thought. She *was* the expert when it came to her children. Most important, it was clear that both Jake and Beverly wanted what was best for their kids. In the neutral zone of my office, perhaps for the first time since they separated, they reached a decision about their children that did not involve a fight, personal or legal.

Why was this important? Because though the divorce had changed these children's lives in countless ways great and small, the most im-mediate and potentially damaging problem was not the divorce itself but the parents' ongoing conflict. Technically speaking, I had one client, Beverly. But divorce is a process that touches the entire family, a family transformed and maybe shaken, but a family nonetheless. I would meet with Beverly and Jake a half dozen times, and it would be a few months before I saw Adam and Hannah relaxed—smiling and laughing—in the presence of both parents, but it happened. My expe-rience with Beverly and her family led to the subject of my doctorate and my career. My work with them also eventually led me to conduct a series of research studies that *prove* parents can work together even in the midst of divorce (see chapter 6)—and that doing so makes a huge difference for their children.

A Better Way

Not long after my experience with Beverly and Jake, I discovered that a handful of professionals also felt the way I did about divorced families, and were creating programs geared to finding new ways of resolving parental disputes. Across the country, forward-thinking mental health professionals and lawyers were starting to treat divorcing parents as two people with a shared interest in their children rather than as opponents in a legal tug-of-war. Mediation, an approach where a neutral third party acts as a facilitator to help parents reach their own agreements in divorce, particularly appealed to me. Mediation reached parents early in the divorce process and tried to contain their conflicts. It proceeded from what then seemed a revolutionary premise: Divorcing parents are the best experts on their own children and they can, with the right attitude and the right help, assume the responsibility for deciding what is best for them. Beverly and Jake showed me how divorcing parents can rise to the occasion, if they know how.

The key to putting children first is reducing parental conflict. Divorce mediation is one way; so is talking over your kitchen table or using lawyers who work in a collaborative as opposed to an adversarial fashion. All the little things that thousands of divorced parents do day in and day out are also incredibly important. They swallow a little of their own pain, anger, and pride, and they find a way to work together in parenting their children. It doesn't even matter so much *how* they get there as *when*—the sooner the better.

My Personal Story

In 1989, my first wife, Jean, and I separated. My experience confirmed for me personally what I had long known professionally: Divorce is incredibly hard. For most parents it is an ongoing and painful struggle to build a new relationship and redefine their roles.

I, perhaps more than most fathers in my position, knew not only what to do but also why it was necessary. Yet nothing braced me for the pain. Nothing prepared me for the realization of how easily my own anguish might have swayed me from saying or doing the right thing. No one told me how hard I would work to put my emotions aside for our daughter's sake. And Maggie's mother probably worked even harder than I did. I had already spent years reading, writing, lecturing about the pain divorce creates for children, but I never truly understood what it all meant until I saw it in my own daughter's eyes.

Fortunately, Maggie was a resilient child—as are most children whose parents divorce. But I never underestimated the real risks our divorce introduced into her life, nor did I forget the pain my divorce caused her at different points throughout her life or how grateful I am that she has grown into a happy, accomplished young woman. But I also believe that divorce was the best decision for me personally at that time.

The Lessons of Divorce

Children are what this book is really all about, although you will be reading more about parents than about kids in divorce for a very simple and extremely important reason: Children can survive and thrive after divorce if parents can find the right way to manage their relationships with their children and with each other. If you, as the parent, can remain effective and loving, your so-called child of divorce (a term I hate to use) will be a child first and foremost. If you can learn the practical and emotional lessons I offer you here, your children can have the childhood that every child deserves. They won't grow up too soon, become the parent to you, or become derailed with problems that cry for help and attention. They'll be regular kids who drive you to distraction one day and make you proud the next. If you can be a parent first, even while facing all the challenges and changes in your life, then your kids will be free to be what you want them to be and what they deserve to be: just kids. Call it your take-home message, your mantra, your affirmation—whatever you want. Just believe it.

CHAPTER ONE

Divorcing Emotions: Riding Alone on the Emotional Roller Coaster of Grief

When it comes to driving and shaping a divorce, for better or worse, nothing is as powerful as human emotion. No agreement, no lawyer, no judge, not even your levelheaded best friend is any match for your unrecognized, unmanaged, and unprocessed emotions.

The feelings stirred up by divorce can be so intense that even rational parents find themselves saying and doing things they never did before, or saying and doing things they promised themselves and others they would never do again. You might bad-mouth your ex to your kids (something you never did when you were together) or find yourself "forgetting" what time your ex was picking them up for the weekend. In the eleventh hour of the divorce negotiations, you might feel compelled to ask for half of that musty old lake cabin you always hated to visit or that painting in the attic you hadn't thought about in the twenty years since his parents gave it to you. You might catch yourself laughing wickedly to yourself over your son's description of how dirty your ex's new girlfriend's house is. Or you might feel inexplicably jealous of how nicely your ex-wife's husband-to-be treats your children. You may ask yourself, how did I get here? Emotions.

Even couples who manage to keep their emotions in check and work cooperatively discover that the psychological uncoupling of divorce can open a Pandora's box of emotional surprises. On top of whatever complaints, transgressions, and failings led up to the divorce, there is the sometimes shocking realization that you and your ex—and how you two saw your marriage—are now worlds apart. You may look at the person you lived with for so long and wonder, "Who is he?" Understanding the dynamics behind what seems like a sudden disconnect between your ex and the life you led together is essential to recognizing your own crazy and confusing feelings and taking the first steps toward building a new relationship with your ex.

Scott's Story

By all appearances, at age thirty-seven Scott had it made. A civil engineer in a large, successful contracting company, he had the friendly confidence of the college soccer star he had been. Outgoing and congenial, Scott had a wide circle of friends who enjoyed his Boston Irish warmth and sly sense of humor.

Everyone loved Scott, yet few people really knew him. The eldest of three brothers in a family fractured by divorce, Scott had been "the man of the house" since his early teens. His father, who drank excessively after the separation, practically disappeared from the boys' lives, so his mother turned to her sons to fill the emotional vacuum left behind. Scott did more than take care of his younger brothers for her; he became his mother's protector and confidant. It was tough, but Scott never complained. Family friends and neighbors marveled at how such an exceptional young man—a straight-A student and star athlete through high school and college—did all that. Bound by a strong sense of duty, Scott never allowed himself to even consider what he might be missing.

Not surprising for a self-described traditionalist like Scott, he met his first serious girlfriend—and future wife—in college. Like Scott, she was different beneath what she seemed to be on the surface. Attractive, energetic, and volatile, Scott's girlfriend soon became emotionally dependent on him, despite her outward independence. From the beginning, she knew that she could count on Scott for almost anything. And Scott, who found her romantically unpredictable and exciting, loved being needed—at first. They married right after graduation, and several years later, after they felt secure in their careers (she had become a lawyer), they relocated to the South and started their family.

"Somewhere along the line—years ago really," Scott said, "something changed. The things about her that I thought I fell in love with—her sharp wit, her honesty, the way she always told you exactly what she thought—started to bother me. Frankly, that's when I started falling out of love."

Despite his new revelation, Scott took pride in "not being a complainer." He believed that he should suck it up and keep going. As a result, he rarely argued with his wife, no matter how relentless her demands or pointed her criticism. "I just couldn't win," Scott recalled. "And I also believed, as we'd said at our wedding, 'for better, for worse.'" Scott said that he "gutted it out for a long time," but he confessed that for years he had been thinking about a separation. About a year ago, he decided that divorce was inevitable, but, typically, Scott kept his feelings to himself and kept plugging away. A little more than a month ago—in the middle of a minor argument, Scott finally told his wife that he wanted out.

Scott's wife didn't believe him at first, and she was stunned when Scott told her that he was "one hundred ten percent serious." A few days later, Scott agreed to try some marriage counseling, but when he attended the first session with me, he politely reminded us that making the marriage work was not on his agenda. His wife desperately wanted to save their marriage, and she worried openly about Scott's mental health. In her words, he seemed like a man "transformed." A few months earlier they had been happily married with three lovely children. Now he was talking about divorce. This just didn't make any sense to her. "Scott," she insisted, "you need some psychological help. Something has changed in you. I think you're depressed—or something. . . ." Her voice trailed off.

Scott agreed that he had "snapped," but denied that he was depressed about anything other than the prospect of putting his children through a separation. What had changed was that he no longer was willing to tolerate "a castrating, loveless marriage." At the same time, he wasn't bolting for the door; he agreed to give couples therapy a try but, as I would later see, only out of a sense of obligation, only because it was "the right thing to do."

As he spoke, Scott's polite manner barely masked his seething rage. In an outburst during our fourth session, he shouted that the marriage was "one-sided" and that he was sick of being "a yes-man." In tears, Scott's wife confessed that much of his anger was legitimate. But when I tried to explore his wife's admission more calmly with Scott, he said that he wasn't in therapy to complain or "waste time" talking about the past. What he really wanted was to "do business"—to get on with sorting the finances and planning for the kids so they could, as he said, "end it." As his wife watched in stunned silence, Scott announced, "This is it. I'm not going to suck it up anymore. I'm moving out at the end of the month, so we better get down to work." I could see that she wanted to say something, but the words died on her lips. As far as Scott was concerned, their marriage was over.

Cindy's Story

Cindy was a bright, attractive, and emotionally intense thirty-eight-year-old woman with a rapier-sharp wit. An only child, Cindy made her working-class Italian immigrant parents very proud: straight As through Catholic school and college and no boy trouble—a "good girl," as her father would say, beaming. Even as a child, Cindy thought for herself, but she still respected her family's values: hard work, honesty, church followed by dinner at home every Sunday afternoon, and mass a couple of times a week in between.

Even as a child, Cindy believed that "real love" was not the fantasy she heard in rock songs or saw in movies. Real love was what she saw at home between her parents: a serious commitment to enduring (rather than enjoying) marriage that was more stable, more "grown-up" than the romantic affection she viewed as "frivolous" and "unrealistic." Sure, her parents fought—heated exchanges followed by a long, silent cool down—but their fighting never scared her because she knew they would never divorce. Now, years later and on the brink of her own divorce, she had begun to wonder if they ever *really* loved each other.

Going into her own marriage to her college sweetheart, Cindy prized her mate's consistency and predictability above what she considered the "Cinderella fantasy" of "living happily ever after." Her father had told her that passion ended "five minutes after a tussle in the backseat of a car," and she believed him. "A couple should work together for the marriage and for the family," Cindy would tell friends. "That's how you show your love for your husband, by raising good kids and making a good life. The passion stuff? That's not really what it's about."

Cindy lived out her marriage according to these values, and in certain respects, her marriage was a success. They had a brood of growing children, two girls and a boy, a very nice home, and a respected place in their community. Despite her strong views on most things, she and her husband rarely fought. Cindy did say that she saw it as her duty to "help" her husband and her children by giving them "constructive feedback." Until very recently, her husband never said that her comments bothered him. She assumed that he felt as she did, that, as she liked to say, "Only your family loves you enough to tell you the truth."

When pressed, Cindy admitted that she felt her husband could have helped more with the children. She also confessed that she was torn between her full-time job and being a mother; she could never attend to one without feeling wracked by guilt over what she wasn't doing for the other. Still, she said, "That's small potatoes. Our marriage was working the way a marriage should work!"

Then one day—completely out of nowhere—Cindy's husband announced that he wanted a divorce. For a moment, Cindy thought that he was either joking or had just lost his mind—this was so out of character. When he persisted, and began talking to her about custody, selling the house, and child support, she panicked. No matter what her husband said to her, Cindy honestly could not understand what he meant or why he was unhappy.

"I have a good, solid marriage," she repeated more than twice when she first called me. I could still hear traces of disbelief as she said, "I have no idea what's happened to him. Why would he do this? He's either having a nervous breakdown or a midlife crisis or something. This just isn't something he would do. It's not him." Sitting in my office during our first appointment, Cindy looked shocked. "All I want to do is save our marriage," she said, weeping softly. "I don't know what went wrong, but we can fix it. I know we can." When a few sessions later, her husband announced that he definitely wanted a divorce, Cindy was stunned. She didn't cry, she didn't scream. She just sat there, frozen.

Would you be surprised to learn that the couple sitting in my office on that day was Scott and Cindy? These are not the stories of two divorces, but of one.

His and Her Marriage: His and Her Divorce

In her influential 1972 book, *The Future of Marriage,* sociologist Jesse Bernard put forth the idea that a couple does not have one marriage, but two: his and hers. Bernard's focus was the typical American marriage of the 1960s (stay-at-home caretaker mother, breadwinner father), and her conclusion—that such a marriage was a better deal for him than for her—struck a chord with women who were dissatisfied with that type of arrangement. Bernard was primarily concerned with a feminist analysis of marriage, and although here we are concerned with the emotional side of divorce, her observation is apt. Couples do not have one marriage. They have two. The differences in perception become painfully clear when a couple parts.

When we are invested in a relationship, we learn to tolerate differences in reality and in perception. Even in the best of marriages, we sometimes pull our punches: We do not always say what we really think or feel. We may even lie to our partner to spare feelings, avoid conflict, or protect the marriage itself. A couple lives together in one relationship, but they experience two marriages. Part of this experience is learning to compromise, but it's also something bigger. We *believe* that our partner is the person we have partly created in our minds. This is probably what most people mean when they say "Love is blind." We accept, distort, and create a relationship, an image of our partners that in many ways is better—as far as we are concerned—than who they are, perhaps better than anyone can be.

Divorce marks the spot where his marriage and her marriage—and all of the beliefs, assumptions, and truths—collide. The blinders come off, and people see their partners' flaws with glaring clarity. Perhaps they are seeing reality for the first time or creating a new, but negatively distorted, illusion. Either way, the reversal of perceptions from marriage to divorce can be dramatic. Many people believe they are discovering their "true" feelings about their partner for the first time, which can result in the familiar "I never *really* loved him [or her]."

It is hard to overstate the emotional devastation some people experience upon learning that they shared what they thought was a loving marriage with a partner who now claims to have never loved them. It is, in some cases, for some people, literally unbelievable.

Cindy would not have recognized Scott's description of their marriage had she not heard him say the words herself. In fact, even after he said it—and said it several times—Cindy was more comfortable believing that he was suffering from a breakdown or had stumbled into some wild affair. She did not recognize or appreciate how much Scott had supported her emotionally or how little she knew about how he felt all those years. She also had yet to come to terms with her own feelings—how, deep down, she resented how much she needed him or that she expressed her resentment through criticizing him.

Scott had his emotional blinders on, too. He knew that he felt unappreciated and burdened, but even in the midst of the separation, he did not recognize his own anger and resentment. He had suppressed his feelings since his own parents' divorce, and in doing so, he had denied both himself and Cindy the opportunity to deal with how he truly felt. There is truth in both Scott's story and in Cindy's, but they are truths for them as individuals. There is no single or ultimate truth for them as a couple.

Married or not, we each bring our own perception to our understanding of everything in our lives. Perceptions are subjective, open to influence from others, and always subject to change. Early in your marriage and your career, you were proud when your co-workers and bosses talked for days about the exquisite parties your wife threw. Ten years and four kids later, you resent the time and effort she puts into playing Martha Stewart. Fifteen years ago, you found the commitment of your promising artist-photographer husband to his muse rebellious and romantic. But the market for the work he does has dwindled, he refuses to do anything he considers commercial, and you are considering filing for bankruptcy. Now you find his stubborn—you would say adolescent—refusal to face economic reality unbearable.

Things change. So do people, and there is no telling how many couples part simply because one or both of them grow away from the other. Even then, however, in the heat of divorce, is it ever that simple? Hardly. Whether we think of it or not, whether we ever articulate it or not, we bring to marriage certain expectations of our partner and of our relationship. Whether from witnessing our own parents' marriage or absorbing what's out there in our culture, we form very strong ideas about what a spouse should be and should do, what constitutes a good marriage, and how we define happiness. Our ideas about all these things may change, too. Some fortunate couples, often with good therapy, can undergo this process and emerge with a better understanding of each other and themselves and possibly even a stronger marriage. But it is rarely easy and not for the faint of heart.

Divorce Rewrites Your History

Most people who divorce will assert that they know why their marriage ended. In Scott's eyes, Cindy drove him away; to hear Cindy tell it, one day Scott just "lost it." After reading their stories, what do you think? If you are like most people, you see shades of truth in both viewpoints.

Whenever trauma occurs, we need to *believe* that we understand why, and so it is with divorce. Our beliefs about the reasons for a divorce are partly based on reality, but they also provide a form of self-protection. They protect us from guilt, shame, and ultimately from responsibility. In order to do this effectively, some of our beliefs will reflect only our interpretation of reality, and, as a result, our beliefs will probably differ from those of our ex.

Not surprisingly, many couples do not agree on why their marriage ended. There may be no dispute over the general cause: They grew apart, or she fell in love with someone else, or they fell out of love. But there is often intense dispute over the events that either directly led up to or set the scene for the marriage's precipitous fall.

Divorce is freighted with anger, grief, and uncertainty. As exes struggle to regain their psychological equilibrium, they develop a version, a history of the marriage that is consistent with their explanation for why it failed. Unconsciously, memories and family stories—which are subject to each partner's different perceptions to begin with—are filtered through the emotional prism of sadness, anger, fear, grief, love, and other feelings. Now he wonders if she ever *really* loved him. Now he "sees" that she always wanted a business partner—not a lover, not a man. Her lack of passion? His problem, she asserts. Didn't he notice—even though she never said anything about it—that his fumbling romantic gestures left her cold?

Didn't she notice, he wonders, that he was frustrated and lonely? That he would have done anything to please her if she had only let him know? "After all, I'm not a mind reader," she said. So did he. The result:

She: We're getting a divorce because he had an affair.

He: I only had an affair because she rejected me sexually and emotionally for years.

She: I was willing to forgive him and admit that I had problems, too, to save our marriage.

He: She *says* she was willing to change, but I've been trying to get her to change for years. She doesn't want to change. She wants to hang on. Yeah, she wants "a husband," but she doesn't want me.

And so it goes. Socially, emotionally, perhaps even financially, it can be easier to blame your ex for his or her failures than to acknowledge and accept your own part in the emotional devastation that is the failure of your marriage.

His and Her Children

The widening gap between his perceptions and her perceptions can grow to include each partner's views of their children. When I finally got Cindy and Scott to talk directly about the impact of a separation on their three kids—Angela, nine; Joey, seven; and five-year-old Colleen—their concerns differed dramatically. Cindy assumed the children felt as she did: angry, devastated, and unlikely to ever recover. Scott projected his own feelings onto his children. He said, "Of course, they'll be sad when we separate, but I'm sure they'll also be relieved by the drop in tension. It will be hard for a while, but they'll be eager to get on with their lives."

When I talked further with each of them alone, Cindy told me that she thought the children would feel abandoned; Scott said he was sure that the kids would finally relax when away from their mother's criticisms. What Cindy and Scott were actually talking about were their own feelings, not the children's. (How many children have you heard say they wanted to "get on with" their lives?)

Even in the best of relationships, the gap between his reality and hers can affect the most mundane things. You think Johnny's advanced-placement calculus class is the challenge he needs; your wife sees only his pencil-chewing stress and wants him to quit. You believe ten-year-old Ariel's obsession with boys is too much too soon; your husband believes that "all kids are like that today" and tells you to chill out. Anger, sadness, love, and grief widen the distance and into it often fall a mother's and a father's respective ideas about their children.

Of course, parents always have some differences of opinion about the kids, but suddenly you are seeing attitudes and behaviors related to or caused by the separation and divorce. Divorce is an emotionally volatile time when two people are going through something together but doing so alone. This helps explain why perspectives and reactions can be so different.

When we feel emotionally vulnerable, one way to feel less so is to feel justified in our thoughts and actions, to be "right." It is easier for each parent to feel right when he believes that the children feel about the divorce the same way he does. Therefore, parents tend to project their own feelings onto their children, to assume that the children share their feelings and their views of what has happened. The truth is, however, that children have their own take on the divorce and the roles their parents play in it.

The Children's Perspective

Without children, you would be a couple divorcing, free to never see, speak, or think of the other for the rest of your lives. Children change all that. My early clients Beverly and Jake, for instance, would both have been relieved to have never spoken to each other again, and that's probably how it would have played out for them were it not for their children. Scott might have left Cindy years earlier, perhaps without a word, if he hadn't had three children.

Families in divorce are a bit like those small, isolated towns in the old Westerns. The classic story line has the sheriff trying to deputize the townspeople to back him up in the impending showdown with the bad guy. Although you may see your ex as the villain, in most cases your children do not. And even when they do, they still feel for him a love and a loyalty that can and should survive your divorce. To them it's not a question of good guy versus bad guy. It's more like being forced to choose between two sheriffs—two good guys—neither of whose posse they should be pressed to join.

The children's perspective may make sense to you intellectually. I have yet to meet a parent in divorce who would not say that the children should come first. Unfortunately and understandably, for many parents the idea of taking the children's perspective does not make emotional sense.

Somehow Danielle and, especially, Frank—who was blindsided by the betrayal of an affair—were able to free themselves from the vortex of their own feelings and focus first on worrying about their son, Sam. But what about Scott and Cindy? Could they make the leap? Unfortunately for their three children, they could not do so readily. They were engulfed in emotions that neither of them understood in themselves or in each other: their devastating, overwhelming, and largely unacknowledged grief.

Understanding Grief in Divorce

To get through your divorce, you must recognize and process grief. *Grief?* you may ask, wondering how you can grieve for a marriage you are relieved to be rid of or a marriage you are fighting to save. Not everyone feels that way, of course, but it is important to bear in mind that no matter what state the marriage you are leaving—or being forced to leave—you are experiencing a major loss.

Grief is a powerful and enduring response to the loss of something we love or something we once loved. For the purposes of this book, grief is a set of seemingly contradictory feelings that are a natural part of coping with loss and, at a deeper level, of trying to reunite with the lost loved one. Grief following theoretically reconcilable losses like divorce is similar to but in many ways more complicated than grief following irreconcilable losses like death.

Most people are familiar with Dr. Elisabeth Kübler-Ross's model of the stages of grief and bereavement related to death: anger, denial, bargaining, depression, acceptance. In this model and from life experience, grief develops on a continuum, starting at point A and ending at point B. This is not to say that people do not experience renewed pangs of grief over time; they do. But for the most part, the most intense grieving ends with acceptance. Perhaps because of the finality of death, the grieving process can come to an "end."

People who experience divorce—parents and children alike—also experience grief, and it, too, has stages, but it is qualitatively different from other types of grief. The main difference is that in the lives of a family, divorce never truly ends. There is always the possibility, however remote, that parents might reconcile. And because of the children, there is *never* a clean break. Through the many tasks of divorce parents and children must accomplish—renegotiating relationships, learning to establish and relate to one another within new boundaries, adjusting to new circumstances, finding a place and an identity within a shifting family "frame"—they face fresh opportunities to revisit old hurts and expose themselves to new ones.

You might have noticed feeling these intense emotions about your divorce. One minute you are furious with your ex—about what, it doesn't matter. Once your anger is spent, you find yourself incredibly sad. Why is this happening? Perhaps as you climb into bed alone, you find yourself longing for a warm body or the sense of security of sharing a bed, a home. What you might not have realized, especially in the immediate emotional aftermath of divorce, is that these seemingly conflicting emotions really are connected. They all are a part of your grief.

The Grief Cycle of Divorce

To more clearly explain this, I have developed a conception of divorce-related grief that differs from those that evolved from the study of bereavement. The key difference is that divorce-related grief does not move in a straight line in one direction. In what I have termed the cyclical model of grief, people instead cycle repeatedly through a three-part phase consisting of love, anger, and sadness.

Here's how grieving relationship loss works: Typically in the beginning, love, anger, and sadness are experienced intensely and only one emotion at a time though in sequence. Cindy offered a wrenching example of the cycle on the day Scott announced he definitely wanted a divorce. A few moments before his announcement, Cindy had been desperately admitting to the many mistakes she had made in their marriage. She made it perfectly clear she was eager to change in order to make things better. But following a few moments of stunned silence after hearing Scott's proclamation, Cindy shouted in fury, "All that talk about your father, and here you are abandoning your own family. Like father, like son!" Despite these bitter words, Cindy was in tears before the end of the session. She was just beginning her rough ride on the emotional roller coaster of grief.

Recently one of my graduate students, David Sbarra, and I showed in scientific research that people really do swing through love-anger-sadness cycles when grieving the loss of an intimate relationship. To study grief scientifically, we picked a group of couples experiencing a significant loss but who were accessible and willing to share their experiences: college students who had been dating exclusively for at least six months and some for as long as two years.

We began following this large group of couples while they were together but focused on only those students who, during our periodic e-mail contact, let us know that things were unraveling in their relationship. Just after the breakup of their love relationship, we gave the couples beepers and carefully structured diaries. Over the next month they reported on their emotions, making notations in the diaries when they were beeped at random times during the day. Sure enough, the young couples' carefully monitored emotional swings between love, anger, and sadness closely matched the cyclical theory of grief.

Over time the intensity of the emotions diminishes and people usually find that the feelings begin to blend. Early on, the grief of divorce is experienced as an intense period of feeling nothing but love, followed by an equally intense period of feeling nothing but anger, followed by an equally intense period of feeling nothing but sadness. During this time, it is impossible to honestly feel what we would commonly call mixed emotions—for example, love tinged with sadness or anger blunted by memories of love. Over time, however, the intensity of the feelings begins to wane, and the cycles of each emotion begin to blur and run into the other two. This overlapping of emotions results in a more realistic, less emotionally painful view of the divorce.

When the blending of emotions does not occur, people get stuck in one emotional cycle or another. Someone who gets stuck on love may deny the reality of the breakup and pine for reconciliation; someone caught up in anger will act out of vindictiveness and a need for revenge; those mired in sadness will assume an exaggerated and unrealistic sense of responsibility for what has occurred.

I am convinced that many of the powerful emotions divorcing couples experience—and the words, decisions, and actions those emotions often drive—can be traced back to their own inability to manage the grief of divorce.

Unmanaged grief can be a powerful, overwhelming force. Divorce is rich in opportunities for parents in the throes of their sadness, anger, or love to act out, to say or do things that feel right in the moment. I am also convinced that these emotions—including even venomous expressions of anger—often are, at a deeper level, manifestations of grief. In fact, angry outbursts often are desperate, if indirect, bids to resolve grief by reestablishing a connection. Getting mad can be a way of seeing if you can still get a rise out of your ex, of finding out if he really is still hooked.

Anger: The Toxic Residue of Unresolved Grief

Like many people in the intense early stages of divorce, Cindy did not recognize her own grief. Once she finally realized that Scott was serious about leaving, her desperation to save her marriage at all costs was transformed—into anger. She no longer focused on her longing; she would not admit to sadness. Instead, her emotional energy fed a blistering righteous indignation over Scott's abandoning her, his children, and his marriage vows. In a fit of anger before she ended our sessions, Cindy said, "If you are going to go through with this, then you are going to pay. You don't know just how much you are going to pay!"

Cindy was true to her word. She hired the most litigious lawyer she could find, and she contested everything—except the possibility that her anger was driven not by Scott alone but by her emotional devastation at the loss of her marriage.

Unlike Danielle and Frank, the couple who openly and honestly expressed their most painful emotions and their less noble impulses during that holiday session in my office, Scott and Cindy had no point of reference, no place to begin the long process of dealing with their feelings. Where Danielle knew she had to accept and absorb Frank's anger, Scott was out of touch with Cindy's volatile emotions—and his own. Where Frank expressed his own hurt and even some plans he knew he would never act out (like keeping Sam from his mother), Cindy refused to admit she had any feelings at all other than anger.

And Scott did not recognize that Cindy's reactions were a part of her grief. Instead, he saw her fury as an extension of her lifelong anger and bitterness. Even more important, Scott could not deal with his long and deeply held belief that he must always put the needs of others before his own. To do so would mean embracing his overwhelming sense of failure and guilt, feelings that stemmed from his "selfish" decision to separate. Ironically, like Cindy, Scott indulged his anger and covered up his grief. The immediate results were sadly predictable for both of them and, more poignantly, were devastating for their children, Angela, Joey, and Colleen.

The Many Functions of Anger

Anger is perhaps the most complicated emotion for former partners to understand and harness in a divorce; it is undoubtedly the most destructive for children. Why is anger so powerful? There are obvious, real-life reasons for the reign of anger—the betrayal of an affair, the threat of losing the children, the loss of a life dreamed about and worked hard for.

But there are also many emotional reasons why anger keeps working its way to the forefront of the relationship between former partners who must find a way to parent. Anger is a part of four more complicated emotional processes: grieving, dealing with hurt, responding to threat, and, paradoxically, hanging on to a loved one.

Although we usually think of anger as unpleasant, in the processes of divorce, anger often is less painful, frightening, and threatening for us to feel. Anger also can allow us to save face in front of our ex or other people. That is why the ball keeps ending up in the slot marked ANGER as we spin through the roulette wheel of emotions in divorce. Emotionally, it can be less painful to indulge your anger than to truly feel your grief, hurt, fear, and longing.

Anger as an Emotional Cover-Up

After Scott moved out, Cindy went into a depression. She lost twenty pounds, complained of being unable to sleep, and spoke gloomily about the future for herself and her children. These are all basic signs of depression, but Cindy lacked one essential symptom: sadness. True enough, when we talked, she often looked or sounded sad. She even cried briefly with me on a few occasions. Yet as much as I encouraged her to express her grief, at the end of a session or a phone call, Cindy always focused her emotional energy not on sadness but on her profound anger at Scott.

Cindy was human. She *was* grieving and cycling through anger, sadness, and longing. (Every time she contacted me, she invariably offered some indirect signal that *she* was still willing to try to reconcile. Again.) But Cindy kept landing on anger, the emotion in the cycle of grief that she was most comfortable with. Her anger protected her from sadness, a feeling she had denied throughout her life. Her anger brought allies to her side in her war against Scott, most notably her family and several old friends. Her anger helped her to save face when Scott ignored her hints at reconciliation. Cindy's anger served its purposes for her, even as it wreaked havoc on the children.

Anger and Pain

Anger helps us to deal with the grief of loss, and it also serves as an emotional Band-Aid in other ways. One of the most basic functions of anger is to cover up pain. (This is why we yell at the furniture when we stub a toe.) Cindy and Scott deliberately hurt each other back because they each were hurt themselves—and out of touch with their deeper feelings. For example, when Scott rejected Cindy's hint about trying to reconcile, she hit a vulnerable spot by saying sarcastically, "Oh yes. You're so *very* responsible. You're willing to abandon your children so you can have a second childhood."

Scott was never as effective in hitting back verbally, but that isn't the point. The point is this: When we are hurt, we naturally respond with anger. We want to hurt back. Yet if we hope to get beyond the Band-Aid of anger, we need to acknowledge the hurt, the more basic, truer feeling.

Anger and Fear

Anger has more in its bag of tricks. Anger also can help to cover up fear. Threatening situations trigger the well-known fight-or-flight response. The fact is that over the course of evolution anger has served the species well in responding to threats. The problem is that outside of truly life-threatening situations, the fight-or-flight response has outlived its adaptive value. In our modern society, it is overkill.

Most people in divorce feel threatened about both specific matters (that she will sue for full custody, for example, or he won't make his child support payments) and about their lives and their futures in general. Threats like these trigger fight or flight. Fear might have dominated Cindy as she sorted through her lists of frightening possibilities while lying in bed trying to sleep. But when, exhausted, she saw Scott the next day, she exploded with the other fight-or-flight option: attack. And Scott did not flee; he fought back. And so it went, on and on.

How Anger—Not Love—Can Keep Us Together

Finally, anger can play one more tricky emotional role, one we may not be fully aware of, one we may deny. Anger can be a way of keeping people in contact with their former partners, of trying to bring them back together. How? Consider this:

Dr. John Bowlby, a British psychiatrist and attachment theorist, studied and wrote extensively about child-mother bonding. Bowlby observed that, when separated involuntarily from their mothers, young children protested intensely. If the mother was available, the toddler's angry wailing brought her running to comfort and protect the child. We have all seen this played out in real life between toddlers and their parents. We know that anger "works" to bring about reunions in this example.

Can anger work the same way in divorce? Absolutely. Anger in divorce can draw exes nearer by getting their attention, prompting responses, and essentially keeping a more intimate, emotional relationship between former partners.

Huh? This can be confusing because, after all, hate is the opposite of love, right? Wrong. As the hit song says and many of us can attest, there is actually a thin line between love and hate. The true opposite of love is something else entirely: indifference. Your intense anger does not tell you that you are done with your divorce. It tells you that you are all *but* done.

If you don't believe this, think about the fourth-grade boy who "hates" girls so much that he spends all his time chasing them; the confused teenager in search of autonomy who "hates" his parents for trying to control him; or how much time and emotional energy you may be spending on "hating" your ex. Think about how different you will feel when, one day, your ex telephones and instead of sending you into a rage, it takes you a few seconds to recognize his voice. The opposite of love is indifference.

It is understandably difficult for most people to admit that they feel compelled to somehow hold on to the person from whom they are getting divorced. How could you ever tell your mother or your best friend that despite everything you have said and done, somewhere inside, you still want him or her in your life? Most people cannot. But you must recognize the emotions that lie beneath the surface of your anger and your ex's.

Children in the Middle

Despite all the problems divorce brings, by far the most serious is parental emotional anger. Why? Because besides the direct disruption to your life and your children's emotional well-being, emotional anger can cause trouble in other ways. In my studies of couples engaged in unresolved custody disputes, I have found that many people contest custody not so much to fight for greater access to their children but as a way of contesting and, in an odd way putting off, the end of their marriage.

Illogical as it might seem at first blush, even disputes that seem to arise out of a need to get back at at an ex may have at their core a need to simply get back—to the person, to the marriage, to a way of life, to a degree of certainty that divorce has blown away.

The fact is that until you have processed all the emotions of divorce, anger will serve the many cover-up functions that nature designed it to. Even irrational anger makes emotional sense. And no one ever said "emotional sense" made sense.

Even the most well-intentioned parents find their emotional anger focused on matters that relate to their kids. Because children are often the one thing in the family that both parents feel so strongly about—and the main thing that ties former partners together after a separation—they can become the focus of conflict and even court proceedings beyond the divorce itself. One parent may punish the other by making a child unavailable or late for visitation; another might launch a custody battle to get back at the ex, as Frank considered doing when Danielle decided to leave, and as Cindy eventually did once she realized Scott was serious about leaving. It is essential to understand that even though real concerns about children are a part of these battles, the deeper, underlying force driving these actions is often unresolved grief, or grief that gets stuck in an early, intense phase.

Living Through the Grief of Divorce

Kids today have a flip expression for dealing with difficult emotions and situations: "Get over it!" But there are some experiences—and divorce surely is one—we can never get over completely. Nor should we. We learn to cope with grief, and we learn to move on, but it would be misleading to say that we ever fully recover from it. As long as our minds remember the love and our hearts can feel it, we have the potential to grieve for years, even decades. To recover completely would mean relinquishing the longing for the happiness and stability destroyed when you lose something you love. To recover completely would mean forgetting the good things as well as the bad.

Despite the prevalence of divorce, even the people who care the most about you and your child may be at a loss for what to say or ways to support you in your grief, regardless of their best intentions. Unfortunately, for many divorced families "support" from others consists of family and friends' taking the side of one parent against the other. Too often, the profound loss and heartbreak are not acknowledged. Too often, we do not recognize our own grief—or our children's—for what it is. Recognizing and consciously working through this grief brings about the ability to process it and move on. The passage of time alone is not enough to smooth the ride, and people who ignore their grief often find themselves—and their children—stuck. This is not like a storm that eventually passes on its own. Getting in touch with and resolving these powerful emotions is hard work, but it is work that must be done.

Grieving Alone

In divorce, many things are lost, and there is often plenty to be legitimately angry about, too. After all, if you cannot be angry when your marriage is wrecked, your children are being divided, your finances are a shambles, and your future plans are destroyed, when can you be? If you cannot mourn the loss of the family home, less time with your children, a reduced standard of living for all of you, a loss of security in the future, when can you?

And that is just what goes on on the outside. What about the deeply personal pain of betrayal or rejection? The sadness over a relationship once bright with promise and hope now lost? The intense self-doubt that often accompanies divorce? The stress that comes with change—even "positive" change—when it feels as if *everything* is in flux and *nothing* will ever be the same again.

Grief and anger are powerful, complex emotions. They are most intense around the time of separation, but they may persist and recur over time. Grief and anger are both natural, appropriate responses to divorce. The challenge of coping with them is that each family member has his perspective on the divorce. This means that every family member will grieve the losses important to her, and that each will grieve differently, about different things, and even at different times.

Danielle may wistfully mourn her lost hopes and dreams; she may even yearn for the happiness she and Frank once had. But while Danielle is reflecting on the past with a mixture of emotions, Frank is fighting for his emotional life. He is struggling not to drown in the turbulent fury of betrayal, the bottomless devastation of a lost marriage, or to be pulled down by the weight of the fear of losing his son, the one person he loves as much as Danielle does. Because we grieve what is meaningful to *us*, it is sometimes hard to appreciate and to support others in their grief, or to get the support from others that we may desperately want.

The Leaver and the Left

If support is so hard to find, why can't former partners support each other through their grief? The answer is because they are likely to be grieving different losses. Think about Danielle and Frank. How can her grief be relatively cool emotionally while his grief is sizzling hot? Is

the difference simply a matter of personality? Perhaps personality accounts for part of the difference, but in my experience, personality explains only a small part of couples' differences in grieving near the
time of the separation. To use a term embraced by young people, a
much bigger factor is who got "dumped."

Who got dumped certainly made a huge difference in how Scott and
Cindy grieved. Scott clearly was sad and riddled with unacknowledged
guilt, but he had been thinking about—and in some ways preparing
for—a separation for years. Though his legal divorce was at least a year
or two away, he had emotionally divorced Cindy years before.

Perhaps Cindy should have noticed, but she didn't. Like many
spouses who are surprised to learn that their marriage is on shaky
ground, Cindy was not looking for divorce on her emotional radar. No
wonder Scott's decision, in Cindy's eyes, came without warning. And
beneath her anger, there is no doubt that Cindy was devastated. Had
their roles been reversed in the decision to divorce, so would many of
their feelings.

Your View from the Grief Cycle

How you see the divorce has a lot to do with where you are in that
grief cycle, and where you are depends on your role in the decision to
divorce. Of course, there are couples who mutually agree to separate
(though I admit I have seen just a few of these in my work). Far more
common are one-sided divorces, such as Danielle leaving Frank because of her affair or Scott announcing he was leaving Cindy, his "only
option" after years of suppressed anger.

Danielle and Scott are typical examples of the person I call the
leaver. Who is the leaver? The leaver can be the husband or the wife
(though, statistically, about 60 percent of all U.S. divorces are initi-
ated by women), faithful or not, loving or not, a "good" partner or
not. What gives the leaver the emotional upper hand is a time-tested
advantage: the element of surprise.

What does that mean? It does not mean that they intentionally sought to gain the upper hand or wanted to surprise their partners. Rather, the leaver—Scott or Danielle—has gotten a head start, so to speak, on the grieving process. He has thought through why he wants a divorce, built up a case in his mind about why his decision is right, and probably even carefully considered where the children might live, how the property might be divided, how his life might be afterward. If there is an affair, the leaver has already made a leap into a future— perhaps even what seems a very promising future—without the current spouse.

The leaver possesses something her partner may need a very long time to develop—a vision of the future, a future outside this marriage. At a comfortable pace, the leaver has already begun cycling through the love-anger-sadness of divorce grief and might have reached a point where he is beyond the most dramatic ups and downs of individual emotions. This might have taken him years or perhaps only months, but he has already started distancing himself from the marriage; he has already begun thinking of it as something that once was—not something that is, will be, could be, should be, might be. Like Danielle, the leaver may even feel emotionally distant enough to feel some sadness and tenderness about what is being left behind.

The other partner is the one I call the left. The left are just like the leavers in many ways: They can be husbands or wives, faithful or not, loving or not, good partners or not. The key difference between them is that, emotionally, they have not taken the first step on the divorce cycle of grieving. Even if they have thought about divorce, they are not as ready and as willing to let their marriage go as the leaver is. As we saw with Frank, and also with Cindy, the pure shock of his partner's decision to separate plunged him into a whirlpool of emotion. Being the leavers, Danielle and Scott already had waded into those churning waters one small step at a time, moving ahead as they acclimated to the chill. Frank and Cindy, on the other hand, felt like they'd been pushed from behind into the deep end.

When the left partner comes up for air, she may glimpse the leaver somewhere downstream. He may be swimming hard in some rough water, but he's not gasping for breath. He knows this part of the river pretty well, and he even might have taken a few leisurely laps further downstream and glimpsed what his new life would be like. The leaver does not feel compelled to fight the currents sweeping them both downstream, away from the marriage; it's the direction he's going anyway.

In contrast, the left partner in the whirlpool is likely to be fighting to get back upstream to rescue the marriage, all the while being pulled under by waves of shock, rejection, and denial. When she looks downstream, all she sees are rapids and bends, and she fears what may be waiting beyond them. Partners in this position, like Frank and Cindy, are likely to feel initially that they would do anything to save the marriage.

The leaver and the left are literally in different places in their grief. They will both cycle through the same emotions of love, anger, and sadness, but they will never be in the same place in that cycle at the same time. Inevitably, one will always be more willing to let go and the other more willing to work it out. One will be overwhelmed with sadness while the other is consumed by rage.

The partners' positions can change only when—and if—the leaver realizes that the decision to leave was a mistake and wants to save the marriage. I have never seen a statistic on how often this happens, but in my experience, it is common. It is also common for the left party to have let go of the marriage by this time, so the only benefit of this reversal of roles is the small solace that the left may get from having the emotional upper hand at last.

The Ties That Bind

Divorce between parents may end their marriage, but it does not end their relationship. From the moment the leaving partner begins to consider divorce, the relationship is changed—whether the other partner knows it or not. Even after the couple has separated, they will find themselves bound in yet another way—what I call the push and pull of grief. I have observed that ex-partners can have a profound influence on each other's movement through the grief cycle. The wave of emotion he is riding typically pushes or pulls her along on her own different wave. Invariably, one partner is always at least one step ahead, and the other one step behind. This is, unfortunately, a perfect setup for conflict.

Here is how it works: Since this push-pull relationship occurs at every phase of the cycle, let's pick a spot in the middle. Here we might find Frank, the left partner, experiencing deep sadness. Danielle had asked for the divorce a few weeks earlier. Because of this emotional head start, Danielle has put enough distance between her feelings and the marriage that she is comfortable recalling with fondness what was good about her life with Frank. She sees and talks with him enough in arranging visitation with Sam to know how sad he is, and this makes her feel guilty and responsible (after all, if she hadn't asked for the divorce . . .). She tries to assuage her guilt by being more caring. Danielle is not about to change her mind and she has no interest in saving the marriage, but she makes a point to say a kind word the next time she speaks to Frank; perhaps when she drops off Sam, she asks Frank how he's doing and maybe even pats his arm.

Danielle drives away feeling like a nicer person; Frank walks back into the house with an entirely different—and wrong—impression: He is full of hope. She still cares, he thinks; maybe the marriage isn't really over. Maybe her other relationship *is* over or turning out to be not all she expected. Acting on his thoughts and fantasies, Frank starts to make more and more friendly overtures toward Danielle. Let's talk for a while. Stay and have dinner with Sam and me. Eventually, he may even suggest reconciling.

To Danielle, who did not intend to make the impression she did and probably does not even realize how Frank misread her signals, Frank is doing this only because he's in denial and refusing to accept reality. He's holding up the divorce, Danielle thinks, and she responds by becoming more righteous about her decision and more frustrated and even angry at Frank's unwillingness to move on. Suddenly, she is less patient when speaking with Frank; she stops asking how he's doing; she watches Sam walk from the car and get safely inside the front door after the next visit, but she pointedly avoids talking to Frank.

Now Frank feels not only rejected but also angry and perhaps even betrayed; after all, Danielle did act like she cared, didn't she? The next time he talks with Danielle, he lets her know how hurt and angry he is. Danielle's guilt kicks in again, and she withdraws further, feeling frustrated and sad that they can't find a way to get along. Frank feels more rejection and sadness because of the growing distance between him and Danielle. The cycle begins again.

Like everything else, grief comes in two varieties: his and hers.

Getting Started with Grieving

How can parents get out of their respective his and hers boxes and start to honestly grieve their losses? My prescription: a small dose of reality and a large dose of responsibility; repeat as needed.

One thing all parents must do is acknowledge the losses of divorce and their own role in the end of the marriage. Divorce offers many enticing opportunities to shirk responsibility: blaming the ex, doing "what is best" for the kids, "letting the kids decide," and playing the victim are just a few. Beware these comfy traps and steer clear. If ending the marriage was your decision, own it. Even if you have a file cabinet of evidence against your ex or just a litany of complaints, no one and nothing else made you decide to divorce.

If ending the marriage was your spouse's choice, remember that every marriage involves two people, neither of whom can be blamed for 100 percent of their collective problems. Your ex made mistakes; so did you. Recognize your shortcomings and try to learn from them. Accepting responsibility is a critical first step in embracing your grief and a giant step toward acting responsibly as a parent in the weeks, months, and years ahead.

You must also come to grips with the fact that your divorce is something you will struggle through largely on your own. Your ex probably is neither impervious to your loss nor an emotional basket case who will never move on. Instead, she is probably just in a very different place with her grief, and it's likely to be fruitless to try to get her to feel how you feel.

Your children also are likely to have very strong feelings about the divorce, but their feelings will not be the same as yours, your ex's, or even their siblings'. Remember that in helping your children cope with their emotions, your job is to understand, accept, and support your child in finding his own way of thinking about, processing, and living with the divorce—a way that may be very different from your own. Your children need you to take care of them. It is not their job to take care of you. If you need a backup, call on your family, your friends, your therapist, your lawyer. Don't call on your ex, and certainly not your kids.

A Final Thought

You may be thinking, If only this divorce could be fixed with an easy prescription, I wouldn't need a book (or a lawyer, or a therapist, or my best friend). Obviously, divorce is not that simple. Filling and taking and refilling my "prescription" demands a lot more than just wanting to do the right thing. Divorce is fraught with emotional distractions and opportunities for everyone to swerve off course. You are allowed to be human. You are allowed to make mistakes. There is no right, or perfect, or, in some people's minds, good divorce. Making your divorce work is going to be up to you. Only parents have the power and the motivation—their children's happiness—to create a better divorce.

CHAPTER TWO

Separate Spheres:
How to Keep Your Emotions
from Running Your Divorce

A s you cope with the realities of separation and divorce (and you may be reading this before crossing those bridges), you may feel like ranting and crying and never letting anyone forget that you have been hurt. When you have children, however, the game of divorce is different and so are the rules. This breakup is not going to follow the same course as others you might have had. You will not have the opportunities to indulge your grief or anger that partners without children have. You cannot refuse to see or talk to your ex for a week, a month, a year, forever. You cannot change your phone number, leave town, or pretend that your marriage never happened. Whether you are the leaver or the left, emotionally on your feet or under the table, as long as someone calls you Mom or Dad, you are on duty.

A Different Kind of Breakup

When you are ending your marital relationship, it is common to wish that you could end your parenting relationship, too—or to wish that your children had a different mother or father. You might resent the psychological presence of your ex, even when he is not physically present. You might get frustrated by the amount of thought that goes into carefully wording questions you ask your children about their time with Dad or Mom.

Difficult as it may be to accept, it is important to remember that families in divorce are still families. Although we tend to think of the tasks of divorce in terms of adjustments in living situations, financial circumstances, and children's access to parents (particularly the parent they don't live with most of the time), the most important challenge every family member faces is not ending their relationships but renegotiating them and redefining them. This includes renegotiating one relationship you probably would prefer to end: your coparenting relationship with your ex.

As you read about building a new relationship with your ex, you may be thinking "This makes sense, but . . ." "But we tried to get along better to save the marriage. Obviously, that didn't work." Or maybe "But we have pressing things to work out, like where are the children going to live? I don't have the time or the inclination to be friends. Not now." Or perhaps "But he's a jerk. I don't want to have anything to do with him!"

These are understandable hesitations, but let me add a "but" of my own: But your children are in the middle. They have no other choice, no other position to occupy. You may not be able to make this a completely comfortable position for your children, but you can make it a less difficult one.

Perhaps you—or your ex-spouse, whom you may not feel comfortable having a lot of contact with right now—are under the impression that to have a successful coparenting relationship, you two must be friends. Maybe the fact is that right now you simply cannot be. You might find yourself thinking that your current relationship with your ex—which can range from ambivalent to openly hostile—is one more thing on your list of ways in which you are failing your child.

Stop. You do not need to be friends. The truth is, parents can find a relationship style that allows them to work cooperatively together without being friends, if they choose not to be.

The first order of business is negotiating a *working* relationship with your ex, or at least setting the groundwork. Just because your new relationship with your children's other parent is being built on the shaky foundation of a failed marriage does not mean that it cannot be an effective working relationship. The three key elements for building a sound coparenting partnership are:

> Understanding Your Personal Emotions
> Managing Parental Anger
> Setting Boundaries

Understanding Your Personal Emotions

We have already explored how and why most separated partners literally cannot understand how the other could possibly feel, say, or do what he or she does. When you and your ex are out of sync, actions are easily misinterpreted. As we saw before, when Danielle is extra nice to Frank, he reads this as a signal for hope in the relationship. Yet she cannot imagine where he got the idea—again—that she would even consider getting back together. She certainly wasn't thinking about it. How can he be in so much denial? How can he be so irrational?

For his part, Frank cannot conceive of why Danielle would be so unusually nice to him if she didn't still love him. He doesn't know about the guilt she feels over his sadness; she doesn't understand how vulnerable he is nor does she appreciate his inability to interpret her actions any other way. All either of them knows is what each sees. To her, he's just clinging, holding on, trying to make her feel guiltier than she does already. To him, she is manipulative, rejecting, and cruel. No wonder the next time they have to talk about who gets Sam over spring vacation, the conversation ends up being about everything but.

Emotional Dynamics

Conflicting emotions are inevitable in divorce. You and your ex are both going to be overcome by feelings at times, and one thing you can count on is that your emotions are not going to be in sync with your ex's. How can parents go on about their job of being parents in the midst of this turmoil? Are you supposed to shut down? Be super-human?

No. The goal for parents is not to become emotional robots. Actually, the goal is pretty much the opposite. Separated parents need to recognize their own emotions and accept that their ex is also likely to feel strongly about the divorce—and very differently. By understanding your own emotional dynamics—and the dynamics between you and your ex—you will be in a far better position to do what you must do for your children: Embrace the truth and complexity of your feelings while at the same time resisting the urge to act on your emotional impulses.

Think about Danielle and Frank again. Frank was honest enough—with himself and with Danielle—to be able to say that he wanted to hurt her and that his first impulse was to do so by taking Sam from her. However, Frank was also mature enough, responsible, and parent enough to realize his emotionally driven motives conflicted with what was best for Sam. Because he recognized and managed his anger, Frank was able to pull back.

Contrast this with Cindy's reactions to Scott: One moment she was pleading with him to come back and the next threatening to make him pay for leaving. Cindy's feelings weren't wrong. In fact, they were much like Scott's. When we are hurt, our natural impulse is to hurt back. Cindy's mistake (and Scott's, too) was failing to understand her feelings, and without understanding, her feelings controlled her instead of the other way around. The real victims of Cindy's and Scott's unchecked anger were not each other but their children. While it may feel adaptive to you, parental anger is *not* adaptive for children.

Harnessing Your Anger

While you are dealing with the emotions that lie behind it, you will simply need to harness your anger. Your anger isn't just going to go away. For the reasons outlined in chapter 1, your anger is serving you too well as a buffer against grief. Unfortunately, your anger isn't serving your children well. Here are some guidelines on managing it I use with my clients:

- Resolve not to get sucked into his or her games. Pride yourself on recognizing the bait as bait. This is far better than biting and then cursing yourself later when you feel the hook.
- Refuse to fight with your ex. It really does take two to fight, and if you can keep your cool, he'll burn out sooner or later. After all, much of his anger is about trying to get a reaction out of you. No reaction? He'll keep trying even harder, pushing the old buttons. But if you don't respond, sooner or later he'll quit—usually when it seems as if he'll never give up.
- Keep your distance physically and emotionally. If you have to, limit contact to a few pleasant or businesslike words. Talk on the phone only by appointment, only briefly, and only about the kids. Keep e-mail and other written communication to no more than four sentences, and *never* use e-mail or letters to vent. Your ex will reread them and brood for days, and your in-box will be full of venomous replies.
- Pick your battles. You aren't giving in; you're just refusing to fight. If it's something really important, you'll talk, you'll negotiate, you'll hold your ground, but you will not fight. Not fighting is how *you* win. More important, though, not fighting is how your children win, big time.
- Around the kids, say nothing if you can't say something positive. Practice that noncommittal, inscrutable Mona Lisa smile. Use that same look with acquaintances and friends, except the couple of really good ones. The others will try to bait you, too. People like a good fight and a good story to tell, as long as it doesn't involve them directly. Smile "that smile" and let them find their gossip elsewhere.
- Face—and embrace—your hurt, your fears, your grief. On the team of emotions, anger is a utility player: It performs its role, but

it also acts out on behalf of its less demonstrative, less vocal team-mates. Work with the whole team. You don't have to *tell* your ex that you're feeling sad, lonely, longing, or afraid. But you can tell yourself you feel that way. Or a really good friend. Or a therapist. Or even just write about your deeper feelings in a journal. Acknowledging the feelings will hurt, but in this case, feeling the hurt is the first step to healing.

- Spend some time looking inward at how *you* can learn from all of this pain, not just at how you have been wronged. In a year, maybe two, you don't want to still be stuck on "he's a bastard" or "she's a bitch." Learn about *your* mistakes, *your* failings, the things *you* can correct.

- Try to find or make a place in your heart for the good stuff—the happy memories, including the children you made together—and also for the sadness at what you have lost, what might have been but isn't. Sadness may not feel good, but it's real and in that sense it's good stuff, too.

The Crucial Work of Setting Boundaries

A big step toward managing your strained relationship with your ex involves setting new boundaries. Boundaries are the rules of relationships. As borders define the geographical boundaries between nations, so emotional boundaries set the parameters of each individual's psychological territory.

We establish interpersonal boundaries over time, over the course of repeated interactions. We may explicitly define a few rules ("I'd rather not discuss my father's death" or "Don't ask me that!"), but typically others learn where our boundaries lie not by what we say but by what we do. Most of us do not need to be told that it is okay to share a confidence with a sibling, a friend, or a spouse, but not the postman, a co-worker, or the boss.

Of course, couples negotiate far more complex, subtle, and meaningful boundaries across the various roles they play individually (spouse, parent) and together (married couple, Mom and Dad). Though couples negotiate some of these rules through direct discussion, more often these boundaries evolve with the relationship.

Without ever discussing it, partners know when and if the other would welcome and reciprocate physical affection and when he would not; when it is okay to share news of your latest problems at work and when it is not; when a complaint is likely to be received as constructive and when it will be perceived as criticism. Partners who are attuned to each other know from a simple glance or a tone of voice that the other needs some space, some quiet, a hug. Together, all of these little rules define your boundaries as individuals in your relationship as well as the boundaries of your relationship as a couple.

On the next level, you form boundaries around yourselves as a twosome. These boundaries help define how the two of you relate to others. For example, as a couple you may have boundaries regarding which holidays you spend with extended family and which you share as a nuclear family. You have boundaries for friends and co-workers, too, which are expressed in terms of when and how you spend time with them, what you share with them. Are friends welcome to drop in unexpectedly whenever they're in the neighborhood? Can co-workers phone at 10:00 P.M. with work-related questions? Do you tell your hairdresser all about your spouse's big mistake on the job, for which he might be fired? Probably not.

Good parents also draw boundaries around themselves as coparents. For example, you may disagree with your spouse about discipline, but the boundaries of your relationship dictate that your children will not be privy to these discussions. Together you present a united front, even if one of you does not entirely agree.

The important thing to remember about boundaries is that they seem to develop all on their own. When couples separate, the boundaries shift and sometimes crumble. Suddenly your most personal secrets as a couple are being shared with friends, family members, lawyers, therapists, mediators, and others. Overnight, you, your ex, or the two of you together have dropped your guard on the parenting front, and your children are seeing and hearing more than you want.

We dot every *i* and cross every *t* in spelling out the boundaries of our relationships with our employer or employees, our landlord or tenant, our teacher or our student. Yet we fail to give much conscious thought to where we draw our personal boundaries or why. They just seem to happen, and so we are often surprised to find that we must consciously redraw the borders between ourselves and someone with whom we might have had the fewest boundaries before.

Boundaries Prevent Confusion

Boundaries let people know where they stand in a relationship—where in your life they may enter and where they may not. A huge problem for families in separation and divorce is that no one—not the parents, not the kids—knows where the new boundaries begin and end. Former spouses have a particularly difficult time with this. They are no longer lovers (usually), but does that mean they cannot work toward reconciliation? Be friends? Enemies? Who knows?

Though this dilemma falls squarely under the heading of adult problems, inconsistency in the parents' relationship (screaming at each other one day, talking about reconciling the next) and uncertain boundaries can be distressing and confusing for children. You will do much to alleviate your children's stress and help them to adjust to the situation if you and your ex can be clear and consistent about what the situation is.

A More Businesslike Relationship

How can you draw new boundaries around your relationship with your ex? What should those new boundaries be? For many former partners, the most workable option is to go back to the beginning and establish a more businesslike partnership.

In the normal course of relationships, people progress from a formal, businesslike acquaintanceship to a more flexible, involved friendship, to an intimate love relationship. When a relationship ends, it is
essential to recognize that the process is like driving on an uphill one-
way street. When the intimate, romantic relationship ends, you cannot
make a U-turn and speed back to friendship or even polite acquaintanceship. You have to drive to the end of the street, make a right turn,
go around the block, and drive all the way back to the bottom of the
hill—and become polite acquaintances—once again.

All that keeps you and your ex involved now is your joint enter-
prise: your children. They are your "business," and you two are "business partners." Accordingly, your relationship should be businesslike,
which means cooperative, formal, polite, structured, limited, and somewhat impersonal, or at least a lot less personal than it once was. This
may be a saddening thought for some, a maddening thought for others, but ultimately it is the best arrangement since it will serve your
children and give each of you the personal distance you need to deal
with your own emotions. You are not lovers and you are not yet again
friends, if you ever truly will be. You are parenting partners in a brand-
new coparenting relationship, the terms of which you will ultimately
define.

Especially in the early stages of your separation, you will both
struggle to define new boundaries. In that process, expect that you and
your ex will violate each other's new rules for relating. It happens. By
being aware of this transitional stage, you may avoid some of the conflict that arises from misunderstandings after a violation. Unfortunately, I see far too many couples who either do not recognize or refuse
to believe that they need new boundaries. I admit that it may seem
awkward to tell the person with whom you once shared a home and
a family and your most intimate thoughts and dreams that she cannot phone you at work, stop by your new apartment unannounced,
or open the mail that's still being delivered to the family home. Yet
you must.

The Value of Clear and Formal Boundaries

The most cooperative coparenting relationships have very clear rules. They remain cooperative relationships because the parenting partners respect those rules and each other's boundaries. Once you have the rules in place and things are working well, you can introduce more flexibility, but not before. And for some of the more strained relationships, maybe never. After all, remember that even though you and your ex still share your children, you do not share a life. Some things that used to be your business—his work schedule, where she spent her last weekend away sans kids—no longer are.

Even Danielle and Frank, who managed to focus on Sam's needs from the outset of their separation, needed work with setting boundaries. Besides caring for Sam, Danielle and Frank obviously cared for each other but, unfortunately, in different ways. Partly out of guilt but also out of genuine affection, Danielle was concerned about how Frank was doing. Frank genuinely cared about Danielle as a person apart from him, too, but at the same time, he desperately wanted her and his marriage back.

Danielle and Frank spent a lot of time talking about their feelings, both because of their good intentions and because of Danielle's guilt and Frank's desperation. At first, it was healthy for them to do some grieving together but as time passed, their concerns for each other got confusing. They would cry together and end up in a loving embrace, one that Frank interpreted as sexual but that Danielle did not intend that way. Frank's attempts to act on his interpretation naturally collided with Danielle's intentions. Not surprisingly, this provoked new hurt, anger, rejection, and guilt.

The solution for them was to follow the plan I outlined earlier. They had to go back to the beginning and form a more businesslike parenting partnership with its clearer and more distant boundaries. Danielle didn't get what she wanted—friendship; Frank didn't get what he wanted—intimacy. Instead, they went back to a relationship that worked for both of them and for Sam: a cooperative parenting partnership with clear rules, expectations, and boundaries.

Understanding the Two Basic Types of Boundaries

We draw boundaries around many different things—our clothes, our friendships, our bodies, our money, our bathroom habits, our thoughts. No matter what they may seem to be about on the surface, all of our boundaries protect just two things: love or power (or both). We set up rules about things we want to control (the checkbook, the social life, the way clothes are arranged in our own drawers), and we set up boundaries around the people we care about. These boundaries let everyone know how much physical affection is acceptable, what personal topics can be discussed, who gets more or less of our time and attention. When people get into conflicts over boundaries, sometimes it's about love; sometimes it's about power; sometimes it's about both. At a deeper level, boundary conflicts are either power struggles or intimacy struggles.

A classic intimacy struggle: She wants him to call whenever he's going to be late from work not because she worries but because she wants to know that he cares enough to call. A classic power struggle: He forgets or doesn't have time to call because he doesn't want to feel controlled by her. To her it's about love; to him it's about power. The key to understanding these boundary conflicts is to look closely not so much at what your ex is doing that is upsetting you but what the conflict may really be about: power or intimacy.

Unfortunately, divorce provides fertile ground for old—or new—power and intimacy conflicts to take root. He wants to stop by to see the kids without notice instead of being controlled by a schedule. This is clearly about power: the power to decide when he will see his children. She wants him to stick to their plan; they're no longer husband and wife and he's invading her space. Here we have a classic intimacy issue. He wants both of them to do a few things together with the kids, to still have a little fun as a family. She wants him to take responsibility for figuring out how to entertain the children on his own.

The solution to these kinds of boundary conflicts usually is to follow the advice I prescribed: Establish a more businesslike relationship. When you both respect the rules, you avoid these problems. If he does not show up unannounced, it's one less opportunity for her to feel that he is invading her privacy. Does this solve all of the problems of divorce? No. But it goes a long way to prevent the creation of additional points of conflict and complications.

For more intense and intractable conflicts, some more detailed analysis may be necessary. If one or both of you repeatedly ignore a more formal, structured protocol and conflicts keep erupting, you need to look at what may be driving this behavior: a bid for love, for power, or for both.

Understand Your Divorce: Your Renegotiated Relationship

People negotiate and renegotiate all kinds of relationships. Every divorce is different, but in my research and experience they each tend to fall into one of three general categories: angry, distant, or cooperative. Your divorce might not match every item under a particular category, but it will probably fall more surely under one than either of the other two.

The Cooperative Divorce

These divorces are ideal but, unfortunately, rare, at least in the beginning. Cooperative divorces generally involve parents like Danielle and Frank, who understand children and empathize with their feelings and who also accept their responsibilities as parents. They have done a good job of protecting children from marital conflict. These parents have learned to stifle their anger and to save their arguments until after the children go to bed or are out of the house.

Parents who have a cooperative divorce are not unemotional or without passion. What's different is that prior to separating, they have usually worked out a lot of their emotions, tempered their passions, and resolved much of their grief, perhaps separately, perhaps together. Prior to the cooperative divorce, couples try to work things out, either to save the marriage or to smooth the upcoming divorce, often with professional help. Parents in the cooperative divorce are grieving their lost marriage and understanding their emotions for what they are. They do not pick up the phone to tearfully reminisce with the ex when they feel sad, nor do they become verbally abusive when they are feeling anger.

If you are in a cooperative divorce, you and your ex have been able to put aside your differences and work hard to be there for your children at birthdays and recitals, holidays, and other family-centered occasions. Even in the midst of occasions that many divorced couples find stressful, you and your ex could be happy individually because you respect the one thing you will always have in common: your love for your children. Because of this, you may or may not be friends, but you have good communication and you present a united front on the major parenting issues.

The Distant Divorce

Parents in distant divorces also keep their marital conflict pretty well hidden from their children, but there often is more to hide. Many parents with a distant divorce are extremely hurt and angry or frustrated and resentful, and the distance keeps their rumbling volcanoes from erupting. Like cooperative divorcers, distant divorcers are child centered and competent parents. In fact, it may be their commitment to their children that keeps them from going to war. The distance enables them to deal with coparenting following the pain of an affair, an ugly separation, or simply the mismatch between two people who once managed to be lovers but were never friends in marriage.

Distant divorcers are definitely not friends, but they avoid becoming enemies—or have learned the painful lesson that distance is far better than fighting. In some cases, distant divorcers are not marked by controlled anger as much as they are by a gradual lack of caring and a growing indifference to each other.

Like cooperative divorcing couples, distant divorcers feel the pain and control their anger, but they do it for different reasons. Often parents with a distance divorce have done less emotional work before separating than people with a cooperative divorce. For this reason, they look back in bitterness, not sadness. They are more resigned to the situation than sorry about it. For these couples, close cooperation may seem—and in fact may be—an unrealistic goal. Instead, they resist the temptation to undermine each other and instead focus on the needs of their children.

Parents in distant divorces must identify the most important tasks of divorce ahead (for example, telling the children, negotiating custody, living with visitation, and so on) and make a real effort to ensure that they can cooperate on these, if on nothing else. Like roommates who don't like each other but find a way to share space, distant divorcers stay out of each other's way. They deal with each other minimally, without much anger or warmth, and keep their focus on their own goals. Distant divorcers feel tied together by necessity or accident, not by choice. But to their credit, they find a way to give each other enough space so that they can make things work for their children.

The Angry Divorce

Couples in angry divorces, like Cindy and Scott, feel rage and pain vividly, have trouble letting go of the marriage (strange as that may sound), and may be so enmeshed in conflict that emotionally they are as involved in each other's lives as they were when they were together. In many angry divorces, there is a good reason why the parents are so embroiled. Everything is new and raw. Maybe the angry divorce happened only recently after an affair was discovered or violence erupted.

Or maybe the partners in an angry divorce just never dealt with real emotions in their marriage and ran away instead—this time for good. Or maybe one or both of the partners has a serious emotional or personality problem—they are narcissistic, manipulative, chronically depressed, or emotionally unavailable.

Parents in angry divorces have perhaps the hardest time because their relationships are the most volatile and the most potentially toxic to children. Rather than having—or being—parenting partners who can put aside feelings for the sake of the children, some exes will not let their partners—and in the worst cases, their children—forget how angry, hurt, and upset they are.

If you are in an angry divorce, your feelings are still married to your ex's. You still think that your feelings are your ex's fault or maybe that your ex's feelings are your responsibility. Your emotions are probably being strongly influenced by your ex because anger draws people together and conflict is difficult to ignore.

If you are a parent in an angry divorce, set your sights on working toward a distant divorce. You can begin by disengaging, refusing to play your part in this game, swallowing a little more of your ex's poison, and resisting the urge to lash out. Perhaps hardest of all for many parents in this type of relationship is refusing to allow the ex's bad behavior to justify their own. Remember that just as two wrongs do not add up to one right, a second act of bad parental behavior just doubles your—and your children's—difficulties. You can minimize the effects of your ex's bad behavior by simply refusing to follow suit.

No Perfect Divorce

There is no doubt that children would benefit if every couple could achieve a cooperative divorce. However, that is not to say that children whose parents remain distant or angry are doomed. They are not. Part of the process of divorce involves striving and struggling to determine what is best for our children, our families, and us. What worked for your sister and ex-brother-in-law or your neighbor or your own divorced parents may not be the solution for you.

If there is one thing most divorced people come away with it is the realization that they cannot force anyone else to change. If they could not change their ex during their marriage, they should not have to be reminded that they cannot change him after divorce. And certain factors that determine whether your divorce is cooperative, distant, or angry may be completely out of your control. Your ex may be a very hostile, angry person by nature. You may feel safer emotionally and better able to cope and help your kids if you keep your distance. Or you may be keeping your distance from an ex who refuses to believe that it is really over and sees in your terse hello an invitation to become closer again.

Your goal is not to attain the "perfect" divorce (impossible for most people) but to look at the resources and limitations you and your ex bring to this new task and to realistically determine what kind of divorce best describes your own. Divorce comes with a long to-do list. Understanding your divorce will help you focus your energy on the options and decisions that are realistic and doable.

Looking Ahead

You cannot resolve your grief or your anger tomorrow, and perhaps your angry or distant divorce will likely remain so for the foreseeable future. Does this mean you will not be able to help your children? Absolutely not. Remember, divorce takes time. Grief follows a natural course over a year, or two, sometimes more. You have a lot of emotional and practical issues to work out. You have to be patient with yourself, and yes, you have to be patient with your ex—even if you thought not doing so was one of the benefits of divorce.

Why? For your children. You do not need to resolve all of your emotions in a marathon therapy session, nor must you shove them away in some closet forever. In fact, you don't want to do either. You want to do your utmost to keep your understandable emotions as a former partner from undermining your actions and responsibilities as a parent. The first step is not necessarily resolving these emotions and improving your relationship with your ex, but being aware of the role your emotions play in your new coparenting partnership and looking realistically at what your new partnership can be, given who you and your ex are and how you see your divorce.

CHAPTER THREE

Children's Realities: The Truth About Kids and Divorce

Divorce represents a loss for almost everyone it touches. As difficult as it is for parents, at least they have perspective. After all, they've lived longer than children. They've endured setbacks and losses before, and most of them come to divorce with some sense of their ability to cope.

This is not true for children. In fact, for most children, divorce will be the first major crisis of their lives. And as if that were not enough, at the same time divorce turns a child's life upside down, it can also undermine a child's relationship with both of his parents and reduce his contact with at least one of them.

How and the extent to which this happens varies from family to family. Still, most children have to adapt to life in two households, even if parents do a lot of shuttling back and forth to ease the transitions. And most children do miss having both parents together.

Children may not be old enough to fully understand divorce or what it means. However, every child needs to have the sense that even though many things have changed, one remains constant: Mom and Dad can still be counted on to be there, wherever that might be. When children feel secure in that, they can shift the focus of their daily lives back to where it belongs: on being a kid, on their activities, friends, and routines.

Divorced Parents *Can* Give Children
a Childhood (or Take It Away)

Fortunately, despite a divorce, loving—and emotionally insightful—parents *can* give their children a childhood. Children from divorced families will be resilient—as most are—if parents truly understand their children's perspective and honestly act in their children's interests. Resilient children bounce back from the struggles of divorce and do well in school, have friends, and do everything else kids do. Yes, divorce is painful even for resilient children. True, some parents fail to recognize the turmoil bubbling beneath the calm surface of a child who only *looks* resilient. Yet if parents do their job of being parents, children from divorced families actually do get to be the kids they really are.

Danielle and Frank succeeded in putting Sam's needs first and their own emotions second every step of the way, from the incredibly painful moment they first told him they were separating through the challenges of moving out, setting up a schedule for Sam, and learning to live and parent on their own. Because they confronted and dealt with their own emotions, for the most part they had a pretty clear view of how Sam felt and what he needed from them. Being committed to doing the best for Sam was not enough. They both did the hard, sometimes painful work of sorting out Sam's feelings from their own. When life demanded that Mom and Dad be present and accounted for, Danielle's and Frank's own emotions got pushed way down on their personal priority lists.

To Danielle's and Frank's amazement, Sam adjusted rapidly to their separation and to living in two households, as do most children whose parents manage a cooperative divorce. Given all of their sadness, guilt, and feelings of failure, Danielle and Frank couldn't yet feel pride in what they achieved. Given the crosscurrents of emotion, I was proud of all three of them and felt that one day they, too, would rightly feel pride about their own efforts.

Unfortunately, Cindy and Scott's parenting contrasted sharply with Danielle and Frank's. They fought constantly in front of the children in the month before Scott moved out. Where Danielle and Frank had carefully planned and set aside a special time to gently break the news to Sam, neither Cindy nor Scott could be persuaded to sit down with the kids to tell them why they were separating or what would happen once they did. They couldn't agree on what to tell the children about anything—not the reasons for their separation nor the details of a schedule, even a temporary one.

As a result, conflict and uncertainty dominated the children's lives. For months the kids didn't know when they would see Dad, and their few erratic visits with him were comprised of fast food and fast fun. Chaos also ruled the children's life with Mom, who was preoccupied with her own emotions and the brewing legal confrontation. Wherever the children were, with either parent alone or briefly with both together, their parents' rancor pervaded their lives.

Cindy's and Scott's actions—and their damaging effects on their three children—serve as a cautionary reminder about how and why divorce poses a risk for children's emotional health. Only parents can protect their children from situations like this by simply putting the children first—*their* questions, *their* feelings, *their* needs. The words you sometimes feel like saying about your ex, the actions you consider taking to punish each other by limiting access to a child or reneging on other commitments—these must all be weighed carefully in light of what they will mean to your child. In such contests, your child should always come up the winner.

The Truth About Children and Divorce

Experts on divorce tend to fall into one of two camps. There are those who contend that divorce inevitably and invariably devastates children and sets the stage for a lifetime of emotional problems, period. In the other camp are those experts who assert that divorce is one of life's challenges that ultimately has little substantial emotional impact on most children. The truth is much more complex and subtly shaded than either extreme.

The opposing sides in the great divorce debate are both completely right and completely wrong. Many children are pained greatly by divorce, and at the same time most of the same children are resilient. So-called children of divorce are not children "of divorce"—they are children of parents, of families, of communities. They are children first, and no more children of divorce than they are children of any other life stress or trauma.

There is no question that divorce has the *potential* to damage children. However, I worry that we hurt children three times in our approach to divorce:

- First, when we cause them to struggle through the pain and upheaval of their parents' divorce;
- Second, when, usually through sensationalistic media or our own hysteria, we lay the burden of carrying a ticking time bomb on kids by inaccurately trumpeting that even if they *seem* to be doing well, children are inevitably doomed or damaged because of divorce; and
- Third, when we fail to appreciate children's courage and strength in facing their family's turmoil.

Are children different than they might have been had their parents not divorced? Certainly. Are they doomed? Absolutely not.

Every child is unique, and so is each parent in terms of his abilities and his resources. We cannot predict exactly how individual children will cope with divorce, because their experience will be shaped by so many factors over such a long time. However, we can help children when we make decisions based on what we know to be true for most of them. Here are some important things we know about children and divorce:

- Divorce introduces huge changes into the lives of most children: direct involvement in parental conflict, economic hardship, changes in residence and school, and damaged parent-child relationships because of lost contact, lost love, and lost parental authority.
- Divorce is a great loss for most children. The center of their

world—their family—is torn asunder. As a result, children must not only grieve, but they must also search for a new foothold as they grasp for the loss of security they once had in their lives.
- Divorce increases the risk for psychological, social, and academic problems among children. This increased risk is a legitimate concern for children, parents, and the community.
- Divorce is painful. Despite your fervent desire to protect your children, you cannot prevent them from feeling the pain of divorce. No matter how hard you try, no matter how much you sacrifice, no matter what you may want, no matter what you are willing to do, this is going to hurt your children.

Compared with children whose parents stay married, children from divorced families are:

- Twice as likely to see a mental health professional
- Up to twice as likely to have problems managing their behavior
- Perhaps 1.25 to 1.5 times as likely to have problems with depressed moods
- Twice as likely to drop out of high school before graduation
- 1.25 to 1.5 times more likely to get divorced themselves

No question about it: For most children, divorce is bad news. But these facts about divorce do not tell the whole story, and statistics tell us precious little about how your child will fare. Parents should not lose sight of the fact that even in the face of stress, grief, and pain:

- *Most* children from divorced families are not at risk.
- *Most* children from divorced families are resilient, although divorce is incredibly painful for resilient children, too.
- Even after a separation, what you do is the most important determinant of whether your children are at risk or resilient. You are still a parent. You and your children still make a family. You and your children's other parent are still the most important influences in their lives.

Before, during, and after divorce, you can make the decisions, take the actions, and create an emotional environment that will reduce stress, lower risk, and foster your children's resilience. These are my broad conclusions based on more than twenty-five years of work as an academic researcher, clinical psychologist, and mediator, and as a divorced parent. Can I support my conclusions with scientific evidence? Absolutely.

The Risks of Divorce Are Real, but Not the Whole Story

We need to add some important context to the scary statement that "divorce increases children's psychological problems." One essential qualification is that despite the increased risk, the large majority of children from divorced families do *not* suffer from psychological problems. A second is that correlation does not mean causation. Divorce is correlated with more psychological problems among children, but this does not mean that divorce caused all of the problems. In fact, scientific evidence indicates that divorce *cannot* be the cause of at least some of children's emotional problems. The final qualification—and perhaps the most important one—is that what parents do *after* divorce can go a long way to eliminating risk and promoting resilience.

One-Fifth Empty, Four-Fifths Full

Research consistently shows that most children from divorced families do *not* have psychological problems. For example, one major national study, conducted by Nick Zill, Donna Morrison, and Mary Jo Cairo, looked at children between the ages of twelve and twenty-one. It found that 21 percent of those whose parents had divorced had received psychological help. In comparison, 11 percent of children from married families had received psychological help. That's nearly a 100 percent increase between groups. That may alarm you until you realize that a statistic like this taken out of context can be misleading for several reasons.

Why? First, seeing a therapist is not necessarily a bad thing. In fact, it can be a *good* thing. (I certainly think it is.) Second, remember that many children from divorced families are brought to see a therapist as part of a custody proceeding or because one of their *parents* has psychological problems. In other words, the fact that these children saw a mental health professional does not automatically mean they had serious problems. They might have been seeing a mental health professional for reasons that had nothing to do with them personally, or they might have been receiving care that helped prevent a manageable problem from blossoming into something more serious. In a nation where, according to the U.S. surgeon general, less than half of all children and adolescents with serious emotional disturbances ever receive professional care, we need to abandon the stigma we attach to mental health care and view such care as an indication of a situation's being addressed, not a problem itself.

We can get even more perspective just by flipping the numbers. If a child from a married home has an 11 percent chance of seeing a therapist, she has an 89 percent chance of not seeing one. A child from a divorced home who has a 21 percent chance of seeing a therapist has a 79 percent chance of not seeing one. This is not just a case of the glass being half empty or half full. We can and should look at the statistics both ways. When we do that, we see that the glass is 20 percent empty and 80 percent full.

The study from which these figures are derived is typical of research on children and divorce. Study after study shows pretty much the same pattern of results—as I have documented in two scientific books and scores of articles on children and divorce. The best scientific evidence consistently points to the same conclusion: Even though divorce increases the risk of psychological, academic, and social problems for children, *the vast majority of children whose parents divorce are functioning with the same level of competency as are children whose parents are married.*

Divorce disrupts the lives of almost every child it touches. Yet the great majority of children successfully sort through the many challenges they face. We need to recognize children's struggles, but we must also applaud and build on their strengths.

Is Divorce the Cause of Emotional Problems?

Many people are familiar with the expression "Correlation does not mean causation," but the logic behind the catchphrase is easy to forget. It means that even though two factors tend to occur together (they are correlated), one does not necessarily cause the other. This warning holds even—especially—when it seems that one thing *must* have caused the other. When we read headlines such as RESEARCH FINDS CHILDREN FROM DIVORCED FAMILIES NEED MORE PSYCHOLOGICAL HELP, we want to jump to the conclusion that divorce caused the children to need expert help with their emotions.

But our rush to judgment is logically—and factually—incorrect. Indeed, scientists have determined that many of the psychological problems found among children *after* a divorce—about 50 percent of them— actually begin *before* their parents ever separate. These psychological problems among children cannot be consequences of divorce because the children's emotional struggles began before the parents ever separated.

How do these studies work? Scientists first evaluate children from married families at a very young age, and then researchers continue to repeatedly assess the children's mental health throughout the years as the children grow older. During the course of these studies, a large number of the children's parents end up getting divorced. This unfortunate circumstance creates a unique opportunity for scientists. We can compare children's psychological well-being after the divorce with how the children were doing emotionally when their parents were still together. What researchers generally find is that about half of the problems found after divorce actually began when the parents were still together.

Why Does Divorce Create Problems for Children?

When it comes to divorce, we tend to focus on its possible effects—the fallout, the aftermath. That is certainly legitimate, but it overlooks the

history and the fact that many couples, probably most, divorce because of serious problems in their marriage. Those problems do not
suddenly arise the moment a couple decides to separate. In fact, those
problems often lead to the divorce. Children whose parents divorce
are not so much children of divorce as they are children of the myriad
circumstances that lead to divorce. Unfortunately, prior to divorce—
sometimes years earlier—the emotional environment in a family can
become toxic.

My former graduate students Daniel Shaw and Michelle Tuer
Martin and I demonstrated precisely this in some of our research. We
conducted one of the new generation of studies looking at how children and families function *while married* in order to better understand
what happens to them after divorce. Sure enough, problems in parenting and marital and family relationships were common long before
parents ever separated. Troubled family relationships before—and
after—parents separate are responsible for many of children's emotional problems.

The truth is that dozens of scientists have shown that the quality
of parent-child relationships and the conflict between parents—*married or divorced*—are the most important predictors of psychological
problems in children. This is true in married families and in divorced
families. Continued problems in parent-child relationships and ongoing parental conflict largely explain why many children's psychological
problems are exacerbated—or developed for the first time—after
parental separation. Again, however, it would be incorrect to say that
divorce caused them.

To some degree, you can control the amount of conflict between
you and your child's other parent. You might feel justified in being angry and in arguing your point. You may even be right about a particular bone of contention. But the moment you begin considering your
children, as all parents should, that conflict must be controlled. And
that means you have to be in control not of your child and not of
your ex, but of yourself—of your emotions, your words, and your actions.

The Toll of Parental Conflict

Sadly, a long time passed before Scott and Cindy learned this lesson. In the year and a half following their separation, they lost themselves in a series of battles that ostensibly were about the children but really were enactments of their own unresolved feelings within themselves and toward each other.

Before they separated, Cindy and Scott each hired a very aggressive lawyer. They both knew of their respective lawyer's reputation, but they both said they needed the "protection." In reality, though, they used their attorneys to attack each other much more than to defend themselves. Even though the lawyers helped to inflame an already volatile situation, their aggressive tactics were not the cause of Scott and Cindy's problems but a symptom of the couple's ongoing hostilities.

The most vexing legal complications pale in comparison to the challenges parents must meet in dealing with their own emotions and their coparenting relationship. Even parents engaged in legitimate legal disputes must realize that it still is incumbent upon them—and essential for their children's emotional health—to keep kids out of the middle of these *adult* conflicts.

Scott and Cindy faced few real legal complications. Their divorce did not have to become a legal battleground. They were financially secure; neither of them was threatening to move out of the area, neither was involved in an affair. If even one of them had seen clear to put the children first, they would have realized they had many workable options for raising the kids in two households.

Unfortunately, Scott and Cindy did not do this. They made little effort to keep their kids out of the middle of their disputes. The two of them fought openly and regularly in front of the children. Cindy generally let loose with emotional, aggressive, and cutting verbal attacks. Scott countered with passive-aggressive tactics. He was full of rage, too, but he vented his anger indirectly through his sullen, uncooperative, and unyielding attitude toward Cindy. In ways that were subtle, and in ways that were anything but, Scott and Cindy pulled their children into an emotional undertow that sucked them all under.

While Scott and Cindy had the power to turn it off with each other—to hang up the phone or dispatch their attorneys to respond on their behalf—for their children, the barrage of their parents' hatred for each other was nonstop. Even when they were alone with the kids, miles from each other, they locked horns in competition to win the children to their side.

"Did you have fun with Dad?" If the kids answered yes, Cindy responded with thinly veiled anger or a look of great disappointment. "Do you miss Mom?" If the kids were lonely, Scott headed to the mall or someplace else for some "fun"; his time with them was designed to make him the more attractive parent.

Cindy's problem wasn't just that she couldn't bring herself to tell the kids she was glad that they had fun with Dad. Lost in her own emotions, she was completely blind to how important their father still was to her children.

Scott was equally lost. Emotionally, he could not fathom why it was normal for the kids to miss their mom, that their longing was not an indicator of his failing as a father and a husband, or that the right thing to do might be to help the kids to telephone their mom for a reassuring chat when they missed her.

How did the children react? Badly, of course, but each responded to the unrelenting anger in his or her own unique way.

Nine-year-old Angela, the resilient one in the eyes of both her parents, showed little outward emotion. Consistent with her personality, she dealt with the turmoil by trying to be helpful. When her parents' fights got nasty, Angela would herd her younger brother and sister out of range by taking them into her room or wherever she might find safety. When Mom's or Dad's temper grew short, she'd help the little kids pick out clothes, pour them bowls of cereal, or do whatever else she could to be helpful.

Angela also took care of her mom and dad. She knew enough to say nothing and stay out of their angry arguments, but she would soothe whomever she was with later by listening to Mom talk about how bad she was feeling or helping out around the house when Dad looked sad and lost.

Seven-year-old Joey's reactions should have smacked his parents in the face (because smacking someone was a common reaction for Joey), but Cindy and Scott clashed vehemently about him. Joey had been diagnosed with ADHD (attention-deficit hyperactivity disorder) a year before Cindy and Scott separated. He had been taking Ritalin, a stimulant medication that helps to manage the behavior problems of children with ADHD, and also had a full behavior management plan in effect at home and at school.

When I first saw them in couples counseling, Cindy and Scott both said the medication and the increased structure at home were helping Joey. But as their marriage came apart, Scott and Cindy disagreed more and more about him. Scott argued that Cindy's hostility was the real cause of most of Joey's problems. And he had some evidence for this because the parents' fighting sent Joey further out of control.

Cindy, who was struggling and often failing to control Joey on her own, disagreed vehemently. She thought that Scott's lax attitude was making Joey worse. Scott said that Joey was fine when he was with him, and as a result, Scott repeatedly "forgot" to give Joey his medication. He said that Joey didn't need the medication at *his* house. Cindy accused Scott of manipulating Joey to score points in a custody battle. Scott countered that his only concern was what was best for Joey. And so it went, on and on.

Colleen, who was five, was the hardest for her parents to read. She was the quiet one in the family, and she grew increasingly quiet and withdrawn as her parents' battles continued. When Mom or Dad got angry or fought with each other, Colleen froze. When one of her parents asked if she was okay, Colleen uttered a quiet "I'm fine" and shut up as tight as a clam. Only Angela saw Colleen cry alone in her room, but even she couldn't get Colleen to open up.

How could Scott and Cindy have failed to see that Colleen was a scared, sad, and confused little girl, and perhaps becoming depressed? How could they have failed to recognize that the *last* thing a boy with ADHD—or any child with a difficult or overly sensitive temperament—needs is to be surrounded by anger and inconsistency? They were, quite simply, blinded by their own emotions. Neither Scott nor Cindy could step back far enough from their own emotions to see what they were doing to the children.

Caretaker Kids: What Resilience Is Not

There is much to say about each of these children. For now, though, I want to focus on something that perhaps isn't so obvious about Cindy and Scott's children, but is critically important: Angela's "resilience." Behavior like hers is *not* what I am talking about when I talk about resilience. This kind of extreme emotional caretaking is developmentally inappropriate and can have long-term consequences on children's mental health.

In the context of divorce, resilience involves letting kids be kids. Resilience does *not* mean turning children into the family caretaker, like what happened to Angela, particularly not making children the caretaker of their parents' conflicts or their parents' distraught emotions. Children in the caretaker role might *look* competent, but this is not resilience. It is anything but. Children who are caretakers are overburdened not so much by extra household tasks but by the developmentally inappropriate responsibility of caring for their parents' uncontrolled emotions.

Stresses like divorce can produce children who grow up too soon, who shoulder—even successfully—responsibilities that are far beyond their years, including responsibilities for their parents. These children may seem to be doing even a better job of coping when, in fact, they are at risk for more subtle emotional problems, especially as they grow older.

We tend to overlook caretaker kids because they seem to be handling it all "so well." They're not crying for Daddy every night, their grades are as high or even higher than they were before, and they seem willing to listen to Mom or Dad rant or cry as the mood suits them. At times, they may seem more like their parents' peer than their child. In fact, this "supercompetence" should be recognized for the warning flag it is—a sign that a child's parents are abdicating too many of their adult responsibilities and not allowing that child to be the child she needs to be.

Resilience is very different than caretaking.

The Resilient Child

- Is still a kid.
- Is basically happy.
- Gets along generally well with friends, teachers, parents, and siblings.
- Does the work expected in school and outside of school.
- Completes reasonable, age-appropriate chores with some grumbling.
- Gets into trouble from time to time.
- Experiences the normal growing-up struggles of children the same age.

The Resilient Child Is NOT

- Above grieving.
- Free from all pain.
- In charge of household and child-care responsibilities that are the parents' domain.
- Responsible for fixing one or both parents' depression, anger, loneliness, or self-doubt.
- Either parent's confidant, ally, or best friend when it comes to the divorce or other adult issues.
- Holding in his or her own feelings in order to protect the feelings of one or both parents or their significant others.
- Unable to express his or her feelings for fear of the consequences.
- Unable to make mistakes out of fear of the trouble they would cause for their parents.
- "Too grown up."

What would happen to Angela if she remained trapped in her care-taker role? I do not have a crystal ball to look into the future, and, frankly, there isn't much research on caretaker kids. Why? Like many parents, psychologists often fail to recognize the burdens associated with the caretaker role.

Still, dozens of Angelas have come to me as young adults and un-burdened themselves about the load they shouldered as children and, too often, are still carrying. (Remember that Angela's angry father, Scott, was a caretaker child himself.) To me, these young adults give voice to—and offer an extremely important caution against—the pres-sures and concerns that little Angelas cannot articulate themselves or really understand.

The Responsible One: A Caretaker Kid Grown Up

A bright, attractive, and engaging twenty-one-year-old college student, Susannah telephoned me for a therapy appointment after one of her roommates told her about a lecture I had given on children and di-vorce. Susannah's parents separated when she, an only child, was five years old. For the next thirteen years, Susannah grew up in a joint physical custody arrangement despite her parents' unremitting hostil-ity toward each another. In the first fifteen minutes of our appoint-ment, Susannah both outlined her experiences in a clear, organized, and articulate manner and dissolved into tears.

"I know I'm the resilient kid you talked about in your lecture," she said. "In fact, Mom and Dad both used that exact word to describe me; 'keep being your resilient self,' they would say." She stopped and a flood of tears followed when I asked, "Why am I getting the feeling that maybe you have been a little *too* resilient?"

Susannah stopped crying after a few minutes and apologized for her tears. "You're totally right," she said, dabbing at her eyes. "I *was*— actually I *am*—too resilient." She cried some more and said, "I really love both of my parents, but I also have a lot of other mixed-up feel-ings about them." She paused. "That's why I came to see you—to finally talk to someone without worrying about making a good impression or thinking about how that person felt."

Both of Susannah's parents were corporate executives. In fact, they both had been rising executives in the same company when they got divorced, and they each refused to leave afterward. After about a year, her mother was promoted ahead of her father, a point that Susannah still heard about from her mother. With this victory under her belt, Susannah's mother felt vindicated and free to leave. She took a job with another large company in the same business. She had made her point.

Fortunately and unfortunately, Susannah was another target of her parents' competition. She said she had no doubt that both of her parents loved her fiercely because they constantly vied for her attention. Yet Susannah was not always reassured by their rivalry.

For as long as she could remember, Susannah spent one week with one parent and the next week with the other parent. If she missed time with one of them, her parents argued and reworked her schedule until they ended up with exactly the same amount of time again. "My father actually kept a spreadsheet, calculating down to the hour how much time I spent with him and then comparing it to how much time I spent with my mother. Isn't that crazy?" she asked.

Susannah hated being in the middle. The more she talked in our first several therapy sessions, the more troubling incidents Susannah remembered. Separate worlds were a given in her life. For example, it became routine for her to say nothing about one parent to the other because every comment led to a quiz or a comparison.

Really big problems arose when her two worlds came together, as they did when—clearly not by coincidence—both of her parents remarried on the same weekend. "Oh, boy. I still can't believe this one," she said. "At seven, I ended up being a flower girl at my father's wedding on Friday night and again at my mother's wedding Saturday afternoon.

"When I think about that, I worry what is going to happen when I graduate from college in a few months. Everyone else I know is looking forward to graduation. All I can do is wonder and worry and feel a knot in my stomach every time I think about it. I mean, this is *my college graduation*. Four years of hard work and great friends. You're supposed to celebrate, right? This is supposed to be *my* big day. But for me, it just means a bunch of anxiety and making another schedule to appease my parents."

As she discussed these various incidents, Susannah said that she was not sure exactly how her parents' actions had affected her. She talked quite freely about being sad and cried easily on many occasions. Yet she clearly was not depressed. Just the opposite. Susannah was upbeat, optimistic, and energetic despite her sad feelings.

Another thing that troubled her was that she had become so uptight and hyperresponsible as a result of her upbringing. She loved being the responsible one, but she dreaded showing her vulnerabilities to her peers, even to close girlfriends or boyfriends. Susannah was great at taking care of other people, but she could not let anyone take care of her.

Anger was yet another problem for Susannah. She denied *ever* feeling angry toward her parents or anyone else. This bothered her because she knew that she must be angry. Her lack of anger—and her lack of passion that somehow seemed connected to this—also had bothered some of her friends. She once overheard a former boyfriend describe her as the "ice queen," a characterization that still upset her two years later.

I agreed with Susannah about almost all of the characterizations of herself. She did have reasons to be angry and sad. She was overly responsible. She did seem to hold herself back a bit, even in therapy. And she was strong—too strong.

At the same time, I also thought that Susannah should be proud of her depth, including her too-well-hidden pain, sadness, and anger. I encouraged her to set a goal—a long-term one—of embracing all of her different feelings. I told her with complete honesty that seeing the "real" Susannah made me like her more, not less.

Was Angela on a similar path as Susannah? I fear that she was. True, caretaker kids could follow a much worse course. Responsibility is hardly a bad quality, and I have seen many former caretaker kids move into successful careers and start their own happy families. However, even though I admire their strength and depth, I mourn the caretaker kids' lost childhood, lost spontaneity, and lost emotional freedom. Susannah could have enjoyed being a kid so much, even a kid from a divorced family. All she needed was for her parents to do a better job of being parents, a better job of being coparents, a better job of dealing with their own complicated feelings. Of course, that's what Angela needed from Cindy and Scott, too.

Trees of Pain in the Forest of Resilience

When it comes to looking objectively at just about anything, the old expression about not seeing the forest for the trees comes to mind. As a parent, your concern is obviously not with the millions of children who together comprise the "forest" of divorce, but one "tree," your child. It is true that for most children, some degree of resilience is the norm. However, we need to remember that even within this forest of resilience, there are trees of pain.

Real resilience means letting kids be kids, but even truly resilient children cannot be protected from the pain of divorce. My daughter Maggie's experience taught me that even for the most resilient children, the pain of divorce never completely ends.

Maggie's Story

In the months and years after my separation, divorce, and eventual remarriage, my daughter Maggie had ongoing questions and concerns not only about the breakup of her mother and me but also about where she fit—and where my love would lie—in the context of my remarriage and her new siblings. Maggie's diary entries from her preadolescent years reflect not only the typical worries about friendship triangles and who dumped whom, but her own thoughts on how to divide and balance her loyalty between two parents, two households, two families, and her fears of losing my love to my new family.

Each new change in our family life challenged Maggie in ways that were a mixture of good and bad. For example, the birth of each of her four younger siblings brought with it a flashback, however brief, of the original pain of her parents' divorce. Maggie experienced anew a paler but no less upsetting reprise of the original hurt with each change in our lives. That such occasions were happy ones for me no doubt made Maggie's feelings even more difficult for her.

In fact, Maggie used her divorce experience as the theme for her college application essay. In it she recalled the anguish we both experienced that day in her sophomore year of high school that she told me she wanted to live primarily with her mother. Prior to that, we had had a joint physical custody arrangement in which Maggie spent Wednesday after school through Saturday evening with me, Saturday evening through Wednesday morning with her mom. The schedule worked well for years, but now with her own increasingly busy schedule, Maggie wanted her stuff in just one place and only one phone number to give to boys who asked. Two years later, in her essay, this is how she described that day:

> I'll be sitting in math class, passing a field hockey ball down the field, driving my car, doing any other normal day-to-day activity. I won't be thinking about my dad, the divorce, or the day that I told him I didn't want to live with him anymore. Still . . . I remember the day vividly, how the wind felt against my face, watching my little brother play with a ball on the lawn, and seeing my dad cry for one of the first times in my life. Feeling the guilt, knowing that it was me who was bringing him to tears. It was something I had to do. A move I had to make if I expected to keep my own sanity, something I needed for my own happiness. . . . I know that moving in with my mom was something I needed to do for me, but at the same time I would like more than anything to be my daddy's girl again.

Even though our family has grown through the divorce, and Maggie has proved to be resilient, I still grieve for her, and for me, when I recall the events, conversations, and intense sadness of that time. Throughout high school, she still had dinner at my house several times a week, but she usually slept at her mother's. Maggie made the difficult decision to have one place to live most of the time, but she always had two "real" homes: Mom's house and Dad's house. She always had, and still has, two parents.

And, as she expressed so eloquently in her essay, Maggie wrestled with making a decision that she knew was best for her but that would prove painful for someone she loved. In that moment, she experienced the grief bound up with guilt that is one of the unavoidable truths of divorce.

Too young perhaps, she learned the hard lesson of the power of love to render us vulnerable to pain. If I did not love her, I would not have been hurt. If she did not love me, her decision would have been far easier to make. In retrospect, it is clear to me that Maggie made the right decision, and my acceptance of it (after much difficult discussion) was the right thing to do. But as families in divorce quickly learn, "right" almost never means "easy."

Children's Pain: Resilient but Not Invulnerable

Until I saw the pain in Maggie's eyes, I admit, most of my scientific research focused on the bouncing back part of resilience, not on the pain caused by the bounce itself.

After recognizing my blind spot, as a scientist I wanted to find an objective way to describe, quantify, and measure the pain Maggie and other children feel about their parents' divorce. I developed, with Lisa Laumann-Billings (a graduate student whose parents had divorced), a new instrument, the Painful Feelings About Divorce Scale, which used a multiple-choice answer format. Respondents choose among six responses, ranging from "strongly disagree" to "strongly agree" or "does not apply" to forty-one statements such as "My friends seem to have happier lives," "I feel doomed to repeat my parents' problems in my own relationships," and "I sometimes feel that people look down on me because my parents are divorced."

One group that we studied contained ninety-nine college students, all of whose parents had divorced years earlier, all of whom were functioning successfully at one of the nation's top universities. Their current high level of functioning in a demanding academic environment was, we felt, a strong indication of their resilience. We also screened our participants on commonly used measures of mental health problems and found that they reported low levels of depressive symptoms and anxiety. However, when we analyzed the study results, we discovered that even the most resilient students reported a significant amount of pain over their parents' divorce. Among our findings:

- 73 percent of young adults believed that they would have been a different person if their parents had not divorced
- 49 percent said that they worried about big events, such as graduations and weddings, when both parents would be present
- 48 percent felt that they had a harder childhood than most people
- 44 percent said that their parents' divorce still caused struggles for them
- 28 percent wondered if their father even loved them

As the father of five children, I was especially bothered by the last finding. Doubting your father's love is not a symptom of any psychological disorder, nor is it an item on a mental health checklist. However, a parent's love is the most valuable and lasting gift a child can receive. Of course, many people grow up just fine in the security of one parent's love, and others grow up successfully with the love of other parent figures or sometimes with little adult love in their lives. But being loved by a parent—ideally, by two parents—is an important end in its own right. Life in many ways is about loving and being loved, and I for one would feel like a failure as a father if my children doubted my devotion to them. They can find me intrusive, but I never want them to find me unloving.

Lisa and I also wanted to be sure that these painful feelings were not simply a reflection of most young people's natural questioning and devaluing of their families as they grow more independent during young adult life. So we recruited another ninety-four students whose biological parents were still married and asked them most of the same questions (though omitting those that pertained directly to divorce).

Of this sample, 14 percent indicated that they believed they had had a harder childhood than other people (compared to 48 percent for the divorced group), and 10 percent wondered whether their father loved them (compared to 28 percent for the divorced group). Of course, we were curious to know what lay behind the pain these students reported, too. If nothing else, their responses indicated that for a significant portion of young adults, emotional pain is part of life—whether their parents divorce or not. However, the findings supported our hunch: Painful memories, feelings, and worries are much more common among young people from divorced families than among those from married families.

The wondering, worry, painful memories, and insecurity these young people reported in our study confirmed what Lisa and I had observed from both our clinical work and our personal experiences. True, pain is not pathology. Grief is not a mental disorder. But it also is true that resilience is not invulnerability. The pain was real, and it lingered. Their resilience grew around that pain, not in the absence of it.

In fact, we suspect—and many social scientists now agree with us—that the difference between resilience and pain explains much of the great divorce debate and should help to resolve it. Scientific researchers like me have generally used objective measures of mental health problems with large groups of children, and these measures lead researchers to highlight the overall mental health of children from divorced families. In contrast, clinical investigators rely on interviews with individual children from divorced families, and they hear reports of painful feelings which lead them to emphasize children's distress. Further, such investigators' findings are skewed because children who are having serious problems coping are overrepresented. At the same time, children who are coping reasonably well tend not to show up in the offices, clinics, and programs from which those investigators draw their data. Again, however, that does not mean that their conclusions may not be valid for particular individuals and that we should not heed their findings. We all need to recognize both the forest and the trees.

The Children's Bill of Rights in Divorce

Divorced parents still must fulfill their responsibilities to their kids, and in my view, children should have rights in divorced families. Here is my Children's Bill of Rights in Divorce. If you can give your children these freedoms, you will have gone a long way toward fulfilling your responsibilities as a parent.

Every child whose parents divorce has:

1. The right to love and be loved by both of her parents without feeling guilt or disapproval.
2. The right to be protected from his parents' anger with each other.
3. The right to be kept out of the middle of his parents' conflict, including the right not to pick sides, carry messages, or hear complaints about the other parent.
4. The right not to have to choose one of her parents over the other.
5. The right not to have to be responsible for the burden of either of her parents' emotional problems.
6. The right to know well in advance about important changes that will affect his life; for example, when one of his parents is going to move or get remarried.
7. The right to reasonable financial support during her childhood and through her college years.
8. The right to have feelings, to express her feelings, and to have both parents listen to how she feels.
9. The right to have a life that is as close as possible to what it would have been if his parents had stayed together.
10. The right to be a kid.

These rights have neither been defined by law nor can they be protected or enforced by anyone but parents. To fully enforce and protect your child's Bill of Rights in Divorce requires your constant vigilance in policing *your* words and actions, *your* unflagging commitment to shouldering the burdens and making the hard choices that insulate your child from the adult issues of divorce. It's a tall order, but your children deserve nothing less.

CHAPTER FOUR

Seasons of Change: The Tasks of Divorce

As you know by now—from this book and from your life—divorce really is a roller coaster of emotions for you, for you and your ex as former partners and as parents, for your children, and for all of you together. The emotions are real, powerful, and at times overwhelming. Despite all this, though, you can't allow yourself to be completely overwhelmed. You have a job to do as a parent, and you have tasks to face as a part of divorce. The tasks are not pleasant, and as we will explore in the following chapters, they can be tricky.

As we move forward to address the tasks of divorce, remember this: Your focus still needs to be on staying in control of your feelings as you confront the social, practical, and legal aspects of divorce. *How you manage or fail to manage your emotions is the most important task of divorce.* How you manage your emotions will make all of the other tasks of divorce far less daunting—or, if you don't, even more complicated—than they may seem right now.

Going Public

Wherever you are on the rough emotional ride, you need to belt yourself in tightly because there is another whole side to divorce: the public side, which means facing the legal, practical, and social aspects of divorce. You have to talk to your children about what's happening, come up with something to tell friends and family members, deal with lawyers and daunting legal issues, devise a schedule for spending time with your children, make some difficult decisions about money, perhaps find a new place to live, maybe look for a new job—while dealing with your ex and your feelings through it all.

Though you might have kept your emotions and your marriage problems pretty much to yourself or between the two of you until now, you may not be able to keep it all under wraps anymore. Your private life is about to go public. You are going to be both the topic of the "news" and the person who writes the press releases.

Actually, it might help to think of yourself as your own press secretary. You may have to respond to false allegations (allegedly made by your ex) and to pointed questions asked by nosy "reporters," people whom you thought were friends but who now seem to be thriving on your tale of misery. The press secretary analogy may be apt because except for letting your hair down with a few people whom you really trust, one of your jobs in the public phase of divorce is protecting your privacy and the privacy of your children. You will need to offer public explanations and answers about your private life, but your declarations don't have to be much more than sound bites, brief stories that will satisfy other people's need to know but won't lead to a feeding frenzy of gossip.

Even if you succeed at keeping what you say aboveboard and discreet, not everyone will always play by the rules. Don't be surprised to read some harsh personal accusations in legal documents or hear unflattering or even untrue things said about you in a court hearing. There your ex—perhaps joined by friends and family members—may utter unbelievable statements about your most private sentiments and actions *under oath*.

Even if you are spared such extreme public embarrassment, you will not avoid some other "routine" but incredibly difficult tasks: looking into your children's eyes as you tell them of your separation; sitting alone at night, when the children are sleeping or with your ex, wondering what in the world to do with yourself; stepping back into a phase of your life you thought was long over: dating.

If this isn't enough, you have to face all of these issues pretty much at one and the same time that you are being jerked side to side and up and down on that emotional roller coaster.

Baby Steps

Even though the size, the number, and the awesome variety of tasks seem daunting, keep this in mind: Divorce does not happen according to a time line or a series of discrete, orderly events. If you commit your energies to speeding through to a final legal settlement, for example, you risk overlooking your children's emotional needs or your own. Rather than taking giant steps toward completing any one task at a time, focus instead on moving forward on several fronts but in baby steps.

What does this mean in practice? In order to be truly prepared to tell your children about your impending separation, you will need to craft an explanation suitable for children, create and agree upon a reasonable but temporary schedule for your kids to spend time with each of you, find a second place for one of you to live, and work out some short-term agreement about money. Each of these tasks has its own list of subtasks and necessary preparations. Where do you start? What are you supposed to do? I lay that out for you in the chapters ahead.

What you do *not* need to do—and what I will urge you not to try to do—is to quickly resolve every challenge posed by any one task of divorce: all of the legal details, all of your children's possible emotional reactions, all of the social fallout of your separation, all of your money problems, and certainly not all of your emotions. Why not? First, it is impossible. Second, you are going to need some time—a year, two years, maybe longer—to truly complete any one task of divorce. (A Yogi Berra warning: It won't be over until it's over, and maybe not even then.) For now, your focus needs to be on taking the small steps in the right direction so that you can take bigger steps down the best path for you and your family in the months ahead.

As we describe the steps you'll be taking, keep in mind that you may not take them in the same order in which they are presented here. Divorce is a dynamic, evolving, highly individual process. Looking back, few couples would agree on the precise point at which their divorce "began." Was it the day he announced his intention to leave? Or the moment years before when she started daydreaming about life without him? That last counseling session? Who knows when the divorce began, and who knows how and when it will all end? You might have already talked with your children; they may be completely in the dark. You might have worked out a schedule easily; you might be locked in a battle over time with your children. You might have decided to keep lawyers out of this as much as possible; you might have just opened the first letter from your ex's attorney. And then, you might have resolved your visitation schedule two years ago, but find you must revisit it and revise it as your children grow older. Wherever you are in the divorce process, you will find guidance in the chapters ahead.

Study the Road Map

I've tried to provide a road map outlining the most difficult, most common tasks of divorce. But keep in mind that this is a map, not a set of directions. You may encounter detours and roadblocks, or smooth passages and shortcuts, where you least expect them. I cannot tell you exactly which way to go because your divorce is, well, your divorce. So while I can't hand you directions to your divorce, I can give you an overview of the three most often traveled "routes": cooperative, distant, and angry. You may choose your route, or circumstances or your ex may do it for you.

Generally speaking, most people will be better off taking the slow and winding route—the more cooperative road. The tour won't be scenic (this is a business trip, not a vacation), but the visibility is good, the curves are wide, and you can brake when you need to for those important side trips—excursions into your own and your children's emotions.

Right now, your emotions may be telling you to get on the expressway. You may want to hurry things up or turn everything over to your lawyer. But I can tell you that this route, if you choose to take it, has low visibility, some slick spots in bad weather, doesn't offer many exits, and is fraught with traffic jams just around the bend. Or you may have the urge to go the opposite direction of your ex, with little interest in traveling to a joint destination of shared parenting. Before you plan your own route, I urge you to study the road map and, when you need to, to ask for directions—from a really good friend, from your therapist, from your mediator, from your lawyer, and, yes, even from your ex. Read about the different tasks, see how different families fared on their divorce journeys, consider new options, and go as slow and steady as you can. Whatever you do, do not let your emotions talk you into letting them behind the wheel. Feelings have a tendency to go in circles.

One warning about reaching the end of your journey: You might not. For many—probably for most—the emotions, obligations, and influence of the divorce remain a presence in their lives long after the final decree is signed. Despite the turmoil of its emotional immediacy, divorce poses major and unavoidable practical obstacles, challenges that you face in the midst of the crisis, but also tasks that might not be fully resolved until that day your youngest child has married and started a family of his own.

How to Manage Your Emotions

You will encounter tasks ahead, and more than anything else, your focus still needs to be on staying in control of your feelings as you confront the social, practical, and legal aspects of divorce. *How you manage or fail to manage your emotions is the most important task of divorce.* How you manage your emotions will make all of the other tasks of divorce far less daunting—or, if you don't, even more complicated—than they may seem right now.

"Fine," you may be saying. "I understand my feelings better. I now realize that I am grieving, that I have to grieve. I'm getting better at recognizing—not always in the moment, but sooner and sooner—when my anger is fueled by underlying feelings like grief, hurt, sadness, or fear." I hope that you also now understand how your ex might be feeling (whether or not you care), and I certainly hope you have a growing appreciation of your children's emotions, how their perspective on divorce differs from both your own and your ex's. I also hope that you now more fully appreciate how and why conflict with your ex is bad for your children.

You also may be saying, "Understanding my feelings and knowing how important it is to keep conflict under control is not the same thing as *doing* it, though. How do I do it?" Good question. How do you keep your understandable anger from polluting the waters of your divorce, the waters your children are swimming in? How do you keep your relationship with your ex from exploding? Follow these two basic rules:

- *Engage your emotions.* Let yourself experience your full range of feelings. Share all of your crazy feelings with a friend or a therapist whom you really trust. Or if nothing else, write about your wildly different, seemingly incompatible feelings in a journal—without a moment's worry about editing yourself as you write.
- *Disengage from your ex.* Establish clear, distant, and formal boundaries in your relationship even if the rules seem silly, artificial, inconvenient, or undesirable. Work on building a businesslike relationship for the sake of your children and let the future decide whether your parenting partnership will grow warmer or stay cool, but remain efficient and effective.

Here's an example of how one couple succeeded in developing a distant, businesslike relationship instead of going to war.

A Distant Divorce: Mapping Out
a Safe and Workable Approach

In the eleventh hour of their divorce, Carlos and Tara came to see me for mediation or family therapy or something; they weren't sure exactly what. By then, they had been separated for about three months and things were going badly for them and their children, fifteen-year-old Carlos Junior and eleven-year-old Isabella. Through their lawyers, the parents had agreed that the children would spend every Thursday night and every other weekend with their father, but neither parent was happy with the schedule. Carlos, a fit and handsome surgeon who carried himself with an air of authority, insisted that he wanted equal time with the children. Tara, an attractive and charming part-time Spanish teacher, countered sarcastically, "You don't spend the time you *do* have with Carlos and Isabella. You change the schedule every time. Is it my fault that you are too busy to spend time with your children?" Carlos looked at Tara coldly for a few moments, then replied in a measured tone that did not completely mask his fury, "Perhaps I would have more time if I wasn't paying your three-thousand-dollar mortgage every month, so that you could keep living in grand style."

Tara took the bait and exploded, "*No!* You will not make me feel bad. You will not take the things from me that I deserve. You will not have your way this time. You have had your way for eighteen years of marriage. You have controlled me. You have controlled our children. You have pulled the strings, but I am not going to dance anymore!"

In response, Carlos half smiled at me and said to Tara in a pleasant but condescending tone, "We will not solve our problems if you talk like this." Not surprisingly, his words failed to soothe Tara. Instead, she succeeded in raising his ire a few moments later when she made a veiled threat about revealing something that obviously caused Carlos great embarrassment. Carlos did not explode, yet I could see him struggling to maintain control as he half shouted, "You will *not* continue to talk to me like this. You will *not* insult me and Dr. Emery in this way."

This was not going to be one of my easier cases. Why would it be? Tara and Carlos had many reasons to be hurt and angry, even though they chose not to share many of them with me. Carlos had moved out of the house after about six months of explosive marital turmoil, turmoil that I guessed stemmed from an affair he was having, although both of them carefully avoided that topic. In fact, they both protected their privacy fiercely, but that mattered little because their bigger problem was right in front of me. Before and since their separation, they raged at each other; in their calmer moments, they just fumed. Although Tara and Carlos lacked the insight or the humility to acknowledge their own anger—Carlos admitted only that he was "frustrated" while Tara insisted that she was finally "asserting" herself—they did admit that their children were caught in their disputes. Carlos Junior aligned himself staunchly with his mother and had become her protector. He was furious with his father for moving out, and the two of them barely spoke. Isabella, who had always been closer to her mother, clearly was working to keep a good relationship with both of her parents. Whether Tara should have or not, she had read Isabella's diary. In it, Isabella confessed her fury at both parents and also her sadness and anxiety about the tension that now filled her life.

Legal tensions further fueled Tara and Carlos's already volatile relationship. Their attorneys had negotiated a short-term schedule for the children, but so far the lawyers had failed to negotiate a complete and final settlement. To move things forward, Tara's lawyer scheduled a trial date, but the earliest available hearing was six months away. When Carlos expressed his frustration at the slow process to his lawyer, she suggested coming to see me. To Carlos's surprise, Tara agreed to come talk with me. To Tara's surprise, Carlos followed through with his suggestion for scheduling an appointment.

Disengaging from Your Ex, Not from Your Children

Couples like Carlos and Tara are not unusual. In fact, they are typical. Divorce might have become a routine part of family life today compared with fifty years ago, but the emotions of divorce remain extraordinary. As we have discussed, people are understandably hurt, angry, and emotionally devastated by divorce. Is it possible for parents like Carlos and Tara to have a cooperative divorce? Probably not right away, maybe never. Is it possible for parents like Carlos and Tara to develop a distant rather than an angry divorce? Absolutely.

How do I know this? Through my research where I randomly assigned couples with an angry divorce—parents who, like Carlos and Tara, had filed a petition for a court hearing—either to continue through court or first to try mediation, to try one more time to work things out on their own out of court. Divorcing couples were divided into one of two groups—those going first to court and those going first to mediation—on the flip of a coin. Literally. What did I find? Twelve years later, *both* parents were far more likely to be involved in their children's lives if the coin came up tails and they went to mediation. Twelve years later, 26 percent of nonresidential parents (those whose children do not live with them most of the time) who mediated saw their children once a week or more compared with 9 percent of parents who stayed in the legal system. (That 9 percent may seem very low, but that's pretty much the national average.) Because it's sometimes hard to see older children in person, I also asked about telephone contact. Of the nonresidential parents who mediated, fully 52 percent talked with their children weekly or more compared with 14 percent who went to court (again on the national average). Finally and most impressive, in comparison to the parents who went to court, the *residential* parents (the parents whose home was their children's primary residence, where they lived most of the time) who mediated indicated that the nonresidential parent remained more involved in virtually every important area of their children's lives over the course of those twelve years.

This evidence lends heartening support to what is perhaps my most basic goal in working with angry parents in circumstances like Tara and Carlos's: to keep them from avoiding conflict with each other by dropping out of each other's lives—and as a result having one parent drop out of his children's lives. Avoiding someone you're mad at is a great way to avoid conflict, unless, like divorced parents, you can't avoid each other.

So how do you avoid conflict without retreating? The alternative to conflict or to avoiding each other is to disengage from each other, to work toward developing a businesslike relationship. In working with Carlos and Tara, I drew a figure illustrating the progression from businesslike relationships to friendships to intimate relationships—and back again all the way to businesslike relationships. It resembled what I describe earlier in this book: a route downhill on a one-way street to intimacy and a trip around the block, back uphill, and another right, to begin again at a more formal, even businesslike relationship. I talked about their importance to Carlos Junior and Isabella, about the need to create clear boundaries in their family relationships, and then instructed them on how to apply the concept in their own relationship.

What were the first rules? Pretty simple, really. If Carlos wanted more time with the children, he first had to show that he could live up to the present schedule. Carlos recognized that clear rules and roles were essential in his work, and this helped him to understand Tara's and his children's need for clear boundaries. So the bottom line about the schedule was: Stick to it religiously; if you have to make a change, give Tara at least a week's notice, take responsibility for finding substitute care for the children if Tara can't accommodate a change, and limit emergency changes to true emergencies—unscheduled surgeries— that would happen sometimes but probably no more than once every couple of months.

We also developed several rules to help Tara establish more businesslike boundaries. For one, when dropping the children off, Tara was not to talk with Carlos about major issues like their divorce negotiations. Instead, she could talk about what the children had packed, upcoming events, illnesses, even the weather, but nothing more serious than that. Tara also agreed to stop making telephone calls to Carlos's home, except for a scheduled call every Sunday night at eight, a call designed to last five minutes, just to check in about the children, the schedule, and other routine issues. Other things—the date of a school play, the results of a soccer match, her worries about either of the children—were to be put into e-mails, *brief* e-mails.

Following these simple rules seemed awkward at first, but soon Carlos and Tara admitted that doing so created a welcome buffer and a sense of relief. Granted, maybe their exchanges were not exactly warm, but that wasn't the goal. The goal was to create an atmosphere in which neither of them had to approach each phone call, meeting, or e-mail wondering what surprise would pop out next. As we will see in later chapters, our initial negotiations started them down a road toward a more distant, businesslike relationship. Their new, distant divorce was not without its problems, but it was far better than the angry divorce that, without guidance, they seemed destined to create. What they came to see—what I hope you can see—is that *how* parents go about resolving problems in divorce is at least as important as *what* the resolution might be.

The Medium Is the Message

In the following chapters, we turn our attention to the specific challenges and opportunities inherent in the most common turning points, or tasks, of divorce. I'm calling them tasks because that is probably the best way to think of them: serious obligations, each with its own particular "how-to" list, deadlines, and checkpoints. You may also notice that I used the word "opportunities," too. That is because each task is a hurdle, but it is also a chance to help your children to maintain or begin to recapture a sense of security, confidence, and trust in you, their family, and the future.

As I told Carlos and Tara, when you approach each of these tasks, you need to pay careful attention to how you go about facing and resolving the conflicts and uncertainties. There is a saying, "The medium is the message," and it means that how you resolve something is as important or more than what you decide. Remember that what you say about, for example, an impending separation and how you go about saying it tells your children not only what will happen in their lives but also what will happen in their relationships with you, their other parent, their siblings, and their family—the family that still is your children's family even though it is being split between two households. The father who moves out suddenly may be trying to send the message to his wife "I'm sick of you and I'm out of here," but he also is sending powerful and hurtful messages he might never have intended to his children: "Dad left without telling me when I would see him, without an explanation, without saying good-bye. Dad left me, too."

How their parents relate is connected in children's minds with who those former partners are, Mom and Dad. This is especially true for children's emotional experience and their understanding of love, relationships, security, and trust. Children in crisis can train a laserlike focus on what really matters. The standard against which they judge your words and deeds is often "If you loved me . . ." When one parent says or does something against the other, we may see it as sending a message to the other parent. In fact, though, children view a parent's behavior as a reflection of the parent's attitude toward them as well, not just their other parent. Even older children who may understand something of their parents' grievances and pain want to believe or expect that a parent's love for a child will form a line of protection around them. Unfortunately, too many children learn that these lines are easily trampled in the heat of divorce. "If they really loved us, they wouldn't have fought for so many years," "How could you just move out like that if you loved your kids?," "He didn't even care enough to pay the child support," "Mom worried more about what her new boyfriend thought than how I felt," and so on are all variations on this far too common theme.

In the chapters to come, I have chosen to focus on talking to children, the basics of legal negotiation strategies, custody and access, co-parenting, and new relationships because these are the universal tasks and potential flash points in the critical relationship between former partners who remain parents. Each poses a new and challenging task in divorce and a new chance to shape or reshape the course of divorce's emotional process. For children particularly, these tasks are linchpins that will define not "divorce" but what divorce means for them, their parents, and their family.

For most children, these turning points mark and define their experience of divorce, not necessarily because children participate in resolving the tasks, but because they experience the consequences of how their parents resolve them and what they decide. Once divorce becomes part of your lives, there is nothing you can do to make it up to your children. However, there is much you can do to ensure that every turning point promotes resilience for your children. This requires not only that you manage your own emotions and make the decisions that are best for your child, but also that you take into account what these moments represent for your child. It demands that you listen with your heart, not just your ears, and that you commit yourself to bearing not only your child's hurt and pain, but also the anger he may feel toward you and the love he should always still have for your ex. Granted, this is a tall order, and to fill it, you need to scout out each bridge long before you or your child has to cross it. These next chapters are about how to cross each bridge without falling off or wanting to burn it once you reach the other side. These chapters are about learning to see these bridges in terms of not only the risks they present but also as points you must cross and can do so in ways that promote— or fail to promote—your children's growth, security, and resilience.

So grab on to the safety bar and take a few deep breaths. In the chapters to come, we are going to face each of the tasks of divorce one at a time, and we're going to outline the steps you need to take to resolve them.

CHAPTER FIVE

Talking to Children About Separation

How can parents tell their children that they are about to separate? That they still will have a mom and a dad but that there will be no more "Mom and Dad"? That the life they have known—the life they believed in, the family they felt safe and secure in—is about to be forever changed?

For some parents, and for some children, separation comes as a relief, a respite from family conflict, turmoil, and perhaps violence. For most parents, though, the prospect of telling their children they are about to separate fills them with remorse, guilt, anxiety, and dread. I felt that way the night I told my daughter, Maggie, that her mother and I were separating.

Maggie's Love of Literature

Even today, that night in 1989 remains one of the most painful memories of my life. I remember every detail. Going to get seven-year-old Maggie from her room upstairs in our two-story brick house. Asking her to come downstairs to the living room to talk with Mom and me about something really sad and important.

Maggie's mother, Jean, and I sat down together and told Maggie of the upcoming separation. Actually, I did almost all the talking. We were unhappy as husband and wife, even though we loved her so, so much as parents, I said. We had been unhappy for quite a while, and we had tried but failed to make things better. Mom didn't want it, but Dad had decided he needed to live somewhere else for a while. He had an apartment. He would show it to her in a few days. Mom and Dad had worked out a schedule so that Maggie would see each of them almost every day. She would have her stuff wherever she was. She would have her friends. Nothing would change about school. And we each agreed that we both loved her more than anything and that that would never, ever change.

I remember telling Maggie that I was no longer happy living with her mother. I remember being careful *not* to tell Maggie that I no longer was in love with her mother. I was afraid Maggie might think my love for her could change, too.

Jean and I were the sort of parents who had done a great job of protecting Maggie from our—mostly my—unhappiness. We shared a deep love for our daughter and worked together in parenting out of joy, not out of a sense of obligation or guilt. One result of our protective parenting was that the news of our impending separation caught Maggie totally by surprise and literally rocked her world.

As incredibly difficult as it was, telling Maggie is not my most painful memory of that night. My most painful memory is the recollection of Maggie's reaction shortly afterward. Her eyes glistened with tears but she did not really cry. She did not ask any questions, although we gave her the opportunity to do so. She did not get mad. Instead, Maggie asked if she could go back to her room, and with our permission, she did.

When I went up to talk with her a few minutes later, I found Maggie reading a chapter book. I had been harping on her about watching less television and reading more. In her uncertainty about what to do with the devastating news, this good, sweet little girl did what she thought she was supposed to do: She read.

That night, Maggie dived into a book. She was trying to cope, trying to be good, and maybe in doing so, hoping to change her life back to what it had been only a few hours before. And Maggie never stopped reading. She read and loved *To Kill a Mockingbird* in fourth grade. By eighth grade, Maggie and her stepmother, Kimberly, were

holding conversations about literature that left me feeling like a for-
eigner seeing American football for the first time. In high school, Maggie's English teachers were her favorites, and she was theirs.

I am awed by Maggie's love and knowledge of literature. But even
today, I cannot help but feel guilt about her passion for books. Was her
passion born of the pain I inflicted that night?

In my heart, I believe that the answer is yes.

A Flawed Script

Even now, I occasionally wonder if I could have done a better job of
talking to Maggie so many years ago. I am sure I could have. Jean and
I could have been less protective, less guilty, when we were still working on the marriage. We could have given Maggie more warning. Long
before that painful night, we could have told Maggie we were having
problems in our marriage but we were trying to work things out. The
night we talked to Maggie, Jean could have said more. I could have
shown more emotion rather than, as always, trying to be too strong.

I could rewrite the script a dozen different ways, and I have done so
in my mind. But every draft is flawed. So let me be clear about talking
to your children: no false hopes. There is no way to do this just right.
You need to spend some time, thought, and emotional energy searching for the right words to say to your children and the right way to say
them. But no matter how you write the script, it will be flawed. There
are no words that can do what you wish they could do—make your
children's pain go away. Still, what you say and how you say it can help
to ease your children's fear, confusion, and anger in the days and
weeks ahead.

Telling Your Children

Talking with your children about your separation is one of the very
first—and most painful—tasks of divorce. Many parents view this

announcement as an admission of failure to the person they believe they have failed the most: their child. Beneath the words "Your father and I have decided to separate" lie layer upon layer of disappointment, not only in your marriage, your ex, or yourself, but in your ability to provide what most parents believe is the basic right of every child: a happy childhood. The announcement of your separation may represent the first time you cannot protect your child through sheer willpower and love.

Because of your worries, you may not only dread talking to your children but you may also seek to avoid it. Yet you can do this, and you must. This critically important task can go a long way toward helping to shape how your child perceives what will come next. It will bear on not only what she thinks or feels about the separation itself, but also about you, your ex, and the other decisions and life changes that will follow.

As you will read in this chapter, how you approach your children depends on a number of factors: your children's ages, the circumstances of the separation, the general tenor of your relationship with your ex, and aspects of the children's future about which you can be reasonably specific and reassuring (e.g., where they will live, when they will see each of you). Your children will benefit if both you and your ex tell them a consistent story, are emotionally present for them, and talk very specifically about how the separation is going to affect their lives, especially their contact with each of you.

Seem like a lot to do? It is. In the vacuum of sure answers, there lurk about a hundred wrong ways to go, and it takes a good deal of emotional discipline and self-awareness to avoid the most common, and potentially devastating, mistakes.

Telling your children you are separating may be your first experience with putting into practice what we talked about in the opening chapters: recognizing and learning how to manage your own emotions, seeing the situation through your child's eyes, and taking actions you will feel a lot better about in two, ten, or twenty years. But trust me: Coping with divorce is a learned skill, like any other. Practice may not make perfect here, but if you can manage to accomplish this first task with a reasonable competence and cool, you will be able to face future issues—those you can anticipate and those you may not—with a degree of confidence and ease that will help not only you but also your children.

Giving Children Some Warning

How much should children know about their parents' marital problems *before* separation is inevitable? One hopes not a lot, because conflict in two-parent families harms children just as much as parental conflict hurts children after divorce. Given that, you might be surprised to learn that parents can do too good a job of protecting children from their unhappiness in their marriage. In fact, some parents do such a good job protecting their children from their own problems that the kids have no inkling that there are any problems until the memorable day when they learn that their parents are separating. Not surprisingly, these children are stunned, greatly distressed, and sometimes even feel betrayed when they discover that life with two of the people they may feel they know better than anyone in the world was not what they believed.

Ignorance can be bliss, but after speaking with many grown-up children who vividly recall the utter shock of realizing that the happy marriage they assumed their parents shared was a front or a sham, I have reached a different conclusion. Children would be better off if their parents prepared them at least a little, if the kids knew that their parents were having some problems, however well controlled.

This is my strong view, and research backs it up. Social scientists have shown that if there was a high degree of conflict in the two-parent family, children fare *better* following a separation in comparison with how they were doing when their parents were together. This is more evidence of the destructive effects of parent conflict on children, and it suggests the optimistic and realistic possibility that a separation can lead to reduced conflict.

But recent studies suggest a new twist on the well-established role of conflict in two-parent families. Scientists have found that when conflict is low in the two-parent family, children have *more* problems following a separation than they did when their parents were together.

This certainly does *not* mean that parents should fight like mad when they are together so that a divorce will be a relief. On the other hand, the finding does imply that some unhappy marriages are good enough from the perspective of children, and perhaps kids in these families would be better off if their parents stayed together. If this strikes you as counterintuitive, remember that children view their parents' marriage differently than parents do.

The research also suggests that for children, a degree of awareness of their parents' problems acts something like an inoculation. For children who have this kind of awareness, the stresses of simply adjusting to the separation are not compounded by what many describe as the unfathomable shock of discovering that your perceptions and beliefs about the two most important people in your world were wrong. If parents can manage to tell children when they are having some serious marriage problems and do so without openly fighting or divulging inappropriate information, it can help to prepare children for the worst. And if the worst never happens, if the parents resolve their problems and stay together, children learn a valuable lesson: Marriage is far from perfect, and one of the most important things about a good relationship is acknowledging your difficulties and finding a way to resolve them as best you can.

A secondary, but no less important, lesson is that a good life for children—a happy childhood—is not necessarily a fairy-tale life. Despite our appropriate attempts to protect our children from the less pleasant aspects of life, we also realize that the difficult moments offer life lessons we all need to learn. Most children have some idea that life is not perfect. Sooner or later, parents have to admit their problems to each other and, yes, to their children. Tempting though it may be to paint a big beaming happy face on this difficult time, resist. The fact is there is no way to get around, ignore, avoid, or distract your child from the fact that his life is changing or is about to change dramatically. Candy coating the situation may buy you some time, but at a high price: your children's trust.

Guilt Leaves No Room for Grief

Anita and Melvin came to see me for some general advice about their impending separation. Anita had rented an apartment and was going to move into it in a few days. They wanted to know what to tell their two girls, Lizzie, age fourteen, and Jenny, age nine, about the separation.

As far as Anita and Melvin knew, the kids thought everything was fine at home, and Anita especially was determined to keep things that way. She was going to make sure that the separation did not disrupt the children's lives in any way. She was even willing to meet their school buses and spend every afternoon with the girls in the family home, a situation that would be both uncomfortable (since Melvin was remaining in the house with the kids) and impractical (since Anita would soon be employed outside of the home). Anita also planned to continue to share many other family activities together with Melvin and the children. Holidays and special events were a given, but Anita also expected the four of them to spend a lot more casual family time together on weekends and at other times.

Anita wanted everything to remain the same, and she dreaded the thought of telling the children about the planned separation. She knew she had to talk to the kids, but she wanted to "keep it light" and Melvin said he agreed with her. Their plan, literally, was to sit the kids down, tell them that Mom was moving out, and then go out to dinner so everyone could, in Melvin's words, "relax and have some fun."

This plan might have worked for Anita and Melvin, who had known about their problems for a long time and who also were racked with guilt and shame. Divorce was unheard of in either of their families, and Anita, who was a traditional stay-at-home mom, had a lot of conflicting emotions about the fact that it was she who decided to end the marriage and she who wanted to move out.

For his part, Melvin worried what his family and friends would think of Anita's moving out. He often wondered if perhaps he should be the one to find a new place, but he loved the comforts of his home. He was also shocked that Anita would seem so comfortable living away from their girls. After all, he had argued many times, girls—especially older girls—need their mother. The prospect of continuing to run his own small advertising business and fill both parental roles—even if Anita was going to be around as much as she wished—frightened Melvin, but he never really could talk about it. After all, he was the man of the house and the father to two daughters he could not help but feel were being abandoned by their mother, no matter how sweet a spin they tried to put on it.

How did Melvin and Anita lock in on such an unrealistic plan? Simple. To their way of thinking, if the children seemed perfectly fine with the separation, Melvin and Anita would not need to feel so . . . terrible and guilty. And as much as they loved their children, Melvin and Anita seemed unaware that keeping it light probably was *not* such a good plan. Even though it had taken the two of them years to come to this decision and months to hash out their plan, neither seemed to recognize that a couple of days' notice before separating was awfully short for the girls, who had not had so much as an inkling that there were problems in the marriage.

Rather than confronting them directly, I asked Melvin and Anita how they would expect their kids to react if one or both of them died. If one of them knew that he or she had only six months to live, when would they tell the children? Both readily agreed that they would want to give their children plenty of time to adjust, so at least several months in advance. How did they think their kids would react? It would be horrible, they said. They were certain that their children would be devastated and conceded that their grief would be a normal, even healthy, reaction. Anita and Melvin said that they would want the kids to move on and resume enjoying their lives before too long, but they certainly would expect them to be upset for a good while.

Of course, exactly the same principles apply to telling children about a separation: It is incredibly hard, it will cause children pain and grief, and it needs to be presented with a fair degree of notice. What could Anita and Melvin have told their children about the problems in their marriage? Maybe something as simple as this:

> We want you to know that Mom and Dad are having some serious problems getting along. We often have been really unhappy in our marriage. These problems are painful and scary for us, so we know it must be painful and scary for you to hear about them now. We are not sure what is going to happen, but you should know that a separation is one thing we are considering. We have not made any decisions yet, and we will tell you right away if we ever decide that separation is our only choice.
>
> Whatever happens, we want you to know that we both love you. You are our kids, and we will always take care of you. You also need to know that we are adults and we can take care of ourselves. Our unhappiness is a grown-up problem, and we will find a way to deal with it. Still, this is a very, very important problem, and we know that our problems affect you, not just us. We want to know how you feel. You can talk with either of us anytime. We will do our best to answer any questions you have.
>
> We are sorry to have to tell you this. That's why we wanted to talk with you now. But whatever happens, you should know that we are always going to be your mom and dad. That will never change.

This conversation does not have to be an hour-long therapy session, especially with younger children. Parents may need only ten minutes for the talk, leaving private time afterward for the kids to let this information sink in and ask questions of either of you individually. The same basic and simple plan applies to talking to children about a separation that is definitely in the works.

When to Tell the Children

What do you do when a separation becomes inevitable? What do you say to your children and when do you tell them? Later in this chapter, you will find detailed scripts on what to say to children of different ages as well as some considerations about how and when to tell younger or older children. As we have just noted, you do want give your children some advance warning about your marriage problems and honestly tell them "maybe" or "I don't know" if they ask if you are going to separate or divorce (unless you know you will not). You also want to promise to tell your children if you reach the decision to separate. But if you decide to separate, do your children need to know right away?

Probably not, for several reasons. For one, you want to give yourself some time to deal with your own feelings about the decision and to plan with your ex about what to say to the children and how to tell them. You also want to make sure this *is* your decision. People usually have a lot of ambivalence about separating, and many parents change their minds—repeatedly.

Most important, perhaps, *before* you talk with your kids, you need to decide quite a few practical arrangements about things like where you will live and when the children will be with each of you. Making these decisions usually takes some time, often a lot longer than parents expect. Finally, you need to remember that children have a far different sense of time than adults. A summer—two and a half months— was an eternity when you were a child, and it still is to your children, even more so to your younger kids. If you tell your children too long before you separate, they might feel trapped in a very uncomfortable situation for a very long time or they may come to believe the separation will never happen.

For these reasons, a month or two is more than enough time for a child of any age to know of an impending separation. In fact, this is probably too much advance warning for children who haven't reached adolescence. For school-age children, a few weeks is likely to be enough time to come to terms with the news, to talk with both of their parents about what is happening, and to get prepared for the practical changes to come. Those preschool age or younger need to know only about a week or two before the separation. Children of this age do not have the cognitive abilities to understand time very well, but they do have the emotional need to know what is going to happen in their lives. So for them, knowing later probably is better than knowing sooner.

What to Say

Once parents muster the courage and resolve to tell their children they are separating, just what are they supposed to say about something so painful, so uncertain, so sad—not only for the children but also for themselves? How do parents frame all of the adult issues—and potentially some very real adult complications—in a way that is both honest and appropriate for children to hear? What do you say? What do you leave out? Today? Tomorrow? Forever?

As much as possible, parents should present a united front to their children, especially when the topic is coming apart. As much as his raw emotions wanted him to do so, Frank realized it would be wrong to tell Sam, "We're getting separated because I just learned that your mother is having an affair." But would it be right to follow Danielle's preference? "Mom and Dad are going to live apart because we haven't been happy living together." This explanation really isn't honest. Or is it? What about all of the unspoken problems in the marriage that led up to Danielle's affair? Should Sam know about these things, too? And even if the parents agree that it is best to leave out all of the R-rated details, should Sam be told that only Danielle wants a separation, a revelation rife with possibilities for vilification of his mother? After all, it is true. But the bigger question is, Would this be fair to Sam? To Frank? To Danielle?

And remember, Danielle and Frank had a pretty cooperative

separation. Imagine the conflict Cindy and Scott faced about the prospect of talking to their children. Exactly why *were* they separating? Because Scott was abandoning his responsibilities as a husband and father? Because Cindy had been cold, cutting, and rejecting for years? Obviously, these are not good explanations to give to five-, seven-, and nine-year-old children, but they do illustrate a common, complicated point. If parents cannot agree between themselves about why they are separating, how can they agree about what to tell the children?

There are still other layers of complications. Parents may not only disagree about the emotions, the grief, and the reasons for the divorce. They also may disagree about what happens next, especially where the children will live and how they will spend time with each parent. As we saw in chapter 3, Cindy and Scott disagreed vehemently about their arrangements for sharing Angela, Joey, and Colleen. As a result, the children found themselves cast into a sea of uncertainty. Surprised and devastated by news of their parents' separation, the children could not even depend on knowing from one day to the next when or whether they would see their father again. Cindy's and Scott's failure to plan ahead and to meet the relatively simple obligation to provide a basic schedule for their children pulled them into the chaos of their parents' conflict—a place where no child belongs.

Keep It Simple

Thinking about, planning, and delivering the news is complicated. However, when you are actually talking to your child, remember this: Keep it simple. Children need simple explanations because they are, whatever their ages, children. Children need and want adult guidance, even when they seem to reject it. This is especially true during times of crisis like divorce. Your explanation should be tailored for *them*, not for you.

These are the basic points you want to keep in mind:

- First and foremost during this time of shock and uncertainty, children desperately need to be reassured that *both* of their parents love them. That is an incredibly important part of this difficult conversation.
- You need to explain why this is happening and how you are feeling and suggest how they might feel, or, more precisely, how they are allowed to feel (which should be however they wish at this point).
- Be honest and accurate, but craft your explanations carefully to be age appropriate for your children. When speaking to your children all together, especially during that first crucial talk, offer one explanation that is suitable for everyone, one that can be understood even by the youngest child.
- Follow up individually and privately with the older children and offer more detailed explanations. When you do, remind the older children that this private conversation is to be kept private. There is a reason why you gave the younger children a more simple explanation. If you do not think your older child will be able to resist repeating the more mature details to younger siblings, then don't provide them. There will be many opportunities to revisit those subjects later.
- Keep in mind that *how* you talk with your children is at least as important as *what* you say. Watch your body language, your tone of voice, and particularly what you are doing and communicating when you are not speaking; for instance, when your ex has the floor if you tell them together or your child asks a question or responds emotionally.
- Keep your explanations brief and straightforward no matter what your child's age. Include only a very limited amount of personal detail, even for older children, including young adults.
- Expect it to take some time for what you say to sink in. Know that there is a difference between your child's intellectual and emotional understanding. Emotional understanding takes more time and ultimately is much more important than intellectual understanding.
- Encourage your children to ask questions now or later, but do not press them for questions now—or try to provide answers for too many unasked questions.

- Be sure to tell your children in as specific terms as possible what is going to happen to them as a result of your decision to separate. Include plenty of who, what, when, where details on the practical implications for your children's life.
- Accept that you have limited control over your children's reactions, no matter how much you tell them or how well you say it.
- Expect that you will be talking about this topic again. Realize that your explanations will become more sophisticated as your children grow older and develop cognitively, socially, and emotionally. Plan for it.

Though this is a big first step, remember that in the long run, what you say will be less important than what you do—the way that you parent and the example that you set for your children in the days, weeks, and years to come.

The Reference Point: Where Do Babies Come From?

How much do children want to know about the details of their parents' lives? Think about the "disgusting!" thought that might have occurred to you as an adolescent: the thought of your parents' having sex. You reflexively purged this thought from your mind—forget about imagining any details—because it was gross; because it was your parents' business, not yours; because you wanted your parents to be parents and not real people.

The same is true about your separation. When it comes to the intimate details of parents' lives, regardless of what some older children and adolescents might say, children want to be treated on a no-need-to-know basis. This applies to most of the reasons behind the problems in your marriage and your divorce.

A good, basic guideline is to talk to your children about your separation in the same level of detail as you would if you were trying to tell them about sex. You do not try to teach a five-year-old girl about reproductive biology. You do not tell a ten-year-old boy details about the pressures, pleasures, and passions of sexuality. You may try to give your fifteen-year-old a more complete understanding not only of reproduction but also of love, sex, decision making, and contraception. Still, you keep the conversation abstract and somewhat superficial. You do not tell a fifteen-year-old—or probably any child, no matter what age—the details of your past and present sex life.

Most parents would consider the guidelines above basic common sense. Unfortunately, for a variety of reasons often related to their own unresolved personal feelings about the divorce, a surprisingly high percentage of parents offer an inappropriate amount of detail—and worse—when talking with their children about their separation and divorce. Although there may be a few exceptions, detailed discussions of matters that were none of your child's business before probably are not his business now. Some parents feel compelled to be honest, and honesty is certainly appropriate. The question, as always, is, How honest should you be? If what you are about to say to your child strays into territory you have never discussed with her before, take that as a signal to stop and reconsider what you are about to say and, equally important, why.

How you should talk with your children and what you should say depends upon a number of things, including how many children you have, how much your children already know, and your children's unique personalities. However, two factors are critical across all situations: your children's ages and the circumstances of your separation.

Talking to Children of Different Ages

Exactly what you should tell your children about the reasons for your separation, and when and how you should talk with them, depends in large part on their age and their level of maturity. There are twelve-year-olds who are more mature emotionally than some sixteen-year-olds. You know your children best.

What follows are examples of what to tell children of different ages. Although each of these scripts reflects the ideal based on my professional experience, I realize that it may not be possible for all parents to offer such a united front, especially in more difficult separations and divorces. Later in the chapter, we consider ways of talking to children under more difficult circumstances while still being sensitive to the children's perspective.

Even if your situation demands some changes in the wording offered here, whatever you say should be measured against these scripts. Whatever the circumstances of your separation, you want to focus on the children's issues and concerns, not your own. You want to tell the children what *they* need to hear, not what *you* want to say. And, again, if you feel compelled to say anything that you know or suspect may be crossing the line, stop, reconsider, and do not move ahead until you are sure that your words serve only one purpose: to help your child.

Infants and Toddlers

Before the age of three, children do not have the cognitive ability to understand what a separation means (or, to refer again to our trusty developmental yardstick, where babies come from). All that children under three years of age can absorb is a very simple explanation like "Mommy and Daddy are going to live in different houses." (This is the equivalent of "Babies come from Mommy's tummy.")

Even simple explanations need to be repeated to very young children. Frequently. The very young child's misunderstanding and questioning is not a sign of some deeper psychological problem. Rather, their questioning just indicates that the child does not understand. It is easy to worry and misunderstand if your three-year-old keeps asking "Why did Daddy move out?" But you need to put this question in perspective. This "why" question is no different—to your child—from the hundreds of other "why" questions he has been asking. The question is much harder for you, of course, but this exchange is not about you; it's about your three-year-old.

Children younger than three years old also cannot grasp the ramifications of a separation for their lives. Very young children really need to experience the changes in order to begin to understand them. Because of their limited cognitive and emotional capacities, infants and toddlers require special schedules for moving between houses, as we discuss in chapter 7. Unlike the schedules for older children, infants and toddlers need a more stable primary home. They also need briefer and more frequent contact with their other parent, so that they will remain (or become) attached to both parents but experience relatively brief times apart from each of them.

Preschoolers (Ages Three to Five)

Preschool children need very concrete explanations about the reasons for the separation and the consequences for their lives. However, preschoolers can begin to understand the explanation, and they can grasp some of its basic implications. Because of this, preschoolers need more detail, but still fairly little and even then it should be limited to information that will help them feel more secure about the impending change. For example:

> Mommy and Daddy have been fighting too much, so we decided that we want to live in separate places. Mommy is going to stay here. Daddy is going to move into a new place. He will take you to see his new house and your new room next week. You are going to live most of the time here with Mommy, but you will live some at Daddy's new house, too. We have worked out a plan so you will never go too long without seeing either Mommy or Daddy.
>
> We also want you to know that you have not done anything wrong. This is not your fault. These are grown-up problems between Mommy and Daddy. We want you to know that we are very sad about this, but Mommy and Daddy can take care of ourselves. We do not want you to try to fix these grown-up problems. That is our job. Most of all, we want you to know that we both love you very much.

An explanation like this is equivalent to telling a preschooler that the baby in Mommy's tummy will be born in a hospital where the big brother or sister will get to see it for the first time. As when a sibling is born, it is important to reassure the preschooler that your love for her will not be diminished by the change in your family, that love does not have to be divided. The explanation also focuses on the practical changes for the preschooler, just as you would want to warn a child of this age that she is going to have to share her room with the new baby or that Mommy and Daddy will be spending time playing with the new baby.

The example is concrete and brief, but even this explanation may be too much for some children, particularly those who are only three or four. You will need to tailor your words specifically to fit your preschooler's age, ability, and personality.

You also will need to "read" your preschooler to make sure that he is understanding you, or to judge if you are telling him too much detail. Look for a blank expression, a lot of squirming, or irrelevant questions like "Can I go outside now?" Again, these are not signs of deeper emotional troubles; they are signals that your preschooler either does not get it or has heard enough for the moment.

Finally, you may want to anticipate your preschooler's emotional reactions, in particular, by including some explanation about the separation's not being the preschooler's fault. Three- to five-year-olds (and many older children) often blame themselves for a separation or divorce because they are egocentric. They think the world revolves around them. Unfortunately, this sometimes means they feel responsible for a separation, especially if they or their behavior have been topics of open conflicts between you and your ex.

You may want to raise the possibility of self-blame now or you may want to wait to see how your preschooler reacts over time. Certainly, self-blame is common, but not every preschooler will come to that conclusion. So you may opt to not present that idea to your child. Again, the "where babies come from" analogy may help you in deciding what to do. Would you try to anticipate your preschooler's jealousy over the new baby? Or would you be more likely to address the problem only if and when it arose?

Whatever you decide to do now, self-blame is a reaction that you should be alert to among preschoolers. The reaction may not be subtle. It could be a burst of tears and a scream, "This is all my fault!" But you may need to ask your child, in a very nonthreatening way, if he understands why you are separating if you want to find out what he believes.

Early School-Age Children (Ages Six to Eight)

Early school-age children have the cognitive capacity to absorb more detailed explanations than preschoolers. Most six- to eight-year-old children understand what the word "divorce" means, and they also probably know some kids from divorced families. As a result, early school-age children are more aware of, and perhaps fearful about, the real or imagined consequences of a separation.

Realistically, six- to eight-year-old children are likely to know that a separation often leads to a divorce. Thus, you need to mention the "d" word, even if you may be reluctant to use it yourself. If you are uncertain, you need to mention divorce only briefly. "We hope that a separation will help us to work things out so that we can get back together. But you should know that we have thought about a divorce. You know what a divorce is, right?"

Although they may have an intellectual understanding of what divorce means, in their fantasies, early school-age children can harbor frightening beliefs about its consequences for them. They may fear that a separation will mean that one or both of their parents will abandon them. Perhaps this is what happened to a friend, was something that they read about in a book or saw in a movie, or maybe the fear merely reflects normal concerns that arise at this age. For example, it is perfectly normal for children this age to develop fears about their parents' death. This is the early school-age child's way of trying to integrate his new, more sophisticated understanding of death into his intellectual and emotional understanding of the world.

Whatever the reasons for your child's exaggerated fears about the meaning and consequences of divorce, in addressing such worries, you do not want to try to give your children an abstract, adult understanding of divorce. Instead, six- to eight-year-old children need some clear explanation about the practical meaning of divorce for their own daily lives as well as for their relationships with each of their parents. You want to explain divorce to your children at an emotional level, not at an intellectual one. Your goal is to reassure your early school-age children that you love them and that you will find a way to manage this new instability in their lives so that they will be safe, secure, and happy.

Besides their practical consequences, a separation and divorce confront early school-age children with an issue relevant to children of all ages, but one that is of particular concern at this age: torn loyalties. Six- to eight-year-olds commonly feel a strong loyalty to both of their parents, even when they are closer to one of them. A separation may make them feel like they have to take sides when they do not want to do so.

To avoid such an unhappy situation, early school-age children may deal with their fears by overcompensating, working very hard *not* to take sides. For example, they may struggle to maintain a perfectly balanced relationship with both you and your ex. This may take the form of always making excuses for you or your ex, feeling the need to always do something (separately) for both of you, or just not being able to express the normal grumbles and complaints that all school-age children voice about their parents.

With these concerns in mind, your explanation about a forthcoming separation to a child this age might include information like:

> You know how Mom and Dad told you that we have been having a lot of problems getting along? Well, we have some sad news for you. Mom and Dad have decided that we just are not happy being married to each other. We have decided that we no longer want to be married to each other. We are sorry to have to tell you this, but we are planning to get a divorce. You know what a divorce is, right? It's like getting unmarried. We both are sad about this, but we think that we will feel better in some ways, too.

We know that you must be sad and scared to hear this news. You may be mad at us, too. However you feel, we want you to be able to talk to us about your feelings.

Anyway, right now you should know that your father is going to move out in two weeks. He has a place even closer to your school than here. He will show his new place to you in a few days. Mom is going to keep living here, at least until the end of the school year. She might look for a new place nearer to your school then, too. So you will still go to the same school, and you will still be able to see your same friends. Plus, you will still see both Mom and Dad almost every day. We have worked out a schedule where you will go to Dad's after school every day, even though you will sleep here most school nights. On weekends, you will be here one weekend with Mom and at Dad's place the next.

We know that these are a lot of changes and that we are telling you an awful lot. We will have time to talk about this more alone in a little while. And we can talk a lot more in the next couple of weeks before Dad moves to his new place. But there is one thing we both want you to understand right now: Mom and Dad both love you very much. And we both want you to know that we want *you* to keep loving your mom and your dad the way you always have, even though we are going to be living in different houses.

Explanations to early school-age children can be longer and more detailed than those offered to preschoolers, but you do not want to give a speech to children of any age. You want this to be a conversation. You want to pause often to give your words time to sink in. You will need to repeat yourself and take turns talking with your ex. You want to encourage or allow your children to ask questions. You want to "use your words," but you also are allowed to show some genuine emotion, particularly sadness, but you want your emotion to be under control. You want your message to be "It's okay to be sad. I'm sad, too, but I can take care of myself, and as best I can, I am going to take care of you, too."

Late School-Age Children (Ages Nine to Twelve)

Late school-age children do not need to be told much more detail than early school-age children. An explanation very similar to the above example generally should suffice as long as it includes one important addition: Nine- to twelve-year-olds will want to know, or they will surmise, who is to blame for the separation. Children of this age typically have developed a strong, and rigid, sense of right and wrong. They are willing to pass judgment on others, particularly their parents. Rather than feeling the torn loyalties of the early school-age child, young people in this age group often are ready to pick sides, typically with the person whom they perceive to be the injured party.

This puts you in a bind if you are the partner who has decided to end the relationship. If you are in this position, I urge you to accept the responsibility in talking with your children. Granted, it is hard to be the bad guy, particularly in your children's eyes. But the alternative may be to play the blame game—where you and your ex try to blame each other for the divorce—and you do not want to drag your children into that divisive, emotionally charged morass.

Besides, nine- to twelve-year-old children are sophisticated. Sooner or later, they will figure out who was responsible for making the decision to separate or whose behavior prompted it. By owning your decision sooner, you will be further along the road toward resolving the issue with your children later.

Accepting responsibility does not mean you have to give the children a lot of personal details. Accepting responsibility may simply involve issuing a clear statement that the separation is something you want but your spouse does not want. "Your father does not want this, but I have given up hope for our marriage. Both people have to be responsible for causing problems in any relationship, but I want to be honest with you. It was my decision that we should separate."

Your clear stand can put you in a difficult position now, but at least you will have put yourself in that position honestly. Though he is unlikely to say so, your ex is likely to appreciate your honesty. Or he may insist that the children know that you were the one who decided to end your marriage. Your hope is that the children will respect your honesty, even if they decidedly do not like your decision.

This is, after all, exactly the same hope we have for children of this age. We want them to be honest with us so we can trust and respect them. We tell them that we expect honesty of them even when (actually, especially when) it will land them in trouble. We usually tell them this as we try to convince them that not being honest in the short run is a morally expensive proposition in the long run. We want them to think beyond the short term.

I am suggesting that you do the same thing. "I want you to know that the separation was my decision, not your father's. I have many reasons why I came to this decision, and most of them concern grown-up problems you don't need to know about. But I did want to tell you this, and to also tell you that one thing Dad and I agree about completely is how much we both love you."

Adolescents (Ages Thirteen to Eighteen)

Adolescents from thirteen to eighteen years old also require a clear explanation about the reasons for the separation and who is responsible for the decision to separate. Contrary to what they might say or what their overall demeanor may suggest, adolescents do *not* need, want, or deserve to be burdened with a lot of details. And even in the rare instances where they do seem eager to hear all the dirt, it is your responsibility as a parent not to provide it. A mature teenager may seem capable of handling this information, but there is a big difference between handling information on a cognitive level (such as what your child probably knows now about sex) and actually experiencing something. This means that other than using more sophisticated language, a parent's explanation to an adolescent does not need to differ much from what they would say to a ten-year-old child. Parents need to maintain the boundary between themselves and their children even when a child is a competent adolescent.

You should be prepared for many possible reactions from your teenager about the news of your separation. Some adolescents show little reaction. Others directly express their relief. More common, teenagers are embarrassed, annoyed, and disgusted about the news. Underneath the flip, angry surface, your adolescent may feel sad and worried, not only for herself, but also for one or both of you, perhaps for younger siblings as well. Still, the main focus of the teenager's reaction is likely to be: How could you do this to me?

Such a reaction can seem incredibly self-focused and obnoxious, but it is a legitimate reaction for children of all ages. When you think about it, what else could they possibly say or think? You need to know that if youngsters this age voted, divorce would lose by a landslide. They know that no matter how valid their parents' reasons for splitting up, divorce *does* disrupt children's lives in many ways. And the potential disruptions can be greater for adolescents because teenagers do have a life. Divorce doesn't just alter their family life, but it may affect their after-school activities, work, relationships with friends, dating, and perhaps even their college plans.

Because they have a life, in talking with adolescents, you need to do more than talk. You also need to listen. You need to seek—and represent—your teenagers' thoughts and feelings about the consequences of the separation for them. In particular, you will want to ensure that your adolescent has a voice as to where she will live, according to what schedule.

We address this topic in more detail in chapter 7, but it is important to be clear about two things now. First, giving your adolescent a voice is not the same as giving your adolescent the authority and responsibility for making this decision. The authority and responsibility remain with you, the parents. This is true even if your decision is to accept and act on your teenager's preferences. Second, because adolescents have their own lives, you need to tell them about an impending separation well in advance. Adolescents need a couple of months, not a couple of weeks, to begin to sort out the practical consequences of your divorce. Of course, sorting out their emotions will take much longer.

Different Scripts for Different Divorces

The circumstances of your separation also are critical to how you talk to your children of different ages and what you say to them. You are likely to follow different scripts if you have a cooperative divorce, a distant divorce, or an angry divorce. In the following sections, we return to these three broad scenarios in considering what to say to your children.

Talking to Children: The Cooperative Divorce

If you have a cooperative divorce, you are the sorts of parents who have done a good job of protecting your children from your marital conflict and unhappiness. For the most part, you have successfully stifled your anger in front of the kids. You saved your arguments until after your children were in bed. Maybe even until you were in the office of your marriage counselor. You and your ex rallied from the depths of your anger and despair not only for your children's birthdays, but also for holidays and other traditionally happy times. Maybe it was easy to be happy at these times, because one of the things that you and your husband or wife have in common—maybe one of the few things—is your love for and joy in your children.

If this is you, like Danielle and Frank, you probably hate the thought of telling your children that you are going to separate. The thought may make you sick. Literally. You may feel like you want to throw up or break down. You do not want to hurt your kids. Maybe the thought of telling your children is so painful that the two of you try, once again, to make things work. You can face the pain yourselves, but you just cannot face your children's pain.

If you can work things out to stay in your marriage, of course that is terrific. But what if you and your ex have tried and tried but failed? You cannot put off talking with the children any longer. What do you do? What do you say?

As we discussed earlier in this chapter, the first thing you need to do—right away—is to give the children some warning. You need to tell your children that you are having serious marital problems. If you have a cooperative divorce, you probably have protected your children well—maybe too well. You will protect them again in the future, but right now, they need to know the painful truth.

When the time comes to tell the children you are separating, you and your ex will want to have a plan about what to say. You will want to talk together with the children, perhaps following one of the scripts outlined earlier. All of the examples I gave earlier in this chapter assume that you have a reasonably cooperative divorce. And whatever words you decide to use, the two of you will want to reassure your children of your shared love of them. You will want to show them in your words and in your tone that the two of you are still working together as parents.

Even though you can cooperate and work together as parents, if you have a cooperative divorce you still should feel comfortable showing your children some of your unhappy emotions. You probably hid most of your feelings from the children until now. You still want to be under control after your separation, but you are human. You do have strong feelings. You are allowed to show some of them at a time like this and, in fact, you probably should.

Your sadness is genuine. Your children should know that you are sad. You can let them see your tears as long as you make it clear that you are still in control of yourself, that you can take care of your own emotions, and—this is especially important—that your children do not need to take care of you. By expressing your feelings but keeping them under control, you can show your children that you are upset but you can and will take care of yourself—and of them.

Expressing your feelings judiciously not only shows your children how you feel; it also shows your children how *they* should feel. By revealing some of your own sadness, you give your children permission to experience (and maybe to reveal) their own feelings. Perhaps, like you, your children have been masking their emotions. Perhaps they have been trying to protect you or protect themselves from their own sadness, anger, and fear.

If you have a cooperative divorce, you will want to present a united parental front in talking with your children together, but you also will want to be available to your children individually afterward. This is true immediately after you tell them your plans to separate and in the days and weeks that follow. The message in your actions is that you and your ex will work together, but as sad as it may be, you are coming apart.

Talking to Children: The Distant Divorce

If you have a distant divorce, you probably have done a pretty good job of keeping your children out of your marital conflicts. Still, you might have struggled at times to contain your hurt, sadness, and anger within yourself and around the children. Or perhaps you have been stuffing your feelings in your distant divorce, because you recognize that you need to keep your children out of the middle. Or maybe you have been swallowing the anger because this is what you have always done. This is what works. Arguing gets you nowhere. Biting your tongue may not solve any problems, you reason, but at least it does not create new ones.

If this is you, your children may not know the details or the seriousness of your marital problems, but they almost certainly know that there are problems. They probably have known this for a long time, possibly longer than you realize. The silent treatment is palpable. Your children can feel the anger and unhappiness between you and their other parent, even if you rarely fight.

Unless they are younger than five or six years old, your children almost certainly have wondered and worried about the possibility that you might divorce. You should not assume they know about your problems. You still need to give them some direct warning about your marital struggles. But you should expect that it may not be a total surprise to your children when you tell them that you two are not happy.

Know that when you announce your separation, your words will come to your children not so much as a surprise but as a confirmation of their worst fears.

Having a distant divorce, you surely are concerned about what to say to your children. You might be just as concerned about what your ex will say. How will you and your ex talk with the children together? Can you avoid a fight? What will you do if he or she says something misleading—or worse—to the children? Do you have to swallow your feelings even when you are telling your children you are separating? For the most part, both you and your ex *do* want to control your feelings, particularly your anger. It is okay to show some of your sadness, and you might even want to talk a little about your hurt and anger. You do not want to withdraw or avoid talking to your children at this important time, but you do not want this difficult occasion to provoke a fight between the two of you, either.

If you have a distant divorce and are facing complications working together with your ex, how can the two of you possibly handle this extremely difficult situation together? The best answer I can offer is that you and your ex need a plan—a very clear, very specific plan—for talking with the children together. You need to agree about what you are going to tell the children and what you are going to keep private. You need to decide who will say what and how it will be said, so that the two of you don't end up contradicting each other in front of the kids. You also need to agree generally about what each of you will say when you talk with the children alone later. Sooner or later, you each will learn what the other has said to the children alone. Work that out now, well in advance. That way, you will avoid some heated conflict down the road, and more important, your children will hear one consistent story from both of you.

If you can agree on a plan, it will be best for you and your children's other parent to talk with them together about the separation. If you cannot agree on a plan, you need to talk with a therapist or a mediator together before you talk with your children. Your conversation with your children should be brief, and it should closely follow the script the two of you work out in advance.

The circumstances of your divorce may cause you to see the earlier examples about how to talk with children of different ages as unrealistically positive. Or they may just not seem genuine. In order to be more comfortable and honest, you may need to tell your children about some of the distance and disagreements between you and your ex. As always, you will want to use your words when you do this. You want to *talk* about your anger and disagreement rather than act it out.

Think about your approach like a rock-and-roll song: Your words are the lyrics and your emotions are the music. You want to tone down the drums and the electric guitar so your children will be able to hear the lyrics, so they can focus on the words you are saying, not the emotions you are saying them with. For example, if you cannot agree on a permanent schedule for sharing time with your children, you might tell a nine-year-old child something like:

Our plan right now is for you to live here with Dad during the school days and to go to Mom's new place on the weekends. But you should know that neither of us is very happy with this schedule. We both want you to be with each of us most of the time.

We are working with someone to help us figure this out, and we will let you know once we agree on a plan. For now, this is a compromise we are going to try. Sometime, after you've had a chance to think about all of this, we would like to know your thoughts. We do not want to pressure you, though. Whatever the schedule is going to be, it will be our decision, not yours. If you have any ideas about what you think you might prefer, we will listen and keep them in mind when we talk. If you just want us to make the decision on our own, that's okay, too. We don't want to put you in the middle, because even though we can't agree about a schedule right now, we both agree one hundred percent about how much we love you and about what a great kid you are.

Obviously, such a statement about your disagreements needs to be presented in a very accepting atmosphere. Otherwise, the children most certainly *will* feel pressured to say something about their preferences.

Your words also will have to be carefully scripted in advance. You need to agree on the details or your attempt to present a united front will backfire. Even something as simple as the consistent use of "we" instead of "I" can be crucially important to your children—and to your ex. Even if you have a distant divorce, you can work together on important issues like this.

Still, cooperation is *not* your main goal if you have a distant divorce. Sure, it would be better if you could cooperate, but right now, cooperation seems unattainable. So instead, most of the time your goal is more modest: to avoid undermining—or being undermined by—your children's other parent. In a distant divorce, you need only to find a way to work together on the really important issues. Telling the children that you are separating certainly is one of these issues. And when working together is difficult, the way to work together is to have a very specific plan worked out in advance, then to stick to it.

Talking to Children: The Angry Divorce

What if you and your husband or wife just cannot seem to sit in the same room together without blowing up? What if all you feel when you are around your ex are overwhelming feelings of rage or hurt? What if you and your ex are so consumed with the immediacy and intensity of all your emotions that you do not know what grief is, because grief requires a degree of acceptance and letting go and you are nowhere close to that? What if you are so embroiled in your conflicts that the idea of moving forward seems foreign or even impossible? If this is where you find yourself, should you and your children's other parent really try to talk with the children together at all?

No, probably not. If you have an angry divorce, the first thing you should do before talking with the children is to look inward—again. And again. Reread the first four chapters of this book and use the information to try to get in touch with some of the hurt, pain, grief, and fear that is likely to be tied up with your anger. See a therapist. Try to find an antidote for the poison of all of your hurt, pain, and rage. Try to find a way to swallow a little more poison from your ex without letting it hurt you. Most important, try to genuinely consider your children's position in all of this mess. Your children probably cannot tell you how they feel. If they can, as in Scott and Cindy's case, you may not be able to hear them. Maybe a therapist or a very close family friend or relative can speak for your children. If they try to, listen. Hear your children's voices even if your children cannot or are too afraid to speak for themselves.

You and your children will be much better off if you can find some perspective, even a little perspective. Your ex may need perspective, too, but you need to focus on what *you* can control: you and, I hope, your children. You have the power to do something right, even when everything seems so wrong in the middle of an angry divorce.

What to Say About an Affair

Here's a tough one. What do you say to your children if your husband or wife has had an affair? What do you say if *you* have had an affair? Affairs often are the immediate precipitants of a separation and the kindling of an angry divorce. This is true even when, like Danielle and Frank, you and your ex disagree about whether the affair was the whole problem or merely a symptom of a longstanding problem in your marriage.

If you were in Frank's shoes, you may be understandably unwilling to tell the children that the reason for your separation is that "Mom and Dad are not happy being married." One problem with this explanation is that it seems dishonest—unless you take the whole history of the marriage into account, and that's far beyond what Sam needs to know, wants to know, or could possibly understand at the age of six. Here's another problem: What if the extramarital relationship is likely to continue? What if, one day, Danielle planned on introducing her lover to Sam as her friend, boyfriend, or future husband?

Danielle certainly was in a bind about what to tell Sam and figuring out what Frank would agree to tell him. But remember, they had a pretty cooperative divorce, and despite the affair, they each harbored some hope that they might eventually be able to save their marriage. As a result, they agreed to tell Sam they were separating because they were having "problems getting along as husband and wife," and Danielle made it clear that she was the one who wanted to separate. (This was critical to Frank.) They agreed to this because of the hope of reconciliation, but they also agreed that if the separation became permanent, Danielle would tell Sam she had fallen in love with someone else. They didn't really expect Sam to understand this at his age, but it was an honest explanation that had Danielle taking responsibility for her actions without dragging Sam into any of the details.

Frank and Danielle's decision about what to tell Sam seemed like a reasonable if imperfect compromise. Remember: There is no perfect script, but there are bad and worse scenarios. What if they had had a truly angry divorce, like Cindy and Scott? The children would have learned about the affair (there wasn't one in their case) like they learned about everything else—from ceaseless volleys of accusations between their parents when they were together or from contradictory and one-sided conversations when they were alone with each of them. As we have seen, some of the effects of divorce on children are subtle, but some of the manipulations parents employ in the service of their own distraught emotions can be anything but.

Obviously, it is extremely difficult to know what to tell children about affairs and especially to agree on what to tell them. Not only is this a huge emotional issue for the parents, but there is also another question: What do the children need to know? Do they really need to know this detail? Perhaps not if the affair has ended, but certainly if the relationship will continue.

So, if the children need to be told, what can parents agree to say that is honest, acceptable to both of them, and does not go into inappropriate detail? Actually, Danielle and Frank came up with a reasonable plan. Perhaps the parent who is having the affair one day needs to tell the children something like:

I need to tell you that a big reason why we are separating is that I have fallen in love with someone else—and I am still in love with her. This is very difficult to tell you. I certainly am not proud of the way that this happened, but I wanted you to hear about this from me. I also wanted to be honest with you in front of your mother. Learning about all of this has been very hard for Mom, and this is part of the reason why we have been fighting so much. I think there are a lot of other reasons, too, but we do not need to go into them now. You can ask me or your mother questions about this or other things alone if you want. But you should know that neither of us thinks that you need to know a lot of details. This really is a grown-up problem. And it is a problem that I am sorry I have created for you.

An admission like this is not likely to solve a lot of problems in an angry divorce but I believe it can be a small step in the right direction. Talking with the children together about this might just be too difficult or impossible in some angry divorces, and in this case, the partner who had the affair would do better talking with the children alone. Still, despite the pain of being present, the other parent might want to make sure their spouse tells the children what they said they would tell them. Hearing the confession may be enough to motivate the hurt parent to follow through with saying little about the affair to the children at this time. And that is what is best because like other problems in marriage, affairs are very much a grown-up problem.

A parent's admission about his affair is likely to be extremely difficult, and the children may well become upset and angry with that parent. As a result, the kids are likely to take their other parent's side. Even children as young as four or five years old will understand that one of their parents has done something wrong to hurt the other parent, and older children, who can understand more of what an affair means, are not likely to forgive easily.

So why tell the children? Honesty. If you have been having an affair, this is a chance to be honest—with the children, with your former partner, with yourself. Why else? Reality. If you have been having an affair, sooner or later your children will learn about it. It is better that they hear about it sooner and from you (not from your less discreet relatives, neighbors, or friends). Any other reasons? Respect. If you have had an affair, you will want to earn back your children's respect, and you cannot begin to do that until you deal with the truth. If you really do hope to start a new life together with your lover, another lesson you will need to learn is patience. If you do not want to divorce your children as well as your spouse, you will need to plan to rebuild your relationship with them as a single parent before you introduce someone new into your life and theirs.

Keeping Kids Out of the Middle

It is a huge struggle to find the right words to say to children in the crisis of separation. Words matter but what you do matters more, and not just on one traumatic day but every day. If you have done a great job of keeping your children out of your conflicts prior to your separation, keep doing it. Though heed one warning: You might be surprised to find that keeping your children out of the middle can be harder to do *after* a separation.

As I discuss in the following chapters, you can expect new and difficult issues to arise about parenting, legalities, money, and new relationships. Because the children are your main point of contact, discussion, and concern with your ex, these new problems can boil over and contaminate a part of your coparenting relationship that has been really strong. So be prepared for some new challenges and maintain your resolve to keep your kids out of the middle, just as you have done in the past.

On the other hand, if you have *not* done a very good job of keeping your children out of your conflicts, now is the time to start doing it right. A separation is incredibly hard on children. Being caught in a war zone is worse. You may not be able to bring a quick end to the war with your ex, but you *can* declare the children to be residing in a demilitarized zone.

Children need and deserve protection from the powerful crosscurrents of their parents' conflict and from the choppy waves of emotion each parent feels separately. Children need and deserve some honest but developmentally appropriate answers about why their parents are separating. Children need and deserve some information about what is going to change in their lives. Children need and deserve some time to come to grips with, to try to understand, this major, unhappy upheaval in their lives. Children need and deserve their parents' understanding and also their love, guidance, and firm, consistent rules. Children need and deserve some space, some separation from all of their parents' stuff.

Helping Children to Grieve

No matter what has been going on around them until now—whether you two were fighting openly and often or you kept your unhappiness neatly under wraps—the news that you will be separating marks your child's first major loss in divorce. The grieving for the life that he or she once knew begins now.

As I have discussed, grief is a primary emotion for *everyone* touched by divorce. That includes your children. Naturally, your first instinct is to protect your child from pain—any pain and every pain, if you could—but that is not possible now. Rather than protect your child from the pain of grief, you want to do everything you can to help your children to grieve.

Note the focus on "help." You cannot *make* an unemotional child grieve nor can you resolve the grief of a distraught child, as much as you wish you could. You also need to recognize that your children may be in an awkward position with you. As a parent, you are likely to be the source of their greatest potential comfort while at the same time, you may be the cause of some of your children's grief—and perhaps a target of some of their anger as a result, since anger is one of the emotions of grief. But there are ways you can help. Here are some essential strategies:

- Minimize your children's losses. Far and away, this is the most important thing you can do. Your child's losses need not parallel your own. Even after a divorce, your child can still have both of his parents, a stable if more complicated life, continuity in schools, friendships, and daily activities, and a continued sense of security. Divorce is a profound loss for your children, but if you can keep their losses to a minimum, you may be surprised how well they cope.

- Allow your children to grieve and to have their own feelings and encourage them to share their feelings with you no matter how they feel. You can and should tell your children that it's okay to feel mad, sad, or wish that things could be the way they used to be. You can and should tell your children that you'd love to listen if they want to talk to you. You can and should tell your children it's okay not to talk if they don't want to, but warn them that you will ask how they are doing from time to time because you worry and you care.

- Help your kids to understand and find words for their feelings. You might do this through conversation, through art projects, or through reading. Many books have been written directly for children of all ages going through divorce and more and more books for children and adolescents—even traditional novels—incorporate divorce, loss, and single parenting into their story lines.

- Share your own feelings as is appropriate. Children look to adults for guidance about how they should feel at times when they are uncertain. Developmental psychologists call this social referencing. You can help your children to know how they should feel by showing them how you feel in limited and appropriate ways. Sadness and longing are two emotions that are healthy for you to share with your children in small doses. The message you want to convey is something like "I feel really sad about this, and it's hard to feel this way. I can take care of myself. It certainly is not your job to take care of me. But I think it's important for you to know that I feel sad and lonely sometimes, too."

Remember: Grief is normal; it is healthy. It hurts you to see your children grieve, but it hurts your children if you do not allow them to have their own painful feelings.

CHAPTER SIX

Keeping Emotions Out
of Legal Negotiations

M ost of us are not comfortable dealing with legal matters, and it is easy to understand why we stress out over a situation that pairs the intimate aspects of our emotional lives with public processes few of us fully understand. Unfortunately, the legal side of divorce cannot be avoided. It looms like a shadow no matter where you are in the process—from the first inkling that you might consider ending your marriage to readjusting a custody arrangement a few years after the final decree.

Because the legal side of divorce may mystify, frighten, or embarrass us, we often are more than willing to hand legal matters over to an attorney. In fact, the first thing friends, families, and even strangers may tell you when they learn you are separating is "Get a good lawyer!" Chances are, you, too, thought about getting a lawyer once you realized that divorce lay ahead. Practically speaking, getting a lawyer is a good idea. It is when we encounter the emotional aspects of divorce that this advice requires further scrutiny and thought.

You already know that unmanaged emotions and parental conflict put the "bad" in bad divorce. What you may not realize is how often "legal issues" may just be your unresolved emotions in disguise. Emotional issues can lead parents to make legal decisions or initiate legal processes that may prove difficult if not impossible to undo. If you and your ex come to a casual verbal agreement and later change your minds, no problem. If, however, you two have handed over responsibility for a key decision such as custody to a judge, later on it can be much harder to readjust your arrangements—or even to discuss them rationally.

Most people will want a divorce lawyer to give them legal advice, review plans and documents they have worked out on their own or with the help of a mediator, to handle complicated legal details, especially regarding financial aspects of divorce. What most people in the early throes of divorce do not fully understand is that no lawyer can solve all of the problems divorce creates for you and your family. No lawyer can heal your hurt, your anger, or your grief. And no lawyer, mediator, psychologist, or judge can tell you what arrangements are going to be best for *your* children.

It is important to understand the crucial difference between seeking advice to help you in the decisions you make and turning over the decision making to someone else. In fact, most good lawyers will tell you exactly this: "You'll be far better off if you can work things out on your own instead of going the legal route"—at least as far as figuring parenting plans, schedules, and decisions about custody. Unfortunately, amid the emotional static, too many parents do not hear or heed that message.

There's a whole array of options that might be best suited for your situation, from "kitchen table" negotiations later reviewed by a lawyer, mediation with a neutral third party, "collaborative" lawyers specially focused on working out agreements without going to court, to traditional lawyers who may take cooperative or extremely adversarial approaches. But before we explore each of these options, let's look at what the impact might be for you and your children in the immediate future and years down the road.

Why You Should Try to Work It Out

In the 1980s, I began studying seventy-one families who were on the verge of going to court in a contest over child custody. Contested custody cases often occur in the angriest of angry divorces, and all of the families in my study had just filed a petition for a court hearing. That meant they had failed to work things out on their own or with the help of lawyers, and they had reached such an unbreachable impasse that they were willing to ask a judge—a total stranger—to decide for them. These mothers and fathers were asking a judge to tell them what to do with their own children.

At this eleventh hour, I asked parents to either join a study of the court (that is, to continue with the legal route but to let me study them) or to try just one more time to resolve their disputes with the help of a neutral third party, a mediator. I assigned families to one group or the other randomly. One of the simplest, most powerful scientific tools, random assignment ensures that what happens either in court or in mediation *causes* any differences I might eventually find between the two groups. Random assignment completely circumvents the real-life complication that couples who are cooperative to begin with might want to mediate while angry couples are ready to fight it out in court. Random assignment assures that cooperative, distant, and angry divorces are equally distributed between the two groups. Couples did not choose what they wanted to do in my study: They were assigned to go to court or to mediation by the flip of a coin.

Using the highest scientific standards in repeated, objective evaluations of these two groups of families, I found that taking control of your own destiny and trying to work things out on your own in mediation led to numerous benefits for children, parents, and families even *twelve years later.* Twelve years after going either into mediation or through the legal process, families who mediated were happier they did what they did. The benefits did not end there. Among the families who mediated, *both* parents were more involved in their children's lives. If their parents mediated, children were far more likely to spend time with the other parent (the one they didn't live with most of the time) and to talk with him or her on the telephone. Specifically, I found that:

- 28 percent of nonresidential parents who mediated saw their children at least once a week twelve years later in comparison with 9 percent of parents who went the legal route.

- In the litigation group, 36 percent of nonresidential parents had *not* seen their children in the last year compared with 16 percent of nonresidential parents who mediated.
- Differences in telephone contact were even greater, an important consideration since many children had left home and many children and parents had moved some distance apart. Among families who mediated, fully 59 percent of nonresidential parents talked to their children weekly or more often compared with just 14 percent of nonresidential parents who litigated.

The increased contact did *not* increase conflict between the parents who mediated. They actually reported less conflict even though they had to deal with each other more. Finally, in comparison with the families who went to court, among the families who mediated, the residential parent said that the nonresidential parent discussed problems with them more and participated more in the children's discipline, grooming, religious training, errands, special events, school and church functions, recreational activities, holidays, and vacations.

Right now, your emotions might sometimes make you wish your children had a different father or that you'd never have to deal with your ex again. But I think that, in their hearts, most parents would agree that the positive outcomes experienced by the families who were assigned to mediation represent the kind of future they would prefer to see for their children. How you negotiate your divorce settlement is going to start you down a path that you will be walking for many, many years.

One more thing: The parents in my study invested very little time up front to reap this benefit many years down the road. They spent an average of only five hours in mediation. In fact, parents randomly assigned to mediation reached agreements in half the time it took to come to a settlement for the families who continued down the legal path. What my study demonstrated and what parents should always remember is that *the legal process can help you to solve your own problems but it can't solve your problems for you*. Whether your family emerges from the legal part of divorce helped or hurt is largely up to you. You cannot blame what happens legally on your ex's problems or your lawyer's bad advice or whatever. In the long run, you have only yourself to blame for how you approach the legal aspects of divorce.

Take the Long View

As you approach the final decision to separate, and ideally before you talk with your kids, think about what you are going to wish you had done when you are sitting at your child's college graduation or some other major milestone event. Picture yourself watching the ceremony with a mixture of relief, sadness, and mostly pride. You let out a sigh, feel your eyes fill with tears, and your heart swells in your chest. Now add your child's other parent to the scene. Is your ex sitting nearby and sharing your pride? Or are the two of you still caught up in the competition, waiting on opposite sides of the stage to see who your kid will hug first? Or is your ex not there at all—long divorced from you and from your kids?

Then think about your child. What would he want on this day? What would you have wanted when you were that age? Perhaps it was something that you did have: two loving parents there beside you. Or maybe your parents were divorced. Painful as it may be for you even now, think about what you would have truly wanted.

Think about how torn up Susannah, whom you met in chapter 3, was about her graduation, and how unfair it was for her parents to still be putting her in the middle. Think about how she was racked with anxiety instead of full of anticipation and pride. Think about whether that's the way you want your children to feel five, ten, or twenty years from now.

You need to also remember that you and your child's other parent are as likely to be brought together again at any moment, without any notice, on occasions that are not so happy. Even the best children from the best homes can encounter difficulties growing up, with school, alcohol, drugs, sex, relationships. It is not pleasant to think about a child's dealing with psychological problems, falling seriously ill, or encountering trouble with the law, the death of a grandparent or a friend, but these things do happen, and in those moments the presence of two parents is even more important.

Finally, and this is the one thing most parents never like to think about, bad things happen to parents, too. Safe in the knowledge that your child is spending most of her time and being raised primarily by you, you may neglect helping your child build a good relationship with your ex. Without even thinking about it, you may be bad-mouthing your ex's new spouse, dismissing your child's new step- or half siblings, or diminishing the importance of the time your child spends with your ex. Stop. Illness, disability, other family crises, or death can happen to anyone at any time. Any one of them could effectively end your ability to parent your child or to retain the same amount of physical or legal custody. Imagine your child suddenly living full time with the ex or the stepparent you have demonized or taught your child, through your example, not to respect.

In approaching legal issues, you should try to work things out fairly and try again. And again. And again—even if things do not work out now, tomorrow, or the next day. That way, even if your ex is not sitting there sharing your pride at your baby's college graduation, you at least will have the solace of knowing that *you* tried. You will know that *you* did the right thing. And so will your child.

Why Your Heart—and Sometimes Your Head— Says, "I'll See You in Court!"

Even parents who believe they have gotten much of the hard emotional work behind them are surprised to feel the hurt, anger, grief, sadness, and, yes, longing raging again when papers are served, the attorney calls, or they have a day in court.

We know that emotions are powerful forces in driving and shaping divorce. However, in the legalities of divorce, parents suddenly find themselves with a new and awesomely powerful tool—an ardent advocate and a new forum for revisiting old issues. Arguing in the bedroom you might have been able to hurt your ex emotionally, but now with the right attorney and the wrong attitude, you can punish your ex in other powerful ways. At a time when we may need to feel right, the thought of winning on a legal point or hearing a judge endorse your side can feel very good, probably too good. For too many parents who have been hurt by divorce, revenge is tempting, and the legal process can be a mighty weapon to that end. But as any judge will tell you, no one wins in a contested divorce, certainly not the children.

Logic and perspective can fall victim to powerful emotions in divorce. For now, the best medicine might be a little reality check. What happens to families, parents, and children in the legal system? Let's revisit our couples to get some general idea. Cindy and Scott's angry divorce differed from Danielle and Frank's cooperative one long before any of them sought out lawyers. We can still learn lessons from their contrasting experiences with the legal part of their divorces.

Danielle and Frank in Mediation

Danielle and Frank each had consulted a lawyer separately before they came to me for mediation just before Christmas a couple of years ago. This was no surprise as I always urge my mediation clients to hire their own, separate lawyers, and most parents do. Many parents, in fact, have a long history with lawyers and litigation, and they seek me out as a mediator only years later—once they have finally learned that legal fights cost an awful lot of money, create tension, and don't give their children what they need: parents who can work together.

Danielle and Frank both were guarded about even admitting that they had seen lawyers, let alone revealing what their lawyers told them. The legal aspects of a separation only added new layers of complexity to the issue of Danielle's affair and to their severely strained relationship. Was their private life about to go public? For obvious reasons,

Danielle didn't want to be cross-examined about her affair in a public courtroom, and she was humiliated by the thought of a lasting legal record of her transgression. In tears, she plaintively asked no one in particular, "Do you think I want Sam to read a transcript about my indiscretions someday?"

Not surprisingly, Frank sympathized very little with Danielle's predicament. His first response to Danielle's question was a sarcastic snort, and then he raged, "Yeah, well, a big part of me *wants* a legal record of your 'indiscretion.' A big part of me *wants* you to suffer the way I'm suffering. I didn't want our marriage to end, and I'd love to be able to tell people why it's really happening—and if they don't believe me, they can check the court record."

What Frank didn't say, but I assume he felt, was that he might feel vindicated, but he would also feel shamed by a public proclamation of this humiliation in his private life. And as Danielle made clear to him in a somewhat veiled statement, she wouldn't be the only one to be humiliated. "Sure, Frank, you could make me look bad, but you know what happened that led up to this, and you know I'd have to testify about that, too."

Divorce and mediation are rife with emotions, and it's never easy. What was remarkable about Danielle and Frank was not how easy it was for them, because it wasn't easy at all. What was remarkable and admirable was their ability to step back from their potent emotions, to get some perspective, and even to admit their shortcomings to each other over several mediation sessions. A few minutes after exchanging threats, they both were on the verge of tears. After a long pause, Frank said, "You know I don't really want to hurt you. I'm just hurt and upset and scared and confused." And Danielle replied simply with a tone that said it all, "Yeah, I know."

I let them cry silently for a moment, then interrupted the pause and asked them what ideas they had for a schedule for Sam. I was careful to point out that I only wanted some initial thoughts and that we'd be spending a lot of time exploring options. Still, Frank immediately went back on the attack. "Well, I'm not about to lose my son just because she wants to end our marriage. I'm not sure what she wants, but one option I'm considering is having Sam live mostly with me—sole custody."

Danielle didn't back down, but she didn't take Frank's emotional bait, either. "That's ridiculous," she said. "You know I've spent a lot more time raising Sam than you have. I'll give you credit. You've been doing a lot with Sam lately, and you're a great dad. Sam needs you, but he needs me, too. What makes you believe I'd even think about letting Sam live with you most of the time?"

This exchange started a long and difficult but productive discussion. The fact that the exchange was productive illustrates a very important point: *Some conflict in divorce not only is inevitable but necessary. The keys to conflict are managing it productively, keeping kids out of the middle, and working to resolve the dispute.*

After much jousting, Frank revealed he didn't really want sole custody of Sam. His real concern was that *Danielle* would want sole custody. Believing this, Frank decided he'd better take a strong bargaining position from the outset, along the lines of the "best defense is a good offense." What Frank really wanted was to make sure that Sam was with him about half the time, joint physical custody. He didn't want to lose his son as well as his marriage, and he truly believed that Sam needed his dad as much as his mom.

To Frank's surprise and great relief, Danielle agreed with him. She said that, as much as she'd miss Sam, this is what she believed was best, too. She thought some sort of joint custody arrangement would be best for Sam and fair to them both. Much to her credit, she also said, "Frank, you know how sorry and ashamed I am about what I have done. But even if things are a mess for us, I don't want to mess up Sam. He's such a cool kid, and you are a great dad. I think I'm a pretty good mom, too. I just want to do whatever we can to not wreck that."

Frank's eyes filled with tears again, and we all spent a few minutes in silence soaking up and trying to cope with the emotion in the room.

All in all, we spent an amazingly productive series of sessions together. (WARNING: Not all mediations move so far, so fast.) Danielle and Frank could have been derailed by their emotions at several points, and they could have been derailed by the legal process. You can guess what might have happened if, instead of recommending mediation, Frank's lawyer had filed for sole custody and Danielle's lawyer had done the same thing.

But as Danielle and Frank admitted toward the end of our first meeting, both of their lawyers had strongly recommended mediation, and they both made it clear that working things out on their own, if they could do it, would be far better than taking the adversarial legal route. As I said before, this is the advice most lawyers give, and it's great legal advice, even if it seems to take matters out of the hands of lawyers.

Cindy and Scott in Court

Cindy and Scott followed a very different path. It was a path of their choosing, but once they were on it, the legal route they chose carried them further and faster down a trail of acrimony that they couldn't seem to turn off, even when they wanted to.

Cindy and Scott each hired divorce lawyers known in the community as hired guns. They were tough, they were out to win for their clients, and win big. The two gunslingers fired their first shots on day one and never seemed to stop. Cindy and Scott worked nothing out on their own—not even a basic temporary arrangement about the kids or managing finances, so Scott moved out without anyone, including the children, knowing when they might see him again. To correct this, Scott's lawyer filed immediately for an emergency child custody hearing. Cindy's lawyer countered by filing (in a different court) for divorce on the grounds of desertion. (Since Scott moved out without a legal agreement, he technically might be viewed as deserting the marriage.)

Each of their lawyers advised Scott and Cindy not to talk with each other during this phase of the legal negotiations, and it was advice they were angry enough to follow. They didn't talk. But how was Scott going to see his children in the two months before the emergency hearing? And how was he supposed to know what was going on with Angela,

Joey, and Colleen if he didn't talk with their mother? I would like to believe that somewhere in their hearts both Cindy and Scott knew that the children were being hurt, but by this time, their anger and their lawyers' aggressive posturing was like a runaway train, smashing everything in its path.

The lawyers exchanged a few threatening letters. Two weeks passed, and Scott still hadn't seen his children. Scott called Cindy repeatedly to demand time with his children, but Cindy ignored him, diverted the conversation by arguing about something else, or just hung up. After another week, through her lawyer Cindy agreed to a brief Sunday afternoon visit—on a one-time-only basis.

In all, Scott saw his children three times for a few hours each time in the first two months following his separation. More important, Angela, Joey, and Colleen saw their dad only three times in the middle of the upheaval of divorce, in the middle of their parents' anger and conflict, in the middle of their own confusion, fear, sadness, and uncertainty. The kids never knew when or whether these visits were going to happen nor did they really understand why Daddy wasn't there.

At the emergency hearing, which lasted an hour and a half, both Cindy and Scott argued that they should have sole custody. In part because the children already were with Mom, the judge awarded temporary sole custody to Cindy and gave Dad visitation every other weekend with the kids. Scott was stunned and furious, but not completely surprised. Within two weeks, his lawyer found a reason to file papers for another court hearing—and on and on it went.

In the year and a half following their separation, Cindy and Scott had five different court hearings, each of which ended with the same general conclusion about the children: sole custody to Mom, every other weekend with Dad. (In the last hearing, a judge also decided financial matters, including among other things an order to sell the family home and divide the proceeds equally.) Cindy and Scott each spent tens of thousands of dollars on legal fees, and the rancor between them escalated, even though it might seem impossible for things to have gotten worse.

What happened to the children throughout this time? Angela continued to be resilient in her parents' eyes, but not so the other kids. Even though Scott started giving Joey his prescribed medication more consistently and maintaining his home routines when they were together, Joey was doing miserably in school academically, behaviorally, and socially. Joey caused a lot of problems at home, too, particularly for his mom who, after all, had Joey most of the time. Colleen grew more and more withdrawn, and a school counselor finally told Cindy that Colleen was acting depressed and needed therapy. Because of the exorbitant costs of the divorce, both felt that they could no longer afford the summer camp for children with ADHD they both hoped would help Joey, and Angela would have to give up either her ballet or piano lessons. It was around this time that Cindy and Scott, who each had been contacting me on occasion, started seriously considering my repeated suggestion to come see me again together.

Be Cooperative, but Be Smart

Of course life is not perfect. Life is not always fair. Doing the right thing can mean taking different routes. Your first instinct always should be to cooperate for the sake of your children, but you need to be aware of your other options. Maybe a distant divorce—like Carlos and Tara's—is more likely to work in your circumstances. Or maybe you need to try to protect yourself. Maybe there simply is no way that your ex—or you—can get past the fact that you are going to have an angry divorce, at least right now. What you want to do is to take the least adversarial approach you possibly can while still protecting yourself and your children.

If you have to take a more adversarial route, you will need to work on distancing yourself from all of the emotions involved. You are not likely to be able to approach the legal conflict the way your lawyer must—like a surgeon. But you will be best off if you can take a more distant, businesslike approach to dealing with your children's other parent during and after the legal process rather than letting the anger spill over into your daily life.

Believe me: You need to follow my emotional advice more than anything else. But, of course, you also need to know about your legal options in divorce. So let's start here with a brief summary of the different ways you can negotiate divorce, beginning with the most cooperative approaches and moving toward those that have increasingly greater potential to turn adversarial.

Negotiating at the Kitchen Table

If you can do it, the simplest and the best way to negotiate a separation or divorce agreement is at the kitchen table. You might be more focused and calm in a neutral and more public environment, for example, a restaurant, but somewhere, anywhere, you and your ex could sit down to try to talk things out on your own.

Doing it yourself is the best approach, because your agreement is about your children, your life. Your separation agreement will spell out how you and your ex are going to raise your children, how you will share the property you have acquired together, and how you will support your children and each other. Do you want someone else to decide how you should raise your children? Spend your money? Dispose of your property? Probably not, and only if you absolutely cannot make these decisions yourself.

Be prepared, though. Even in a relatively cooperative divorce, your emotional stuff is still likely to complicate your discussions with your ex about the legal side. Before you try to negotiate a separation agreement at the kitchen table, you and your ex almost certainly will need to have talked out many emotional issues at that same table or maybe in a therapist's office.

If both of you are emotionally ready, you will almost certainly learn that the legal issues in your separation and divorce are quite straightforward. One exception is if you are very wealthy and have complicated trusts, inheritances, and marital property. If this is you, you

■ SEPARATION AGREEMENTS

What is a separation agreement? A *separation agreement* is a document that you and your ex sign outlining the details of how you will manage your separation. Your separation agreement may be a very informal agreement that you and your ex work out over the kitchen table; a detailed document written up by your lawyers listing the specifics of how you will manage your separation (as well as a lot of legalese); or, in the states that grant a legal separation, a formal instrument filed with the court and ratified by a judge.

Your separation agreement may address the five big legal issues you must decide in a divorce: physical custody of your children, legal custody of your children, child support, alimony, and property division. Or your separation agreement may address none or only some of these issues and do so informally or temporarily. The simplest separation agreement says merely that the partners agree to separate.

Especially when it comes to your children, you may find it close to impossible to commit to writing what is best to do *for the rest of your children's childhood*. Actually, I generally don't advise that you *should* try to do this. I recommend first agreeing to a reasonable and well-thought-out parenting plan, but a temporary one. That way, you will have a chance to see how your children react—and plan for fixing any problems—before you lock yourself into a legal agreement that can be difficult to change. Such agreements can be far easier to reach, and as I discuss in chapter 7, they have other advantages, too.

You should know that a separation agreement often becomes the basis for an eventual divorce settlement. If you hammer out a lot of details now, you should do so very carefully. And before signing any separation agreement, even an informal one, you should have a lawyer review it. Your lawyer will advise you both about the general terms of the agreement and about specific language that may have a special meaning in the law.

probably already are used to having lawyers involved in your life. Otherwise, the legal issues concerning your children are all about parenting. The financial aspects of divorce law either are very straightforward or so vague that you will be better off resolving them on your own.

You also will learn that a number of things that are incredibly important to your children are *not* addressed in the law. For example, the law does not require you to decide whether or how you will pay for your children's college education. Still, paying for college is something you would be wise to address now, as are several other issues that are *not* mentioned in the law but should make your list of a dozen legal topics that matter most for children.

A Lawyer Can Help You to Negotiate on Your Own

Even if you are comfortable negotiating on your own, you would be wise to consult a lawyer either while you are negotiating or after you have an unsigned draft of an agreement. Once you sign an agreement, it is all but impossible to get out of it, so you want to be sure you really have thought things through carefully before signing. A lawyer can alert you to problems you may be overlooking, inform you about local practices (for example, the preferences of local judges for sole or joint custody), and help you to make sure you are not striking a bad bargain driven by guilt, fear, or misinformation.

Later in this chapter, I'll talk more about how lawyers are trained to approach divorce and other legal negotiations. But let me offer a few words to the wise now. You may feel that when it comes to this divorce, you and your kids are in this together; that anyone who represents you is also representing and concerned about your kids. Unfortunately, this is not the case when it comes to lawyers in divorce.

It is important that you understand that a lawyer's job is to advocate for you, the client, *not* for your children, your family, or your coparenting relationship. Some lawyers take this to mean that their job in divorce is to get the best possible deal for you (for example, the most time with the children or the most money) regardless of how this might affect your ex, your relationship, or your kids. These lawyers are ardent advocates for you and you alone, and they show little interest in your family relationships or the long-term emotional repercussions.

Many lawyers do moderate their adversarial approach when it comes to divorce. Legally, though, a lawyer who takes this more cooperative approach is still your advocate and only your advocate. But like Danielle's and Frank's lawyers, most divorce lawyers I have encountered will urge you to work things out on your own, to take the long view, and to consider how your legal negotiations might affect you, your children, and your ex. Figuring all of this out is not your lawyer's job, but these more "holistic" lawyers will raise emotional issues for you to consider. Because some lawyers are more adversarial or more collaborative, you would be wise to check out your lawyer's reputation in advance so you'll know with whom you are dealing.

A lawyer's job is also to spot problems with agreements, to point out how things—anything and everything—*might* go wrong. If you employ a lawyer to review your agreement, do not expect a pat on the back and a rousing "Great job!" Instead, you'll hear what's missing, what's worded improperly, how something might be misinterpreted.

Even after hearing such legal advice, you may still prefer to use your own words and follow your own agreements. A moral contract with your ex can be stronger and more enduring than any legal contract your lawyer can devise. Other parents want to get the legalese just right even though they drafted their own agreement. You should think about what you might want in advance, and you definitely should be prepared for your lawyer to criticize your agreement rather than praise it. Once again, that's a lawyer's job.

If your relationship is very cooperative, you and your ex might want to consider consulting a lawyer together. But you should be aware that the same lawyer cannot represent both of you. She or he may talk to you both, but lawyers cannot engage in *dual representation*—representing both sides in a dispute. Technically, a lawyer you consult together must either represent just one of you or act as a neutral mediator.

Finally, you probably will want a lawyer to file the papers for a legal divorce if and when the time for that comes. Typically, lawyers will file papers for a modest fee if you and your ex are in agreement about the terms of your divorce. If you want to file papers without a lawyer, it is possible to get a pro se divorce, in which neither you nor your ex has a lawyer. Several Internet Web sites can guide you through the pro se process in your state. You also can call the family court in your community. Some courts actually have kits that lead you step by step in filing papers for a pro se divorce in your jurisdiction.

Mediation

If talking on your own is not working or if you just do better when a third party is present, you and your ex may want to consult a mediator. Mediators are neutral third parties—usually mental health professionals or lawyers—who facilitate negotiations, but mediators have no power to make a final decision if you cannot reach an agreement on your own.

Mediation usually is confidential, but not always, and you need to know what kind of mediation you are entering into at the start. If it is confidential, if you and your ex fail to reach an agreement, mediators cannot make a recommendation to a judge about how you should settle your differences. If it is confidential, you should view mediation as a chance for you and your ex to work out your own agreement, much like sitting at the kitchen table. The difference is that the mediator is a neutral expert who will keep things calm, facilitate your discussions, and offer you some expert guidance and advice.

You should find out right away if you are participating in mediation that is *not* confidential. In some court-connected programs, mediators *do* make recommendations to the court if mediation fails. In this case, mediation is more like arbitration—where the neutral third party *does* impose their decision on you. The mediator's recommendation can be a powerful influence on judges, who commonly accept and act upon it.

If your mediator is going to make a recommendation and you want out of mediation, what do you do when the mediator says,

"Fine. You can stop. Mediation is voluntary. But if we stop now, you should know that I will recommend against your getting custody." That is *really* different from negotiating around the kitchen table, so if at all possible, make sure your mediator can guarantee confidentiality.

Selecting a Mediator

You want to select a lawyer or a therapist with great care, but you want to be even more careful in selecting a mediator. In some states, mediators might not be required to have a professional degree and might be certified after just twenty hours of training. You should look for someone who is not only a mediator but who also is a lawyer or a mental health professional—a psychologist, psychiatrist, social worker, or counselor. Some mediators actually work in male-female, lawyer-mental health professional teams, an ideal but more expensive combination.

Not surprising, lawyer-mediators are more knowledgeable about the law, and they usually are less sensitive to emotions, more directive, and more focused on the details of your written settlement. Mental health mediators are more familiar with the psychological issues in divorce, and they typically are more sensitive to emotions, more supportive, and as focused on addressing the psychological aspects of your separation as on working out the legal details. You may prefer a mediator with one type of background or the other or a male-female team.

As with selecting a lawyer or therapist, it also is a good idea to shop around until you find an individual you like and trust irrespective of his or her professional credentials. In looking for a mediator, you want to pay particular attention to your mediator's style as well as professional background. Some mediators give a lot of direction and advice; others focus only on facilitating your discussions. You want to pick a mediator whose approach makes you feel comfortable and confident.

Some court-based mediation programs are one-shot deals that last no longer than a couple of hours or a day. With private mediators, you should expect negotiations to take place over the course of a few months, for a total of perhaps ten to twenty hours of mediation. How long me-diation will take depends on how complicated your circumstances are emotionally, practically, and financially.

You also should know that it is quite common to return to media-tion over time to revise your agreement concerning your children. Your agreements about your children are never 100 percent final in the law, and you may find that arrangements you designed for your three-year-old boy and seven-year-old girl are not working as well when your children are eight and twelve years old or eleven and fif-teen years old. (In chapter 7, I'll talk very specifically about what kinds of arrangements work best for children of different ages and for different divorce styles.) You may also want or need to rework your parenting arrangements as you and your children get involved with new activities, relationships, and obligations, or in the event that one of you relocates out of the area or incurs other familial or financial obligations.

In short, you should view whatever custody agreement you reach as a living document, something you will change as needed to better meet your children's changing needs. In fact, in my study comparing the effects of mediation and litigation, one of the positive effects was that parents who mediated changed their child-rearing arrangements more often than parents who went to court. Most parents who medi-ated made only one or two changes over the course of twelve years, and they typically rearranged things informally in order to accom-modate their children's and their own changing needs. Parents who went to court almost never altered their custody arrangements, even over the course of twelve years. Once you set off down the legal path, it really is hard to change direction and become more flexible again.

Finally, as with negotiations around the kitchen table, you would be wise to consult a lawyer outside of mediation during the process and certainly before signing off on any agreement. Your mediator should advise you to consult a lawyer and can give you the names of lawyers in your community if you do not already have one.

Lawyers

You should hire a lawyer to review any agreement you reach in mediation or around the kitchen table. But if negotiating on your own or in mediation is getting you nowhere, you may need to hire a lawyer to do some negotiating for you. If you just *think* the more informal process is not going to work, give it a try—a really good, honest attempt—before you scuttle it. Once shots are fired, it is harder to call a truce. You always can get more adversarial after trying to cooperate, but it is hard to step back and try to cooperate once you are embroiled in a legal battle.

Whether or not you pay your lawyer a retainer is one practical difference between asking your lawyer to consult with you or negotiate for you. A *retainer* is a substantial amount of money that you pay to your lawyer in advance. Several thousand dollars is a typical retainer in divorce, and the money is used to pay attorney's fees as they accrue. Any unused balance will be returned to you. If you want your lawyer to take over your legal negotiations, many attorneys require you to pay a retainer up front. On the other hand, if you simply ask an attorney to give you advice or to review an agreement, you usually can pay by the hour.

You should know that it may well take you longer to reach a settlement if you use lawyers rather than negotiating yourself or through a mediator. In my research, parents who mediated reached an agreement in half the time it took parents to achieve a settlement through their lawyers and the courts. And statistics showed that parents who mediated were happier with the whole process and its effects on their family than parents who used the traditional route through lawyers and the courts. Parents who mediated were happier right after they reached a settlement, one and a half years later, and twelve years afterward. And remember: The design of the study demonstrated clearly that mediation *caused* parents to reach a settlement sooner and to be happier with the process.

What if you just cannot reach an agreement on your own or in mediation? Maybe your ex is being unreasonable, is unwilling to compromise, or just can't get past his or her emotions. Or maybe you just don't feel strong, confident, or emotionally in control enough to negotiate on your own. Or perhaps you are facing legal complications that just seem, well, too complicated. In circumstances like these and in situations where domestic violence is part of the history or a real possibility, you might want to hire a lawyer to negotiate for you.

If so, one option you may want to consider is trying to work out any disputes you have about your children together with your ex (with or without a mediator), but let your lawyer take the lead in negotiating financial matters. This way, you will be taking advantage of everyone's expertise—you know what's best for your children, but your lawyer is likely to be more sophisticated about financial as well as legal matters. This is exactly what the families in my study did. We mediated issues concerning the children, but the lawyers handled the financial matters.

Vigorous Representation

If you ask a lawyer to negotiate for you, remember that any lawyer's ethical obligation is to represent your interests, and only your interests, and to do so vigorously. But lawyers can differ greatly in how fervently they embrace their obligation of vigorous representation and in the aspects of the legal process they consider their forte. While it is true that lawyers settle more than 90 percent of divorce disputes out of court, just like your kitchen-table discussions, your lawyer's settlement negotiations can be friendly or vicious.

Some lawyers go to court in a lot more than 5 percent or 10 percent of their cases. These trial lawyers are experts in litigation; this is what they are most comfortable doing and what they believe is in their clients' best interest. As a result, they may not focus much on negotiating, or on you, until the time to go to court nears. Other lawyers feel their expertise lies in negotiation and that litigation represents a last resort. They will spend more time and energy on negotiations.

How do you know when you might need a really tough trial lawyer instead of a more cooperative negotiator? A lot depends upon you and your ex. First and foremost, you want to get a really aggressive lawyer only for *practical* reasons, not for emotional ones. And there are lawyers out there, albeit a minority, who do encourage their clients to channel their emotional turmoil into aggressive legal tactics. Emotional reflexes—hurt feelings and that primitive human desire to hurt back—propelled Cindy and Scott to hire their very adversarial lawyers. We can conclude from the results that neither of their lawyers had much interest in persuading his client to disengage the emotional gears from the big legal engine carrying them all away.

You do not want to make the same mistake. Although many people (like Scott) may believe that their ex's hiring an aggressive lawyer forces them to do the same, it is not really the case. Your reasonable, mild-mannered negotiator can be effective against your ex's attack dog of a lawyer. Refusing to fight while refusing to give in is a response that can help you preserve a reasonable, if distant, working relationship for the future.

This may be particularly true if your ex is being driven into a legal fight by his or her emotions. As discussed in chapter 2, your ex may be fighting to get a reaction out of you or, perversely, as a way of trying to hang on to you. If you don't fight back—if you can be patient enough to give your ex (and yourself) adequate time to grieve and gain insight into his emotions—you may be able to avoid having those unresolved emotions played out in a legal fight.

I have just given you two circumstances when you should *not* hire a really aggressive lawyer. When *should* you? Only in the most dire circumstances: When you believe your children are truly threatened, when your spouse has a long history of running over people (inside or outside of court), when you have been abused, threatened, or beaten down to the point where you can no longer stand up for yourself.

Even in incredibly difficult circumstances like these, sooner or later, you're going to have to find a way to stand up to and deal with your ex. Your lawyer isn't going to move in with you to help you handle the day-to-day conflict that may be in your future. And although you may hope that a court hearing will end the conflict, nothing is ever final—not even a judge's orders—in a truly angry divorce.

Collaborative Divorce

Many divorce lawyers will tell you that they prefer to negotiate cooperatively, but they are hamstrung either by the adversary legal system or by the lawyer on the other side. They will tell you that they want to negotiate, but will warn you that your ex's lawyer is a piranha, a pit bull, an ogre bent on eating the flesh off your bones. Your lawyer may say that he or she needs to be just as tough in order to protect you.

This can be true. The American system of justice is based on a model of competition, not cooperation. Think of the terminology— "legal battles," for example—and the fact that the contest is supposed to end with a winner and a loser. Still, you should know that many excellent and very strong lawyers do find ways to negotiate cooperatively. In fact, there is a new movement called *collaborative divorce* that is designed to promote more cooperative lawyering among members of the divorce bar.

Collaborative divorce lawyers agree to represent you only as long as there is a collaborative lawyer on the other side. Collaborative lawyers agree to negotiate cooperatively with each other and in good faith. They also agree to settle your case outside of court or to no longer represent you if they fail to do so. Because the collaborative divorce movement is new, it may be difficult to find two collaborative divorce lawyers outside a major metropolitan area. Still, collaborative divorce is an option worth considering and one that tells you pretty clearly what can happen if your legal negotiations become very adversarial. After all, lawyers, not psychologists, started the collaborative law movement.

The bottom line about lawyers is this: You are likely to need a lawyer for advice, to help you file papers, and perhaps to take over your negotiations for you. Most lawyers will tell you that you'll be better off working things out on your own, but, if necessary, they will take over the negotiations. In this case, most lawyers will take the long view and negotiate more cooperatively so that you and your ex can at least have a distant divorce and parent your children together in a businesslike fashion. But if everything gets worse once the lawyers get involved, ultimately, it is your problem and your fault. Your lawyer works for you, not vice versa.

Neutrals in a Custody Battle: Evaluators and Guardians *ad Litem*

If legal negotiations are failing and you are preparing to go to court, a custody evaluator or a guardian *ad litem* might get involved in your case. Custody evaluators are mental health professionals, often employed privately but sometimes employed by the court, who evaluate you, your ex, and your children with the goal of making recommendations to the court about how your children should be reared after your divorce.

Your lawyer may hire a custody evaluator as an expert witness for your side but, if so, you can expect your ex to hire a different expert who will counter your own. The result is likely to be a battle of the experts that can cause a judge to discount both professional opinions. It will be much more helpful and productive to have a neutral custody evaluator, either someone whom the court appoints or someone agreed upon by you, your ex, and your lawyers.

Guardians *ad litem* are advocates appointed by the court to represent your children's interests in your divorce. Guardians *ad litem* usually are lawyers but in some jurisdictions, they might be specially trained nonlawyer advocates. In theory, guardians *ad litem* advocate for your children's interests in divorce, potentially taking a third adversarial position in a custody dispute. In practice, however, many guardians find that they serve children best either by acting as mediators or as neutral eyes and ears who help judges sort through the conflicting evidence that is sure to be presented if your case goes to court.

Judges, Arbitrators, and Parenting Coordinators

If you cannot reach a settlement on your own, in mediation or through your lawyers, someone will make a decision for you. If you need a third party to decide how you and your ex should raise your children and deal with your finances, you almost certainly have an angry divorce—or soon will. Most parents get to this point only if they are having a great many problems in their relationship and going to court will not make things better. The evidence presented in court can be extreme, with a dramatic "spin" put on it to make one side look good and the other look bad. Hearing testimony about your failures as a spouse and parent from your ex—and possibly from family and friends—hardly soothes the hurt, anger, and pain of divorce.

Face it: Court hearings are expensive and divisive, and as Cindy and Scott learned, it usually takes an awfully long time to schedule and prepare for court. You may not be able to get a hearing date for six, eight, or ten months or longer. Meanwhile, life goes on. Your children and your relationship with them don't get put on hold while you are waiting. What are you supposed to do in the meantime? I can tell you what family court judges hope you will do while you are waiting: work things out on your own.

Hard as it may be to imagine on the day you order your lawyer to fire off the first angry volley, tomorrow, next week, or next month, you may see things a bit differently. Most judges believe even more strongly than lawyers that it is essential for parents to come to terms on their own about raising their children in divorce. Why? Because like your children, judges are in the middle of your dispute, and that's a very uncomfortable position. Most judges know that no amount of wisdom can solve your family problems better than you can.

Because of the divisiveness and long delay in getting a court hearing, if you really can't work things out on your own, you may want to consider some form of arbitration as an alternative. Some jurisdictions have *special masters* who will hear evidence much as a judge would, but the case is tried more quickly, less formally, and with a binding decision presented more rapidly. You should know, however, that the decision of a special master may be subject to appeal in court.

Other arbitration alternatives include *minitrials*, private trials that are run according to terms that both sides agree to in advance; for example, that the judge's decision will be binding. Retired judges often hear minitrials and render a verdict soon after the conclusion of the trial. Private mediators also may offer arbitration services where the presentation of evidence is less formal than in a minitrial.

Parenting coordinators are a relatively new type of arbiter in separation and divorce, and they usually get involved only in very high-conflict cases. Parenting coordinators usually are mental health professionals either employed privately or by the court. They meet informally with the separated parents to try to help them resolve day-to-day childrearing disputes as they arise.

Parenting coordinators do what is sometimes called *med-arb*, mediation that can turn into arbitration. One difference from mediation is that if the parents cannot agree themselves, a parenting coordinator will become an arbiter and he or she will make a decision for you, either on the spot or shortly afterward. Typically, parenting coordinators hold the authority to make only limited decisions; for example, resolving conflicts about the children's schedule during an upcoming holiday or school vacation.

No Pain, No Gain

The idea of negotiating the legal details of your divorce with your ex probably makes you feel angry, frightened, sad, hopeful, guilty, unsettled, or all of these feelings at once. The idea of actually reaching an agreement surely provokes strong feelings, too. You may be afraid about agreeing to something that might be unfair, may not work, and cannot be changed. Depending upon whether you were the leaver or the left, the thought of reaching an agreement may make you feel relieved about the prospect of ending your legal negotiations—or despondent about the prospect of ending your marriage.

Despite the potential benefits of cooperating, all these feelings may drive you toward a more adversarial approach. As with Cindy and Scott, your raw emotions may want you to scream at your ex, "I'll see you in court!" Or maybe you just do not want to deal with the negotiations because you are afraid of making a mistake. Or maybe you do not want to sit down at the table with your ex because he or she still does not get it about your feelings. Maybe you are devastated about ending your marriage while your ex seems only too happy to be wrapping up the legal details. Or maybe you want to do business— finally—and your ex keeps dragging his feet and bringing up the past.

I need to be honest with you, and you need to be honest with yourself. For you, and for your ex, too, negotiating more cooperatively is probably going to be harder emotionally, not easier, than a more adversarial approach in the short run. Negotiating cooperatively goes against the grain of your grief. Working cooperatively with your ex does not let you settle on the anger that protects you from your hurt, the anger that can give you the distance and help you to heal.

Negotiating cooperatively forces you to deal with your ex, and doing this is likely to kick up a lot of emotional stuff for you. Some of the stuff will be hurt, some will be anger, some will be guilt, and some will be sadness. Ambivalence is another feeling that negotiating cooperatively is likely to bring up. If you can work out a settlement cooperatively and work together for your kids, you may grow more uncertain about whether or not you really want to end your relationship. After all, you may wonder, if we can work this out, why couldn't we have saved our marriage?

In other words, negotiating cooperatively may temporarily impede your moving forward in your grief. It may raise old questions and old feelings, even old hopes and dreams, that you thought you had left behind. Even after a year or more of negotiating, as you're about to sign off on a final agreement, you might find yourself asking, "Should we *really* be doing this?" In fact, this powerful underlying feeling may cause you or your ex to find something wrong with the agreement, not because there really is anything wrong, but so you can put off making your settlement (and your divorce) final. So you can put off dealing with your grief.

These paradoxical reactions do not mean that you are making a mistake about your divorce or that you have done something wrong. They are the natural emotional consequences and reactions of this life-altering and difficult process called divorce. These responses tell you that what is happening matters to you, that you are taking your decisions and your responsibilities seriously, and that you are allowing yourself to do the hard emotional work that must be done. If you can learn to anticipate your feelings and understand, you will be more likely to respond in a way that you will be satisfied about now and tomorrow. In the long run, your short-term struggle, discomfort, doubt, sadness, and worry will pay dividends for you, your ex, and especially your kids. No pain, no gain.

CHAPTER SEVEN

Parenting Plans

Making decisions about where children will live undoubtedly is one of the most frightening and difficult tasks of divorce. The prospect of no longer being with your children *all* the time is bad enough. The thought of losing your children can be terrifying. The fears—and the conflicts that can stem from them—often are compounded by traditional legal language: One parent wins custody while the loser is reduced to periods of visitation with his own child.

Good parenting isn't a contest. Parents can take a different, more child-friendly approach to both legal negotiations and the child-rearing agreements they construct. Like many experts, I prefer to think about this challenging task as devising a *parenting plan,* a legal agreement that spells out a clear, specific schedule for children as well as guidelines for each parent's coparenting responsibilities and role in decision making. In fact, it may be completely unnecessary to use terms like "custody" and "visitation" in a legal agreement if you can work out a detailed parenting plan.

In this chapter, I will outline issues parents need to consider in devising a parenting plan and discuss the pros and cons of alternative arrangements, particularly schedules for children of different ages and for parents with a cooperative, distant, or angry divorce.

One of the most important considerations is *how* you approach your negotiations, which is why I discussed this before talking about *what* issues need to be decided. Decisions and arrangements that seem desirable or workable on their own can be made or broken by several important factors: the emotional tenor of the divorce and the coparenting relationship; the developmental and emotional needs of the children; the simple logistics of the lives you, your ex, and your children now lead. There is no perfect, one-size-fits-all solution to any problem of divorce or coparenting. Everything is trial and error and compromise. The sooner parents can learn to live with the situation's inherent shortcomings and imperfections, the more quickly they can move on to truly making the best of things for their kids and for themselves.

A critical goal in developing your parenting plan is to understand and contain your volatile emotions well enough so you *can* think clearly and objectively. You may not be able to fully trust your judgment, particularly on such an important, emotionally charged issue as your children. You may be uncertain *what* to do or your intuition may be tainted by your own hurt, loneliness, jealousy, or anger. Here is where research on families who have gone through this before can help.

For example, consider the much-discussed option of joint physical custody, where the children live with each of their parents somewhere close to half of the time. Is joint physical custody good for children? Well, many things go into deciding whether or not joint physical custody is feasible, let alone beneficial. Important considerations include practicalities: How close do the parents live to each other? To the child's school? What type of child-care options are available when a parent cannot be home? How old are the children? Research has demonstrated clearly that joint physical custody is much too disruptive for very young children, and it can interfere with the busy schedule of older adolescents.

But the most important ingredient for making joint physical custody work is a reasonably cooperative relationship between the parents. Research shows that, on average, joint custody is associated with a modest increase in children's well-being as measured in various ways, including their psychological health and the quality of their relationships with both parents. However, on closer inspection, joint physical custody really is the best *and* the worst arrangement for children. Joint physical custody is the best arrangement when parents can cooperate well enough to coordinate rules, schedules, schooling, and frequent transitions. It's the worst arrangement when it puts children smack in the middle of their parents' war zone. Remember Susannah's sad, bitter memories of growing up as the prize in her parents' joint physical custody competition and how this taught her that her parents' feelings mattered more than her own.

You need to bring several crucial elements to your parenting plan: consideration of your children's perspective, a degree of flexibility, and a commitment to developing a reasonable, working, businesslike relationship with your children's other parent. Here are some research-based, commonsense rules for devising a parenting plan:

- When you first separate, think of your parenting plan as a temporary arrangement. Short-term plans give you the chance to *see* how your children are adjusting to the schedule, not just to guess about how they might do. After a reasonable trial (probably a few months), you can tweak the plan to better meet your children's needs or, if necessary, go back to the drawing board.
- Think about your time with your children in terms of months and years, not hours and days. Remember the spreadsheet that Susannah's father kept to ensure he got equal time down to the minute? This is *not* what you want to do to your children. Why do I say years? Because a plan that works well for your four-year-old son may not be the best arrangement when he turns seven, twelve, or sixteen. And the possibility of making changes might make it easier for you—or your ex—to accept an imperfect parenting plan now.
- Integrated parenting plans require cooperative coparenting relationships. If you have an angry divorce, your children are likely to fare better with a more traditional schedule where they live primarily with one parent, spend some regular time with the other parent, and do not transition between homes very often. If you have an angry divorce and you *want* a more equal parenting plan, work on building a better, businesslike relationship with your ex.
- More complex and integrated schedules challenge the resources of children who are anxious, difficult to manage, or have learning,

emotional, or social difficulties. If your child has emotional or learning problems, you probably need either a pretty simple schedule or a very high degree of cooperation with your ex.

- The same schedule does not always work for children of different ages. If you have a good businesslike relationship with your ex, you might be able to devise schedules that differ slightly for different children. Part of this individualized schedule might include precious alone time for you and your ex to spend with each of your kids.
- Infants and toddlers benefit from having a primary home and frequent but briefer visits with the other parent. The goal is for the very young child to be away from either parent only for relatively short periods of time.
- Preschoolers and school-age children can manage longer periods of time with each parent, and longer times generally are a plus because they mean fewer transitions for children and for parents.
- Adolescents require the integration of three schedules: Mom's, Dad's, and their own. Because teenagers have their own busy lives, parents should not be surprised if a complex schedule creates problems for them.
- Siblings with good relationships can help to buffer transitions for one another. It may be easier for a younger child to transition between homes or be separated from a parent for somewhat longer periods of time if he has older siblings going back and forth with him.
- Parents should listen to children's input about the schedule, but the final decision is a parent's responsibility, not a child's—or a teenager's. Parents may believe they are asking for only a child's input, but when you ask your twelve-year-old daughter what *she* wants, you often inadvertently make her feel like she is being asked to choose between her parents.

Do You Need a *Final* Parenting Plan Now?

Before either of you moves out of the family home, is it essential to have a final parenting plan in your separation agreement? Do parents have to work out *all* the legal details just as they're about to embark on what may be the bumpiest part of their emotional roller-coaster ride? Are the days, weeks, or months of those first breathtaking emotional ups, downs, and hair-raising turns the best time to put together such a plan? Many parents believe so, though sometimes that is because this is what their lawyers tell them. These parents believe that in the midst of their turmoil, they must work out a parenting plan that will work *for the rest of their children's lives.*

Seem like a lot? It is. My view—one that I share with many lawyers and mediators—is that it's way too much to ask and not necessary. During this difficult time, you *don't* have to work out a parenting plan for the rest of your children's childhood, especially if you have or believe that you can develop in the near future a reasonably cooperative coparenting relationship. And note the words I use: "reasonably" (as in not perfect) and "cooperative" (also as in not perfect). In fact, you should *never* try to make decisions for the rest of your children's lives in your legal agreements. You really do want your parenting plan to be a living agreement.

Put aside all the fears and legal technicalities that might be racing through your mind for a moment and think like a parent. Approach these decisions the same way married parents make important decisions about raising their children. No parent would want to make a final decision about choices concerning a child's college education—public versus private and which school?—and commit to paying years of tuition bills when that kid is just five, or nine, or even fifteen.

The choices you make about your children in divorce are the same. Your child will change, and so will you. What seems impossible today may be easy next week, next month, or a few years down the road. Similarly, today's perfect situation simply may not exist in the future. No one, least of all judges, lawyers, psychologists, mediators, and certainly not even the best parents, can decide at one difficult moment in time what is going to be best for a child's entire childhood. This is why some flexibility is essential in any divorce.

A Tentative Plan for Your Children

In my experience in mediation and therapy with hundreds of divorcing families, parents have worked out all sorts of initial parenting plans. Some parents—Frank and Danielle, for instance—refuse to sign a legal agreement when they separate (even though they agree about the schedule), because they want to see what is going to work first and because they believe that their moral commitment as coparents is stronger than any legal agreement. At the other extreme, some parents insist that they must work out every legal detail before they can separate. I have watched many of these parents occupy the same house for months, a year, or longer in a war of attrition while they negotiated their settlement.

Most common, parents follow the middle road. They negotiate a limited separation agreement, a brief and often informal document that includes a statement about the partners' agreement to separate (to protect against a potential charge of desertion), a detailed but temporary parenting plan, and perhaps a brief financial agreement.

Although you may assume that this would blur the boundaries I encourage families to set, such plans have built-in flexibility. They leave room for families to make changes and adjustments to meet unknown or unexpected future needs and circumstances. The stability a child requires in divorce comes not from having the same visitation schedule from day one until they move away from home. It comes from knowing that their parents can meet their needs, and children's needs—like parents' needs—can and do change.

This approach leaves you with the much easier, more realistic task of coming up with a plan worth trying right now. As a result, parents find it much easier to agree to a temporary, more flexible plan than one that is supposedly final and inflexible. If they can muster the minimal degree of cooperation necessary to do so, parents feel much more comfortable with a plan they can reevaluate, a plan that can grow and change along with their children's needs and their own changing circumstances.

This responsive approach to creating a parenting plan is particularly important for infants and toddlers. Ideally, parents of very young children will negotiate a series of temporary agreements, adjusting them as needed every six months or so until the child becomes a preschooler. Once the child is three, four, or five years old, a schedule—anything from fifty-fifty to something fairly traditional—can work for several years, perhaps longer. For example, here is the parenting plan that was a part of a mediated agreement for a six-month-old baby:

> We agree that our six-month-old son, Daniel, will benefit from having a primary home now, but we also agree that it is important that he spend an increasing amount of time with each of us as he grows and becomes a toddler. Over the next six months, Daniel will live primarily with his mother, but he will spend every Monday and Wednesday afternoon with his father from 4:00 P.M. until 7:00 P.M., as well as every Saturday from 9:00 A.M. until 5:00 P.M. During this time, we may try having Daniel spend an occasional overnight with his father. When Daniel is one year old, we will revisit this agreement in order to rework the parenting plan to best suit Daniel's needs. Our goal is to increase the length of time Daniel spends with his father. Eventually, this will include regular overnights and perhaps joint physical custody if it will be in Daniel's best interests.

Taking a Risk on Working Together

Negotiating a more flexible parenting plan certainly feels a lot nicer than hammering out an ironclad final legal document, but is there a downside to the responsive approach? Honestly, yes. For one thing, the two of you working out such an agreement together will raise red flags for most attorneys, and the most adversarial among them can be expected to argue that you should not sign such a document.

In the case of baby Daniel, here's what the attorneys for Mom and

Dad might say. The mother's lawyer might point out that she is taking a risk if she agrees to a flexible, responsive schedule. Why? Because the best time for the mom to win in court is now: She is breast-feeding and has been taking care of the baby almost all of the time, and, besides, judges tend to be extremely reluctant to interfere with the attachment relationship between a mother and an infant. If she wins custody, her lawyer might counsel, she can be flexible later if her baby's father deserves her cooperation. But if she agrees to be flexible now, she might be in a difficult spot if her ex acts like a jerk and she later decides that her child will benefit from continuing to live with her most of the time.

This is good enough legal advice, but here's the problem: What is the *father's* lawyer likely to tell him? The father's lawyer may point out that he, too, is taking a risk if he agrees to the responsive approach, though for different reasons. Right now is the best time for *him* to win in court: No schedule has been established for very long, the baby's mom is about to go back to work, and, besides, children are attached to their fathers, too. Judges today look favorably on fathers who *want* to be involved, especially in light of the many fathers who don't. If Daniel's dad gets joint custody, he can be flexible later by not insisting on disrupting his baby's routine too much. But at least he would be compromising from a position of significantly more power than he would if he and Daniel's mother simply agreed to make changes as the baby grew older. If he agrees to be flexible now, he might be in a difficult situation if his ex backs out on the deal and later decides that their child should stay with her most of the time. A precedent would be set, and that might give the mother a strong case.

This, too, would be pretty good legal advice, but the problem is obvious. There is going to be a fight of one sort or another if the parents act out of such defensive positions.

There is no doubt about it: You *are* taking a risk if you try to work with your ex by taking a responsive approach to your parenting plan. But you also are taking a risk—a risk of wrecking your coparenting relationship—if you jump into the adversarial approach. There is no way to avoid risk, no matter what course you take. Risk is inherent in divorce. However, my experience and the results of my research show that parents are likely to reap benefits if they take the risk of working together.

You *can* experiment until you find a schedule that works for your children before you sign off on a final parenting plan. And let's be realistic. Part of the experiment is seeing how your children react, but part of it is also learning how well you and your ex can coparent together. The adversarial approach and the advisers to help you take it are not going away anytime soon. If things should go awry and you need to take a more aggressive posture, the lawyers to help you will be there.

A Responsive Approach in a Distant Divorce

Tara and Carlos, the Spanish teacher and the surgeon with two adolescents and a distant divorce, took a risk on working together as coparents even though their divorce was far from friendly. Carlos had been fighting for joint physical custody of fifteen-year-old Carlos Junior and eleven-year-old Isabella while Tara scoffed that Carlos did not keep to their present agreement of having overnights with the children every Thursday and every other weekend.

In mediation, Tara and Carlos learned to establish rules that defined clearer, more businesslike boundaries. One of several rules was to stick to the present schedule rigidly for several months as outlined in a temporary agreement. After this, we would revisit the arrangement and consider increasing Carlos's time with the children.

When Carlos and Tara came to see me again after a few months, each started off with a list of complaints. Tara pointed out that although Carlos had pretty much adhered to the schedule, he had rearranged a recent weekend so he could attend a conference. Afraid that he was backsliding, she was also angry that he hadn't told her about the conference in advance. He obviously had to have known about the meeting months ago.

Tara also accusingly raised several concerns about how Carlos was acting with the children. He was too hard on Carlos Junior and he needed to be more sensitive to Isabella's preadolescent emotional struggles. "And when you are with the children, you need to *be with* them. They don't want you running to the hospital, reading journals, or talking on the telephone. They want you to be there *with them!*"

Carlos became agitated in his controlled, dignified way. He responded with his own litany of complaints about Tara: She was quizzing the children about him, she was continuing to undermine him, and she was trying to control *his* relationship with *his* children. "Yes, I should have given you more notice," he said. "But I knew you'd get angry—just like you are right now. I only wanted to avoid a fight, but it looks like that isn't going to happen no matter what I do."

Things were starting to heat up when I asked them if over the last months, they had been following the rules they had agreed to. There was a pause, and then they admitted that they generally had followed the rules and that there had been far less conflict. I reminded them that there was a *reason* for putting distance in their relationship: to avoid conflict. It was all right to blow off a little steam in mediation, but I didn't expect everything to be great between them, and this wasn't just a gripe session. I did wonder, though, if the children seemed more at ease without all the fighting. In fact, they both agreed that Carlos Junior was not as angry with his father or as protective of his mother, and according to Mom, Isabella's diary entries indicated that she thought her parents were getting along better.

What did they want to try to work on next? Tara turned to Carlos, bracing herself for his joint physical custody argument, the one he mounted whenever Tara attacked. Much to her surprise and mine, Carlos didn't make a case for joint custody. Instead, he said that he wanted to visit his aging parents for a week. "It is my right to bring the children to see their grandparents during their school vacation!" Tara argued about whether having the kids during spring break next month was Carlos's "right"—as he had to know she would—but she soon agreed to the plan. She had always gotten along well with her former in-laws, and she thought it was important for the children to spend time with them.

We agreed to keep the temporary agreement the same and scheduled another appointment in a few months. At that time, Tara and Carlos told me that their attorneys had negotiated an acceptable financial settlement, and they also had agreed to incorporate their current, temporary schedule (every Thursday and every other weekend with Carlos) into their final agreement. Even though their earlier schedule became their final one, as is often the case, going through the process of abiding by the terms of an agreement that the two of them had shaped together gave them confidence and control over not only the outcome, but also over a broad outline of their coparenting relationship. Clearly, Tara and Carlos were not going to be friends again anytime soon, if ever. But they had proved to themselves and to their children that they were serious about creating a sound coparenting relationship.

Having worked out their legal agreement, too many couples figure they have done their work and leave it at that. Tara and Carlos wisely continued with mediation, coming to see me at the beginning of every semester in their children's lives—near the beginning of the school year, around the first of the new year, and before summer vacation started. Mediation gave them a place to deal with the differences they couldn't manage on their own, and it was a place to sort out any upcoming changes in the schedule: holidays, summer vacations, business trips, and things of that nature. Their relationship remained distant and strained, but it worked far better for them and for their children.

What Those Scary Legal Terms
Really Mean for Parenting

Divorce brings many people into the legal system for the first time in their lives, and for many parents, dealing with lawyers and legalities is anxiety provoking, to say the least. The unfamiliar legal jargon, the lawyers' warnings about everything and anything that might happen, the feeling that control of your life is in the hands of others—all of these things contribute to the heightened sense of wariness, fear, and uncertainty of divorce.

When you submit to a surgeon's care, you sign a consent form that not only gives the doctor permission to perform the procedure but that also spells out in detail every known thing that can possibly go awry. The good news with most surgery is that you sleep through the most uncomfortable parts of the operation, and, if all goes well, you wake up and eventually feel better.

Unfortunately, your divorce lawyer isn't like the surgeon who does all the work while you lie there unconscious, blissfully unaware of the pain and other unpleasant details. Your lawyer is more like a physical therapist who may offer helpful guidance and good tips but who reminds you that ultimately the really hard work—and your successful recovery—depends on you.

Since you are going to have to do the work anyway, and some of it will hurt, it helps to understand what you need to do and why. Once you learn what the legal terms *really* mean, you will discover that the legal matters concerning your children in divorce are all about two things: decision making and a schedule for sharing time with them.

These are things you understand as a parent, and, in fact, some parents choose to circumvent legal terminology completely and in their legal agreements simply refer to how they will share and divide decision making and time. Along these same lines, a number of states have replaced the confusing and loaded term "custody" with more palatable legal language, such as "parental responsibilities" or, my preference, "parenting plans." (Divorce laws differ from state to state, and although parents face the same issues about decision making and sharing time wherever they live, learning about the particular laws in your state is one reason why you should consult with a lawyer.)

Terms matter: Few parents want to think of themselves as just "visiting" their children. And because terms matter, I want to explain the most commonly used legal terms concerning children and parenting in divorce. But I also want to be clear about the bottom line: Words are just words, even when phrased as fancy legal terminology. Good parenting in divorce isn't about carefully framed words. Good parenting in divorce is about having a clear schedule for sharing time with the children and clear rules about which decisions parents make alone and which they share. Good parenting in divorce is about maintaining a reasonable, working coparenting relationship with your ex.

Sole and Joint Custody

State laws vary, but the term *custody* probably is most familiar and is used most commonly. Many laws distinguish between legal and physical custody, and this is important. *Legal custody* refers to parents' legal responsibility for their children, particularly the authority to make major decisions about their children's lives. *Physical custody* refers to where children will live and according to what schedule.

Parents with *sole legal custody* have sole responsibility for making major decisions in their children's lives. Parents with *joint legal custody* share these decisions. Parents with *sole physical custody* have the children living with them most of the time. Parents with *joint physical custody* divide the time with their children more equally.

If you have a distant or an angry divorce, the idea of making all of the child-rearing decisions on your own may sound appealing—or the prospect of having to make every decision together with your ex might sound impossible. But winning sole legal custody does not free you from your ex, and sharing joint legal custody does not condemn you to an endless series of day-to-day conflicts.

Why? Because only a few decisions typically are shared in joint legal custody while parents who don't have legal custody still are parents. They are still involved in their children's lives. In fact, joint legal custody normally means sharing decisions only about:

- Elective medical care
- Schooling
- Religious education

That's it. Joint legal custody does *not* mean that you and your ex have veto power over each other, the right to constantly second-guess the other parent, or an equal share in the hundreds of decisions parents must make every day. Some parents with angry divorces do try to veto, second-guess, and micromanage, but joint legal custody does not give them the license to do so. Instead, parents with joint legal custody decide together when a child should get braces or see a psychologist, whether a child will attend private or public school, or if a child will be raised as Christian, Jewish, Muslim, Hindu, agnostic, or some combination of the above. Of course, children benefit when parents can agree generally on similar rules and routines in each of their households, but joint legal custody does not mean that parents *have* to agree about these things.

Exactly what is joint physical custody? The dividing line is not always clear, but an arrangement often is considered to be joint physical custody when the children spend at least one hundred overnights per year with each parent (an average of at least two overnights per week). The number of overnights can be important because some states reduce child support payments when the joint physical custody threshold is reached. Still, joint physical custody does *not* necessarily mean dividing time with the children exactly fifty-fifty.

Should You Expect to Have Joint Custody?

Twenty years ago joint legal custody was a new idea, and many legal professionals viewed the arrangement with skepticism. Today, joint legal custody is the rule, not the exception. Why? The arrangement doesn't typically cause problems, and the term can help *both* parents to feel connected to their children. Think about it this way: No one wins joint legal custody. Parents share decision making in marriage, and if someone ends up with sole legal custody, what really happens is that the other parent loses the parental authority he or she once had.

For this reason, retaining joint legal custody may be—and usually is—emotionally and symbolically important to parents. Research shows that the symbolism can translate into action. In comparison with parents who have lost legal custody, parents who retain joint legal custody spend more time with their children, pay more child support, and pay child support more regularly. If anything, joint legal custody leads to fewer problems between parents, not more.

What about joint physical custody? In many ways, joint physical custody is the ideal arrangement for children because they still have two parents very much involved in their lives. But, as I have pointed out, joint physical custody requires a good deal of parental cooperation. Joint custody without parental cooperation can become the worst setup for kids. And here is a reality check in thinking not only about your divorce style but also about the practical challenges of joint physical custody. Only a minority of parents and children from divorced families—my best estimate is 5 percent to 10 percent—succeed in maintaining a joint physical custody schedule.

There are many reasons for this low success rate. Number one on the list is that joint physical custody requires a lot of cooperation, emotional restraint, and patience for logistical complications. If you think you might be able to manage joint physical custody, try it. Just be prepared for the emotional and practical hassles. Before you decide what kind of custody arrangement seems right for you:

- Think very seriously about joint physical custody if you have a cooperative divorce. As long as you can keep your children out of your conflicts, your kids will benefit from a more integrated physical custody arrangement where they see both you and your ex a lot of the time.
- Think very seriously about sole physical custody if you have an angry divorce. If you and your ex cannot distance yourselves from your conflict and anger, it is sad but true that your children are likely to be better off seeing one of you less often. At least this way, they will not be in the middle of your conflicts so much of the time.
- If you have a distant divorce, joint physical custody can work as long as you can muster the necessary businesslike attitude toward

your ex. But beware that the challenges of joint physical custody may further strain a troubled parenting partnership.

Alternative Schedules for Your Children

Joint physical custody is an uncommon arrangement for children, and hundreds of different parenting plans can work well for children and for parents. Because parents' divorce style is critically important to the success of different parenting plans, I suggest different schedules for parents with angry, distant, and cooperative divorces. But keep in mind that these are *options* to help you think about alternative plans. *You* are the leading expert on your children, and you should be the one to craft a plan that you think will work best for them. The child development principles noted on the following pages are well grounded in scientific research, but there is little solid evidence about how alternative schedules actually affect children of different ages. As a result, some professionals disagree about what arrangements are best for children of different ages or for children whose parents have angry divorces. For example, some experts believe children cannot manage overnight visits until they are around four years old; others believe that infants are unharmed by regular overnights and this arrangement helps children by promoting their attachment to *both* parents. Similarly, some professionals are adamantly opposed to joint physical custody under virtually any circumstance while others believe that the arrangement benefits children even when their parents have an angry divorce. The schedules outlined here are intermediate between these extremes and are grounded in the best available research.

Another consideration is that it works better, if possible, to keep the schedule the same for children from week to week. We all think about our schedules in terms of days of the week, not in two-week blocks, although the two-week period is inexplicably common in custody arrangements. For most kids (and most parents), one week is a smaller, more manageable, and simpler chunk of time. It is easier for a child to know "If it's Thursday, I'm at Dad's." The alternative is having to remember if *this* Thursday is Mom's or Dad's or to figure out whose Thursday it will be in three weeks—the date of your big away game, field trip, or award ceremony. Kids get used to calculating, so this isn't a huge problem as long as the parents are willing to take a role in keeping track of events and to be flexible as needed. Still, simplicity is always better than complexity when it comes to managing children's lives and our own, particularly with all of the complications introduced by divorce.

Equally important as simplicity, a schedule that stays the same from week to week means that children are apart from their parents for shorter periods of time. As a result, parents have greater opportunity to be involved in their children's daily lives. For children, especially younger ones, life seems to run on a weekly schedule: new spelling words on Monday, test on Friday; many major school vacations are Monday through Friday, as are schedules for things such as summer camp.

Finally, as you read the schedules for successively older age groups, keep in mind that they serve two purposes. You will want to consider schedules that fit your child's current age, but you may also want to read ahead to older age groups. This suggests how you may adapt the schedule as your child grows older, and, as you will see, there are more options open to parents with cooperative than with angry divorces.

Infants and Babies: Birth to Eighteen Months

One of the most challenging and controversial schedules is for very young children, from birth to about eighteen months. Special difficulties arise for a number of reasons. The parents of very young children might not have a well-developed relationship with their child or each other, especially if this is their first child and/or the parents are unmarried. These parents lack history, precedent, commitment, and trust, yet despite the fact that the relationship may be new, when parents conceive a child they have tied themselves together for a lifetime.

Another problem is that the best arrangements for very young children involve frequent, brief contacts between each parent and the child, which also means that angry parents will be dealing with each other more than they might like. Finally, experts and parents alike may not agree on how much importance to place on one of the most basic psychological tasks of this developmental stage, a stable *attachment relationship,* the special bond formed between an infant and his caregivers.

Mental health professionals agree that babies benefit from having at least one *secure attachment*—a parent or caregiver who provides the baby with a sense of security growing out of a history of consistent, sensitive, and responsive care and comfort. More controversial is the extent to which babies need a single, primary attachment relationship, whether regular separations from the primary attachment figure sow the seeds for later emotional problems, and the extent to which substitute attachment figures ease the distress of separation.

Controversies about attachment relationships have led to debates about many topics (for example, care in orphanages, medical care for babies, infant day care), including appropriate parenting plans for very young children. It is prudent to support a baby's relationship with a primary attachment figure during the first year to eighteen months of life, but it is equally important to encourage the development of a secondary attachment relationship. The best way to do this is to devise a schedule where the infant has a clear and consistent primary home and frequent but relatively brief contact with the other parent.

If a baby can develop a secure attachment relationship with each parent—even if one parent is the primary attachment figure and the other parent is the secondary attachment figure—parents can move more quickly toward more integrated schedules (if this is their goal). They also may be able to make occasional overnights (perhaps one per week) work well for a baby younger than eighteen months old. After all, many lucky parents have their babies spend occasional overnights with loving grandparents, an arrangement that apparently benefits everyone.

Attachment relationships are perhaps the major psychological consideration for infants, but there are other important issues including encouraging the infant's rapidly changing physical and cognitive development;

the provision of adequate physical care, health, and safety; the incredible importance of eating and sleeping routines for babies; practical issues such as the need for extra cribs, car seats, and other essential infant gear; and infant day care, which may be a challenge or an opportunity in devising a parenting plan. If a baby is in child care full time or close to it, the schedule can tolerate fewer disruptions. However, the day-care time gives the other parent many opportunities to spend time with the baby, provided that his or her schedule makes that possible.

Of course, the parents' work schedules and the distance between their homes affect how creative they can or cannot be. Two parents who both work 8:00 A.M. to 6:00 P.M. have fewer options for sharing time with a baby than do parents with more flexible hours or parents who work different hours. The sample schedules listed here assume some flexibility in at least one parent's schedule, but when, how, and whether parents can find free weekday time obviously depends on their work commitments or their willingness or ability to alter their work hours.

Besides day care, the other major opportunity for real creativity in the schedule involves spending time with a baby in his primary home. The familiarity of the environment enhances a baby's sense of security, and thus makes other changes less challenging. The problem, of course, is that parents have to have a pretty cooperative relationship, since this essentially places exes in regular close contact in one of their homes.

With all of these considerations in mind, here are some possible alternative schedules for children younger than eighteen months old:

Traditional Options for an Angry Divorce
- Every Saturday from 11:00 A.M. until 5:00 P.M., including an afternoon nap.
- Every Saturday from 9:00 A.M. until 1:00 P.M.; every Wednesday from 3:00 P.M. to 5:30 P.M., picked up at day care and returned to other parent's home.

More Integrated Options for a Distant Divorce
- Every Saturday from 11:00 A.M. until 5:00 P.M., including an afternoon nap; every Wednesday evening from 4:30 P.M. until 6:30 P.M., perhaps spending some time at the residential parent's home.
- Every Saturday from 2:00 P.M. until 6:00 P.M.; every Monday and Wednesday from 3:00 P.M. to 5:30 P.M., picked up at day care and returned to other parent's home.

Closely Integrated Options for a Cooperative Divorce
- Every Saturday from 11:00 A.M. until 5:00 P.M., including an afternoon nap; every Monday and Wednesday evening from 4:30 P.M. until 7:30 P.M.; some contact/feeding/bedtime takes place at residential parent's home.
- Two weekdays from 8:00 A.M. until 1:00 P.M. (substituting for child care); every Saturday from 11:00 A.M. until 5:00 P.M.; occasional Saturday overnights if the baby seems to tolerate them well.

Toddlers: Eighteen Months to Three Years

For toddlers, attachment relationships continue to be a key consideration. Toddlers have formed attachments to their primary caretaker, the residential parent. Toddlers also should be attached to the nonresidential parent provided that their contact has been regular and responsive to the baby's needs. Toddlers will prefer their primary attachment figure, especially in times of distress, but secondary attachment figures can comfort and soothe toddlers, too.

Because of this, most toddlers can manage longer separations from their primary attachment figure, including a regular overnight if it is part of a very clear, consistent routine. When experimenting with overnights for toddlers, parents need to communicate closely before, after, and perhaps during the toddler's overnight away from the primary residence. Hearing a parent's voice on the telephone may be reassuring to an anxious thirty-month-old, or the parent who is new to overnights may need to learn about the routines that work best for eating, sleeping, and toileting.

One of the major new psychological issues for toddlers is the emergence of the "terrible twos." Temper tantrums and the word "no" can become the toddler's favored negotiating style beginning around eighteen months and usually ending between the third and fourth birthdays. Part of the challenge in dealing with this behavior is that parents need to learn how and when to say no themselves while also respecting the toddler's growing sense of autonomy. It would be emotionally unwise (for the toddler and the parent) to treat every temper tantrum as an act of rebellion, so parents need to pick their battles wisely. Coparents can benefit greatly if they can consult each other about the behavior they observe, the limits they set, what works, and what doesn't.

Additional considerations for toddlers include the increasing need for intellectual and sensory stimulation: books, play, and peers, the new challenges of toileting (expect slow progress and lots of accidents if potty training is inconsistent across households), the toddler's continued need for routine, and perhaps the emergence of some challenging social behavior, which may include anything from hitting or biting to extreme shyness to developmental delays. Such concerns might affect what kind of schedule works, and they definitely are managed best if coparents can work together. Some sample schedules include:

Traditional Options for an Angry Divorce
- Every Saturday from 2:00 P.M. until 6:00 P.M. Overnight until 10:00 A.M. on alternate Sundays.
- Every other weekend from 2:00 P.M. on Saturday, with an overnight until 11:00 A.M. on Sunday. Alternate Monday evenings from 5:00 P.M. until 7:00 P.M. on the Monday following the weekend spent with the residential parent.

More Integrated Options for a Distant Divorce
- Every Saturday from 9:00 A.M. until 5:00 P.M., including a nap. Overnight until 9:00 A.M. on alternate Sundays. Every Wednesday evening from 4:30 P.M. until 6:30 P.M.

Closely Integrated Options for a Cooperative Divorce
- Every Saturday from 10:00 A.M. until 10:00 A.M. Sunday. Every Monday and Wednesday evening from 4:30 P.M. until 7:30 P.M.; some contact/feeding/bedtime takes place at residential parent's home.
- Two weekdays from 1:00 P.M. until 5:00 P.M. (substituting for child care); every Friday from 1:00 P.M. until 12:00 P.M. on Saturday.

Preschoolers from Three to Five Years Old

Children between the ages of three and five years old usually have multiple attachments to the various caregivers with whom they interact on a regular basis: both parents, teachers, regular babysitters, older siblings, and extended family members. During times of distress, a preschooler may strongly prefer one or perhaps either of two alternative attachment figures. Still, the number of different attachments both reflects and encourages the preschooler's budding independence.

Another big change is that children typically have developed a clear gender identity by the age of three, even though play with the opposite gender continues (typically ending around age six). Preschoolers might become particularly invested in acting like their same-gender parent, and if that relationship is weak (especially if the child has no other same-gender adult to identify with), this can cause questions and doubts for children but perhaps more so for parents.

Preschoolers can ask questions that seem laden with deep meaning but are probably pretty straightforward in their mind; for instance, "Jeremy lives with his daddy. How come I only see my daddy once in a while?" The appropriate answer to a question like this is not therapy for your three-year-old son but something straightforward like "Your daddy lives far away. It's sad that you can't see him more, but he loves you very much—and I love you more than anything! Do you want to call Dad tonight or draw a picture for him right now?"

Other important developmental changes for preschoolers include their increasing need for peer contact and their growing imagination. Peer play offers your preschooler stimulation and the opportunity to learn critical social skills like sharing and cooperation. Peer play also makes time pass much more easily—and quickly—for preschoolers, so plan to include friends during some of your time with children of this age. A preschooler's growing imagination is reflected not only in increased interest in stories and games, but also in fears of monsters and the dark, issues that may need to be managed across households. A four-year-old's sudden but persistent concern about monsters in the closet is normal and not a fear planted by a malicious coparent!

Even with the terrible twos behind them, preschoolers still need discipline. Many rules concern social relationships, everything ranging from learning to share to basic manners. A broader socialization task for preschoolers is beginning to learn how to control and regulate their emotions. "I know you want to ride Billy's tricycle, John, but that would make Billy sad. Why don't you play with the ball now and maybe Billy will let you have a turn in a little while?"

Preschoolers are developing a rudimentary sense of time that can make separations less anxiety provoking. Still, three-year-old children do not know how to measure time apart from their experience, so consistent schedules and routines remain critical. Even five-year-olds who are learning how to measure time cannot yet relate this abstraction to their experience. A five-year-old may know that Saturday comes in three days, but she will need frequent reminders and concrete guidance about what this means; for example, "First, there is today, Wednesday, then Thursday, then Friday, *then* Saturday."

Transitions between households can be difficult for preschoolers. Parents may experience transition troubles with preschoolers not only when exchanging the children, but also when dropping them off at preschool. As with the school drop-off, transitions between houses will be easier if they are positive ("You're going to have so much fun!"), relatively quick, and smooth—free of conflict or distress. And, of course, children three to five years of age can vary widely in their development. Less integrated schedules are likely to work better for a young three-year-old while an old five-year-old child is prepared to manage more integrated schedules. Here are some options:

Traditional Options for an Angry Divorce
- Every Saturday from 11:00 A.M. until 2:00 P.M. on Sunday.
- Every other weekend from 5:00 P.M. on Friday until 1:00 P.M. on Sunday. Alternate Mondays from 5:00 P.M. until 7:30 P.M. on the Monday following the weekend spent with the residential parent.

More Integrated Options for a Distant Divorce
- Every Saturday from 11:00 A.M. until 2:00 P.M. on Sunday. Every Wednesday evening from 4:30 P.M. until 7:30 P.M.
- Every other weekend from 5:00 P.M. on Friday until 3:00 P.M. on Sunday. Every Monday and Wednesday from 11:00 A.M. to 1:00 P.M. picked up and returned to day care.

Closely Integrated Options for a Cooperative Divorce
- Two weekdays from 1:00 P.M. until 5:00 P.M. (substituting for child care). Overnights every Thursday night. Every other weekend Thursday from 1:00 P.M. until 2:00 P.M. on Sunday.
- Every Thursday from 5:00 P.M. until 5:00 P.M. on Saturday.

Early School-Age Children from Six to Nine Years Old

Early school-age children still find security in their relationships with their attachment figures, and by this age, most children are able to seek comfort from other adults (for example, teachers) when their parents are unavailable. Six- to nine-year-old children also are much better able to regulate their own emotions than preschoolers, thus they are less dependent upon attachment figures. One consequence of their increased ability to understand and control their feelings is that early school-age children also begin to learn how to mask their true feelings. They may not want to "look scared" or "act like a baby" (cry). Gradually, and in many ways, sadly, school-age children learn not only how to control but also how to cover up their true feelings.

Because of their increased independence and capacity for emotion regulation, however, most early school-age children can easily manage separations of a few days and perhaps as long as a week if they are quite comfortable in their alternative environment. The early school-age child's growing understanding of time also makes separations easier. By the time they are six or seven, most children not only have learned the labels for time concepts—telling time, days of the week, months of the year—but they also have a concrete appreciation of the passage of time.

Still, parents need to recognize that time passes much more slowly at the age of seven than thirty-seven. Being two hours late may seem like nothing to a parent, but two hours is *two hours* to a child. (Remember how long time lasted between the end of school and dinnertime when you were six?) A week may be a very long time for a six- or even an eight-year-old to be away from a parent, thus some early school-age children struggle with seeing one parent only every other weekend or with being apart from each parent for long blocks of time in a week-to-week joint physical custody schedule. Telephone calls can help to bridge the distance of time, even though school-age children usually are not terribly good at making conversation over the telephone.

School, schoolwork, and, with luck, an eagerness to learn are the major developmental tasks for children this age. The central importance of the school routine can create problems for parenting plans (weekday visits and overnights can be more difficult) and requires increased parental cooperation to make weekday transitions work. Most seven-year-olds cannot independently organize their school materials, let alone get all of their stuff back and forth between houses, so parents need to carefully monitor and help manage the organizational effort.

Parents also need to coordinate and communicate about the children's schedule—after-school activities, special school events, basketball practices, piano lessons, award ceremonies—for logistical reasons and so they can both enjoy these special events and support their children's efforts and successes. I discuss potential problems (can angry parents sit together?) and effective strategies for managing these real-life complications in chapter 8.

Finally, many early school-age children have a well-developed (some would say overdeveloped) sense of fairness. They are learning rules in all areas of their lives, and they are more aware not only of their own emotions but of other people's feelings. This can make an angry divorce or a misunderstood parenting plan particularly hard on six- to eight-year-olds who may feel strong loyalties to both of their parents and torn about how to balance them. With all of these considerations as a backdrop, here are some alternative sample schedules:

Traditional Options for an Angry Divorce
- Every Friday from after school until 5:00 P.M. Saturday.
- Every other weekend from 5:00 P.M. Friday until 4:00 P.M. Sunday. Alternate Mondays from 5:00 P.M. until 7:30 P.M. on the Monday following the weekend spent with the residential parent.

More Integrated Options for a Distant Divorce
- Every Friday from after school until 5:00 P.M. Saturday. Every Monday evening from 4:30 P.M. until 7:30 P.M.
- Every other weekend from 5:00 P.M. Thursday until 4:00 P.M. Sunday. Alternate Thursday evenings from 5:00 P.M. until 7:30 P.M.

Closely Integrated Options for a Cooperative Divorce
- Every Thursday from 5:00 P.M. until 5:00 P.M. on Saturday.
- Every Wednesday from 3:00 P.M. until 5:00 P.M. on Saturday with one parent; every Saturday at 5:00 P.M. until 3:00 P.M. on Wednesday with the other parent.
- Every Monday and Tuesday with one parent; every Wednesday and Thursday with the other parent. Alternate weekends from Friday through Sunday with each parent.

Late School-Age Children from Ten to Twelve Years Old

Most theories of child development place six- to twelve-year-old children in the same developmental category because there are no major shifts in development in this age range. Still, in comparison with first or second graders, older elementary and middle school-age children have far more experience with school, peers, and separations from their parents, and they are far more deeply embedded in the culture of their schools, extracurricular activities, and peers. In a co-operative divorce, late school-age children are better able to manage a week-to-week schedule with each parent, but their own schedules are getting busy, which places new demands both on children and parents.

Late school-age children also are likely to have mastered modern methods of communication. The telephone is a central part of the lives of many ten-year-olds, and a good number are asking for (and perhaps getting) their own cell phones and e-mail accounts. While they pose a new set of problems (including monitoring the Internet), these new tools allow parents and kids to maintain closer and more frequent contact even when they are not together. Of course, there is no substitute for actually being with your eleven-year-old son, even though hugging him is now out of the question!

Like early school-age kids, late school-age children still talk about fairness a lot, but they increasingly are concerned about what's fair to *them*. After all, adolescence is only around the corner. As a result, children of this age are increasingly likely to voice opinions, often strongly worded, even angry ones, about a variety of matters, including their parents, divorce, and perhaps their schedule for spending time in two households. Parents should listen carefully to children's opinions whatever their age, but however well-articulated or strongly felt a child's opinion may be, remember that making decisions about the schedule is the responsibility of a parent, not a child.

Traditional Options for an Angry Divorce

- Every other weekend from 5:00 P.M. on Friday until 4:00 P.M. on Sunday. Alternate Mondays from 5:00 P.M. until 7:30 P.M. on the Monday following the weekend spent with the residential parent.

More Integrated Options for a Distant Divorce

- Every other weekend from 5:00 P.M. on Thursday until 4:00 P.M. on Sunday. Every Monday evening from 4:30 P.M. until 7:30 P.M.

Closely Integrated Options for a Cooperative Divorce

- Every Wednesday from 3:00 P.M. until 5:00 P.M. on Saturday with one parent; every Saturday from 5:00 P.M. until 3:00 P.M. on Wednesday with the other parent.
- Alternate weeks with each parent with exchanges on either Fridays or Sundays.

Adolescents Age Thirteen to Eighteen

By the time they become teenagers, children have developed "adult" intellectual capacities in their ability to reason, understand, and learn. But adolescents not only have limited experience *using* their ability to reason; they also are riddled by emotions and peer influences that commonly cloud clear thinking. There is a good reason why society only gradually gives adolescents increasing citizen rights—to drive, to vote, to purchase alcohol—and parents need to issue revocable "learner's permits" as teenagers test their own and their parents' limits in virtually every area of their life.

The focus for most American teenagers is on their own increasing independence, not on their family life. Because of their self-focus and their own busy schedules, some adolescents prefer to have one house as headquarters, even if they previously lived comfortably in joint physical custody. It also is not unusual for adolescents who have lived primarily with one parent to wish to make a change in their primary residence, especially if they move in with their same-sex parent.

Adolescents also often want and are able to manage more flexibility in their schedules, particularly after they get their driver's license. Of course, an adolescent's request for flexibility can be a means of manipulating parents to get more freedom from *either* them as well as a sincere desire to have a less scheduled routine.

Communication between parents, clear rules, and presenting a united front are even more important when it comes to disciplining a teenager. Parents also will do well to remind themselves—and it often takes a conscious effort to do so—that balancing autonomy and relatedness is the goal in parenting the adolescent. Teenagers naturally want more freedom, but they also want and need relationships with their parents, though your adolescent may be unwilling to admit this.

If they are unhappy with the schedule, teenagers are more likely than younger children to voice their preferences about changing it. Perhaps this will come in an angry outburst or perhaps as a serious and well-reasoned request. Parents should consider their teenager's requests very seriously. One reason is practical: It may become impossible to force a teenager to live by a schedule he hates. Still, parents should make the final decision about changing the schedule, even if their decision is to accept the teenager's request. This way the parents not only shoulder the burden of responsibility, but they also maintain authority and control. You will listen but you, the parent, are in charge. Some parenting plan options to consider:

Traditional Options for an Angry Divorce
- Every other weekend from 5:00 P.M. on Friday until 4:00 P.M. on Sunday. Some flexible contact is possible during other times.

More Integrated Options for a Distant Divorce
- Every other weekend from 5:00 P.M. on Thursday until 4:00 P.M. on Sunday. Dinner on the "off" Thursday, plus some flexible contact during other "off" times.

Closely Integrated Options for a Cooperative Divorce
- Every Wednesday from 3:00 P.M. until 5:00 P.M. on Saturday with one parent; every Saturday from 5:00 P.M. until 3:00 P.M. on Wednesday with the other parent with more flexibility to meet teenager's own needs.
- Alternate weeks with each parent with some flexible contact.

Holidays and Vacations

Working out the details of how children will spend holidays and vacations—or, more precisely, with which of you they will spend them—is one of the most difficult decisions parents face. Parents actually hate the thought of it, and, given the emotional aspect of most holidays and our ideas about how families ideally spend their vacation time—"together"—it's easy to see why.

Because it's a hot issue, working out vacation and holiday schedules is one task you may want to leave until it's time to negotiate your final agreement. However, remember that life will not go into suspended animation until then. Mother's Day, Father's Day, children's birthdays, summer vacation, and the really big holidays will keep rolling along. Without even the most basic agreed-upon guidelines about which of you has whom when, you may find yourself entering into discussions on a nearly weekly basis. Sooner or later, you will probably come to appreciate the benefits of working out a clear schedule for these times.

Bear in mind that what you decide, like any custody or visitation arrangement, is subject to change over time. For instance, many parents celebrate some holidays or birthdays together, particularly soon after they separate, and this can be a terrific short-term strategy. Celebrating a child's birthday or a special holiday together shows (and requires) a degree of cooperation, and a joint celebration can ease the pain of feeling alone during special family times—even though a shared holiday usually is a poignant reminder that the divorced family is different from what the married family had been.

But most divorced families cannot continue to celebrate holidays together over the long term. Sooner or later, parents and children move on, as they need to do. Joint celebrations can become complex and often untenable once parents become involved with new partners, who may have their own children (or children they have had together) and extended-family commitments of their own. What will you do when your new husband wants to go to his parents' for Thanksgiving, as he has always done, but for years you and your ex have been eating turkey together with your children?

Holiday schedules are rarely simple, and you may expect some hard-core negotiating around these deeply symbolic "bonus" times. However, the benefits of having a clear holiday schedule months (or years) in advance cannot be overstated. The result for most families is significantly *less* conflict in the long run. You do *not* want to be trying to negotiate a schedule with your ex as the days tick off toward the countdown of some very special event. Having a schedule, or at least having agreed on some basic principles (for instance, Mother's Day is spent with Mom; Father's Day with Dad—regardless of the inevitable flak from the other "honorees" of the day on either side of your respective families), will not only ease the transitions but make any time spent with either of you all the more enjoyable, too.

What is the best kind of holiday schedule? As with the weekly parenting plan, parents can and should take advantage of their opportunity to be creative, and here "creative" means simple, not complicated. That said, most holiday schedules are variations on one of three basic alternatives.

First, parents should easily be able to trade off holidays that are more important to one parent than the other, including each parent's birthday, Mother's Day, and Father's Day. If parents hold different faiths, they also may easily divide up certain religious holidays. A word to the wise if you find yourself wanting to be petty about these kinds of obvious trade-offs: don't. This isn't fair to anyone, especially your children, and the *last* thing you want to do in divorce is to pick unnecessary battles.

The second option is dividing some holidays and vacations. Summer vacation is the most obvious holiday to divide. For example, each parent might be allowed to take the children away for one, two, or three weeks of vacation, depending on the parents' work schedules and the ages of the children. Children younger than four or five are likely to have a difficult time spending more than a week away from their primary residence, although there still are options for creativity. Older siblings or familiar relatives, for instance, may go along on the vacation, and this can make the separation more manageable for younger children.

I also know many reasonably cooperative coparents who vacation together but separately. In this arrangement, the primary attachment figure travels to the same general destination, and she is available to young children as needed or perhaps makes a plan to see the children briefly once or more during the holiday. Whatever the details, summer vacation dates should be finalized by April 1 or May 1, and parents are wise to include a provision for doing this in their parenting plan.

In addition to the summer vacations, some parents also prefer to divide major holidays. Some parents might divide the Christmas holiday and school vacation so that the children are with one parent from the beginning of the school vacation through 1:00 P.M. on Christmas Day, and with the other parent for the rest of Christmas Day through the remainder of the school vacation. This arrangement may stay the same from year to year, or parents may alternate who gets the first half and who gets the second half of the holiday.

Alternating is the third basic option for dividing holidays, as many parents prefer to rotate who the children spend their holidays with from year to year. In some cases, one parent may have Rosh Hashanah and Hanukkah in one year while the other has Yom Kippur and Passover. The next year, the parents switch who has what holidays, alternating back and forth in successive years. And, of course, some parents combine trading off, dividing, and alternating; Mother's Day, Father's Day, and birthdays with the appropriate parent, dividing the Christmas school vacation, and alternating Thanksgiving and spring break from year to year.

The holiday schedule overrides the regular week-to-week schedule, and parents probably should make this clear in their agreement. Some parents try to make up missed days by subsequently altering the weekly schedule, but counting and reworking is complex, can create conflict, and is contrary to the spirit of holidays. However, parents must also be reasonable. If you and your six-year-old son have been gone on summer vacation for two weeks, be reasonable and let him see his other parent soon after you return home, even though this may be outside the regular schedule.

Finally, let me suggest one exception to the rule that it is best to follow a schedule for celebrating special events separately. I like to think that parents can find a way to celebrate part of their children's birthdays together. Attending the same birthday party or other important events that you both will want to attend is something you and your ex might consider doing now and continuing until you toast your son "Happy Birthday" with his first legal drink. Look upon this as great practice for other important events: your child's confirmation, bar or bat mitzvah, sweet sixteen, high school or college graduation, wedding, or your grandchild's birthdays.

More Considerations for Your Schedule and Your Parenting Plan

Some parents object to spelling out the details of weekly or holiday schedules because they want to be more flexible. Flexibility sounds great, but it can be a recipe for disaster. In order to be flexible, parents need to communicate with each other openly and frequently, whether they feel like it or not. They also have to be willing and able to deal with ambiguity and change.

Circumstances like this are likely to cause conflict even for parents with a cooperative divorce. My advice is to work out a very specific schedule so that boundaries are clear, expectations are clear, and the need for communication is minimal. Once you have a schedule in place, you can try being more flexible. If it works, good for you. But if it doesn't, at least you have a plan to fall back on. In fact, a good strategy for avoiding conflict is to include a number of additional arrangements related both to time and decision making in your parenting plan. Even though you might not be legally required to address many of these issues, some of the most important things to include are:

- *Consider creating different schedules for the school year and the summer.* Your children, and probably you, too, can be a lot more flexible during the summer than during the school year. You can use summers to be creative in your schedule, for instance, by moving from sole to joint physical custody during the summer, or even by reversing the schedule or changing the primary residence for the summer. Creating different schedules for the summer and school year is likely to be one of your few available options if you and your ex live a long distance from each other.
- *Consider contacts with your children in addition to the schedule.* You can bridge the time you and your children are apart with other kinds of contact, such as telephone calls, e-mail, letters, or brief visits when you visit your child's school or attend extracurricular activities. Because telephone calls can be intrusive, these generally should be limited to once a day at a set and mutually agreed-upon time.
- *Be specific!* You can avoid a lot of conflict if you are. You should discuss what joint legal custody does and does not mean with your ex: which decisions you will share and which you are free to make on your own and perhaps commit your joint understanding to writing in your agreement. You also should spell out your visitation and holiday schedule in detail. What do you mean by "Thanksgiving"? One day or the four-day weekend? Thanksgiving Day and the evening following? Where does the night before fit? What do you do if your child has the Wednesday before off from school, too? Spell out those details, including the hours, as shown in the various sample schedules.
- *Establish a method for communicating routinely about parenting with your ex.* A detailed parenting plan will save you headaches and heartaches, but you cannot anticipate everything in advance. This means you *will* need to communicate with your ex routinely. But

until communication becomes comfortable and easy, you should establish a plan for talking with your ex about your children. You should *not* plan to talk when exchanging the children. This time tends to be rushed and full of distractions, and you do not want to end up fighting in front of your kids. Instead, plan a regular but brief weekly telephone conversation with your ex at a mutually convenient time before exchanging your children. Talk for five minutes from work every Friday at noon or for five minutes at nine on Sunday night, after the kids are in bed.

The topics of your conversation should be straightforward: medications your children need to take; problems they are having within themselves or with each other; critical homework assignments or problems in school; and special achievements like a great test grade that you both want to be sure to praise. If talking on the telephone is too difficult, e-mail or voice mail is an acceptable alternative. A brief e-mail or telephone message also is often the best way to let your ex know about an upcoming special event. *But keep it brief and factual.* If you vent your anger in an e-mail or a telephone message, your ex will brood about the message and perhaps reply in some way that will escalate the conflict. Or maybe you will discover your message becoming a part of a legal proceeding.

- *Anticipate how you will make future changes, not what changes you will make.* In thinking about changing the schedule as your children grow older, focus on creating a plan for *how* you will make changes, not on *what* changes you will make at some unknown point in the future. You cannot know what kind of schedule will work best in the future, but you can plan to review the schedule and change it as needed.
- *Anticipate future disputes.* You can be certain about one thing even after you have worked out a detailed parenting plan: You will need to change it in the future. For example, the possibility that one parent will relocate causes great concern for many divorced parents, and the reality of relocation can be a real problem practically and legally. You cannot decide now what will happen in the event of relocation because you don't know whether this will happen or what

options the future might hold. However, you can anticipate how you will work to resolve the problem if it arises. Your agreement could indicate that either parent would give the other at least six months' notice of a potential relocation and indicate that parents would first attempt to resolve the issue themselves and then in mediation before going the legal route.

• *Perhaps include a statement of your general parenting philosophy.* Finally, you and your ex may want to include some statement about your parenting philosophy in your parenting plan. For instance, your commitment to supporting each other's parenting or perhaps your Children's Bill of Rights, based on the one you can find in chapter 3. A philosophical agreement like this is probably too vague to be legally enforceable, but the commitment you and your ex make as coparents is a moral force, particularly when committed to writing.

CHAPTER EIGHT

Coparenting for Resilience

Parents' struggles through divorce are understandable, but they come at a time when their children need their parents to be more—not less—available to them. It may take former partners a year or two, even longer, to renegotiate their relationship with each other, but children can't wait that long. In order to promote resilience, children need their parents to be parents *right now*—even in the middle of the crisis of divorce. With so much changing, children need to be able to count on Mom's being Mom and Dad's being Dad—and on Mom's and Dad's being Mom *and* Dad.

Before parents can really help children with their feelings, they have to recognize and contain their own emotions. Think of that safety announcement the flight crew makes before every takeoff: If the oxygen masks drop, put on your own before helping your child with hers. It is the same in divorce. You have to take care of your own feelings before you can best help your children with theirs.

This is one of the main reasons why in earlier chapters I discussed *adults'* hurt, anger, and grief, and the need to set new boundaries around old relationships—and around legal negotiations. Mastering or at least beginning to master these emotional and practical tasks is essential to effectively promoting resilience in your children after divorce.

These are not, however, the only hurdles divorcing parents must clear for the sake of their children. The task of parenting apart presents a whole new set of emotional challenges. Many of these emotions differ for parents depending upon whether the children are with them most of the time or only a relatively small amount of time, or whether the parents share joint physical custody.

Challenges for Residential Parents

Residential parents—those who have the children living with them most of the time and whose home is the children's primary residence—face a pretty basic practical and emotional challenge: the hard work of raising children alone. You might have thought you were busy raising your children *before* you separated. Now, you are juggling more balls and faster, trying to keep them all in the air with both hands *and* both feet.

For residential parents, even little things like shopping for groceries cease to be little. When you were together, you might have shopped when the kids were in school or on the weekend when your ex could watch the children or on your way home from work. Now, you may buy groceries on your lunch hour, if you can manage that, or else you may have to haul the kids to the store with you after work.

Then there is getting the kids dressed, fed, and out in the morning, and then fed, undressed, and back into bed at night. In between, residential parents worry about things like school, shuttling the kids to wherever they need to be, their homework, their fighting, and their feelings. Residential parents also get to do everything else involved in managing children and a household all alone—doing the dishes, cleaning house, mowing the lawn, shopping, paying bills, and repairing whatever breaks. And they feel the stress of doing it all on their own with only one head, two hands, and twenty-four hours in the day.

When the children are off with their other parent, residential parents often feel relieved to have the house and a little time to themselves. But this "free time" is often consumed by doing the chores that could not get done before. Whatever relief residential parents feel often is tainted by feelings of loneliness and anxiety. You may feel like someone has ripped a hole in your life when your children are gone, or maybe you just are uncomfortable not knowing exactly where your children are and what they are doing. You also may worry about your ex's parenting, perhaps for good reasons.

When your kids return, overtired, overindulged, sad, quiet, or just "off," you are confronted with another, unwanted challenge: dealing with a break in the stability that you so desperately want for your children. If things go well with your ex, you may wonder who your children would rather be around—you or your ex. If they don't go well, you may worry and ask why you are left cleaning up another of your ex's messes.

Challenges for Nonresidential Parents

Contrary to what some assume, life is not one big party for nonresidential parents, those who do not have their children living with them most of the time. Their exes sometimes think that nonresidential parents are living a party life, and in some cases that may be true. Nonresidential parents certainly have more free time—probably too much free time. Many nonresidential parents literally do not know what to do with their free time without the kids around to fill it.

You may feel lost about what to do in little ways, like not knowing or caring about what to make for dinner, and in big ones, like wondering who the heck you are now that you are only a part-time parent. Your life—and your identity—was structured around your marriage and your children, and now that structure has crumbled. While residential parents never for a moment question whether or not they are still parents, those who see their children less often may wonder.

For parents whose children are with them only every other weekend or so, the hole in their life can be a yawning abyss, not an occasional void. Many parents in this circumstance realize that they need to construct a whole new life for themselves, but they wonder, "What should that life be?" One benefit of being frantically busy with children is that there is no time in the planner or PalmPilot for existential crises. For better or worse, your children fill—and define—your existence.

Without the structure and meaning of having children, nonresidential parents need to find new answers to old existential questions. The search for answers may cause some parents to cut loose in ways that they have not for years, but the partying—and perhaps the promiscuity—soon loses its appeal. Instead, new activities and brief new relationships become superficial ways of trying to fill the emptiness. A better way to fill the void may be to work harder or to get back in shape, but your motivation as a nonresidential parent often is just not there. What you really want, what you are really missing, are your kids.

Nonresidential parents often long for that feeling of family when they are away from their children. Unfortunately, sometimes these parents don't feel like they are part of a family when they are with the children, either. When you finally see your kids, you may find it hard to connect during such a short, unnatural amount of time. Maybe you try to cram two weeks' worth of life into every other weekend or to make up for whatever time you have lost. If so, your ex may complain that you get to have all the fun with the kids, but you probably feel empty, not happy. Wild weekends with the children do not fill the lonely void any better than wild weekends on your own. The frenzy does not fill the hole; it just covers it for a while.

Some Challenges for Joint Custody

Parenting apart also presents a challenge for parents with joint physical custody. With joint custody, parents face some of the problems of both residential and nonresidential parents. They juggle like mad when the kids are with them and then wonder what to do with themselves when the children are gone.

Parents with joint physical custody also often struggle trying to find a rhythm in the calendar not only for their children but also for themselves. They sometimes feel like a yo-yos and fear that their children feel the same way. Just when you settle into a routine, the kids are yanked away to be with their other parent. Joint physical custody preserves a child's close relationships with *both* of her parents, but parents with joint custody sometimes wonder if there is sufficient stability and continuity in their child's relationship with *either* parent.

If you have joint physical custody, you knew beforehand that it would require extra effort. Now you know that the effort is *work*. Maybe the clean clothes you send with the kids always come back dirty or their stuff ends up scattered between two households. When the kids need their cuddly toy, homework, or sports equipment, it always seems to be at the other house, and you and your ex have to make an extra trip and have an extra exchange. Parents with joint physical custody also have to work constantly to coordinate parenting across two households, doing things such as sharing a babysitter, finishing homework assignments begun elsewhere, or extending discipline from one house to the next.

These are all major challenges of joint physical custody when parents have a cooperative coparenting relationship. When the coparenting relationship is distant or angry, either every complication leads to an argument or parents with joint physical custody just do not bother to try to coordinate things for the kids. Joint physical custody may keep things balanced for the kids, but it is much more complicated to share parenting across two households than to base it in just one.

Meeting the Challenges of Parenting Apart

Parents have their own strong and pressing feelings in divorce, but sometimes parents must put their own feelings on the shelf—at least temporarily—so they can better meet their children's needs. Not only must parents manage their emotions, but they also may have to learn new ways of managing their children. Parenting alone can require more energy, patience, and confidence than parenting with a partner, and it may mean that parents have to learn new roles, too. Some parents need to learn how to discipline on their own; others how to show affection; and most must master the tasks (cooking, cleaning, yard work, repairs, finances, arranging playdates) that their partner fulfilled in managing a household while raising children.

Parenting can be complicated but the goal of good parenting might be less complicated than you have been led to believe. In the emotional turmoil of divorce it's important to remember the basics of parenting. According to leading experts in developmental and child clinical psychology, there really are only two critical aspects of parent-child relationships: love and parental authority.

Reassuring Children That They Are Loved

If we were fortunate to have had loving parents, feeling loved is our most treasured memory of childhood. Unfortunately, following separation and divorce many children question their parents' love. So now is the time to reassure your children of your abiding love for them. You want to affirm your love because it is wonderful to hear "I love you," even when you feel secure. You also want to affirm your love because, due to the divorce, your children may be confused, frightened, or harbor hidden insecurities about your love or the love of their other parent.

Saying "I love you" is always nice and often reassuring but the little things that parents do, and do regularly, are what really demonstrate their abiding love for their children. Children always are comforted by routines and rituals, and predictable activities are especially reassuring during this tumultuous time. Children of different ages are reassured by developmentally appropriate routines, such as always being tucked in with their security blanket, being read a story at bedtime every night, always finding a special treat in their lunch box, having a parent there to help them with homework every evening, or even just regularly watching a favorite television show with them.

Family rituals also are important, particularly for older children. Family rituals may include sharing certain meals together, regular visits with relatives, attending religious services, taking vacations together, or celebrating holidays and special events as a family—even if this means inventing new celebration rituals now that you are on your own. And let's not forget the special memories we treasure from our own childhoods: an affectionate nickname, that special greeting, or a funny incident that brings a smile thirty years later.

Children feel secure when a parent who cares for them most of the time maintains old routines or creates new routines and rituals. This does not mean that routine and ritual are unimportant to children in their relationship with a parent whom they see less often. Actually, just the opposite is true. If your children are with you less often, they need the boundaries of your parental love to be even *more* clear and consistent. If you see your children every other weekend—or according to whatever schedule—you probably know how hard it can be to show your love from a distance. Because it may be hard to communicate your love, you need to show it all the more clearly.

How can you do this? One way is that, until your schedule is second nature for your kids, they need you to be absolutely rigid in sticking to the plan for picking them up, making telephone calls, whatever it is you are supposed to do. You may not like the restrictions of parenting on a schedule, but particularly soon after your separation, your children need you to be faithful to the routine. Your consistency helps your children to feel secure in your love. It reminds them that even though there may be physical distance between you, you are still thinking of them, and they are still your top priority, no matter where you are. Being late, missing phone calls, or otherwise breaking promises (and you should view things like visitation schedules as promises, even if you feel they were foisted upon you by your ex or the courts) sends the message that there is something else in your life that means more to you than they do. Needless to say, this is neither a healthy nor a happy thought for a child who misses a parent's presence.

Children also need clear and consistent parenting if they are living in a joint physical custody arrangement. Particularly for the first several months, children will feel more confident and comfortable if parents adhere closely to their joint custody schedule. This is true even if their parents' ideal and eventual goal is to be more flexible. During this time of uncertainty, children's needs for predictability and stability are greater than parents' wishes for flexibility and accommodation.

If you have joint custody, you and your ex also will need to work with a good deal of cooperation to foster your children's sense of security by establishing similar daily routines across two households. You may instinctively balk at having even a simple daily routine dictated to some degree by what your ex does in his home, but remember, this is about the kids, not about you. If your ex insists on having your ten-year-old in bed by 9:00 P.M. on school nights or makes time each week for your seven-year-old's reading tutor, you probably should do something pretty similar, too.

Especially when children are younger, consistency is not only comforting; it simply is much less confusing for children to operate under one set of rules and routines rather than two. This does not mean you have to do everything exactly as your ex does, or vice versa, but if you have joint physical custody, you at the minimum want to consult about these sorts of things. That way, you'll at least understand why your son is exhausted in the mornings before school when he is with you or why your daughter's reading grades aren't improving as they should.

Discipline Is Loving

Following a separation, many parents struggle to determine when and how to discipline their children. This is true even of parents who consider themselves firm but fair disciplinarians. Something about the many changes and stresses of divorce leaves many parents either less certain about their parenting skills or too emotionally or physically drained to devote the same energy and attention to the task that they did before.

Sometimes it's a combination of all of the above. Some parents excuse themselves from their parental responsibilities by saying they just want to enjoy their children, and discipline seems like an intrusion on their precious time together. Other parents know it is important to set limits, but when their children misbehave following a divorce, they no longer are sure how to respond. Does Jessica need discipline or patience and understanding? You certainly do not want to discipline your children if their misbehavior is a symptom of a deeper emotional concern, and you may be uncertain about what is a symptom and what is simply obnoxious behavior. (Let me reassure you: Children in the throes of divorce are still capable of simply being obnoxious!) Still other parents know their children are misbehaving, but they are not sure how to discipline, they do not have the confidence to follow through, or they try but their discipline does not work.

Finally, let's not forget that prior to your separation, you and your ex were parents together. Maybe one of you played the good cop and the other played the bad cop. Perhaps little Kyle or teenage Amanda knew to listen to you because it was a more attractive prospect than having to deal with parent number two later on. Or maybe your child complied more readily then because it seemed like a fairer system overall. To some kids, a second parent functions as a walking court of appeals, someone who might temper or soften the first parent's judgment and, if they're really lucky, overturn it "on appeal."

Before your separation, your children probably had a reasonably good idea of where the two of you stood on a range of issues and how you could be expected to respond. Now, however, even you may not know how you feel about, say, staying up late on school nights when it's one of their precious nights with you or about talking back, since you may be able to empathize and believe they do have something to be upset about.

In the wake of so many changes, you can be sure that your children have been watching you and your ex like they never did before. Your inconsistencies in enforcing rules, changes in parenting style, and differences in tolerance levels for certain behaviors have been duly noted and filed for future reference. Just as you might feel obligated to somehow make up for the difficulties of divorce, your child may also feel that he or she is due something in exchange for the emotional upheaval and many adjustments this change has demanded. I do not mean to suggest that children are coldhearted and calculating about this—they aren't. But it is human nature to desire some acknowledgment or compensation for our troubles, especially those we did not cause.

If you are struggling with discipline for whatever reason, you do need to find ways to discipline your children fairly but firmly. Even though, like many divorced parents, you might be more concerned that your children feel loved, your children still need your consistent and reasonable discipline. They need you to maintain, reestablish, or, for the first time, develop clear boundaries that demonstrate your parental authority. Your rules need to be clear, your ex's rules need to be clear, and to the extent possible, the two of you need to work together to set fair rules for your children and enforce them across two households.

Most important, you need to follow through. You can say that there's no eating in the den a hundred times a day, but if your children eat in the den without incurring consequences, you have not made a rule—you have just been talking. And kids know the difference.

Children need discipline to teach them how to behave and to understand and learn to take responsibility for the consequences of misbehavior. As much as children (especially teenagers) may protest otherwise, they also need discipline because limits are comforting. A little freedom from authority can be fun, but as most of us remember from our own youth, too much freedom is frightening. Clear, firm, and reasonable parental discipline marks a boundary of parental love as much as of parental authority. Parental authority teaches children how to behave, and it also makes children feel more secure.

The Goal: Authoritative Parenting

So what makes a good parent? You certainly have heard or read an abundance of advice about parenting in books, magazines, or on television. You probably have been told how to be a better parent by your mother, your grandmother, your next-door neighbor, your children's teachers, or maybe by a stranger in the supermarket. Maybe even your kids have had a few suggestions. Your ex also might have told you what you need to do differently as a parent.

The range of advice we all hear about parenting reflects the many challenges of being a parent, our imperfections in doing the job, children's cleverness in outsmarting us, and our own insecurities as parents. And divorce casts a long shadow across many fields of competence. The emotions of divorce may make us question just how good we really are as friends, lovers, spouses, and, yes, even as parents. Many people feel like they have failed in their marriage because of divorce, and in their minds this means they have also failed their children. In short, they feel hopeless and helpless. They wonder, "What else could go wrong?" or maybe, "Can I do anything right?"

Parenting is a big job, and probably the most important responsibility in your life. But let's put it in perspective, too. Parenting can be a source of anxiety even for the most secure, happily married among us. Do not be surprised if especially now you find yourself doing a little—or maybe a lot more—wondering, wavering, and second-guessing.

Parenting is challenging, but as I said, good parenting really is less complicated than many would have us believe. Good parenting really is all about finding the right balance between love and discipline. In fact, the leading method of classifying parenting styles places parents in one of four categories based on whether or not parents are warm and loving on the one hand and firm and fair disciplinarians on the other hand.

The best style of parenting, *authoritative parenting,* is to be both loving *and* firm with discipline. According to leading researchers, whether married or not, a parent's goal is straightforward: to establish clear boundaries of parental love and parental authority with your children. The value of this advice is evident in the benefits for children. The children of authoritative parents tend to be independent, responsible, and self-confident. This is true whether their parents live together or not.

In contrast to authoritative parents, *authoritarian parents* are strict in discipline, but they also are autocratic and offer their children relatively little love, understanding, and support. The children of authoritarian parents tend to be well behaved but less self-assured and socially competent than the children of authoritative parents. Later in adolescence, the children of authoritarian parents may rebel against the oppressive regime of parental control.

Indulgent parents are the opposite of authoritarian parents. They give their children a lot of love, but for one reason or another, indulgent parents don't really bother with discipline. As a result, the children of indulgent parents are likely to be self-confident but also selfish and impulsive. In short, the children of indulgent parents don't learn to respect other people's boundaries.

The last group of parents are *neglectful parents*, people who generally show meager interest in their children. Neglectful parents offer their children little in the way of affection or discipline. The children of neglectful parents are the most likely to suffer from extreme problems such as child abuse and juvenile delinquency.

In order to promote resilience in your children through a divorce, you want to be an authoritative parent—to maintain, create, or reestablish clear boundaries of your parental love and parental authority. You also need to do everything you reasonably can to help your ex be an authoritative parent, too.

Learning to Be an Authoritative Parent

Many divorced parents need to learn new roles in parenting in order to offer their children clear boundaries of both love and parental authority. This certainly was the case for Tara and Carlos, who each needed to find new ways to relate to Carlos Junior and Isabella.

As a result of their work in mediation, Tara and Carlos resolved the biggest problem their divorce created for their children. They succeeded in turning their angry divorce around and creating a more distant divorce that worked better for everyone. The distance—actually the reduced conflict made possible by Carlos and Tara's more businesslike relationship—made family life much easier for all four of them. The clear and more formal boundaries in their relationship freed Carlos and Tara from the stress and distraction of constantly anticipating and preparing for a fight. As a result, they were able to focus on parenting their children rather than on feeding their anger. The drop in tension relieved Carlos Junior from his role as his mother's defender, and the truce allowed Isabella to end the high-wire act in which she watched her every step, delicately balancing her relationship with each of her parents.

This all sounds great, doesn't it? But there was also a catch. The new, welcome distance in their relationship created problems in parenting that Tara and Carlos never faced when they were together. When they were married, Tara and Carlos each specialized in their parenting roles. Tara was more of an indulgent parent. She gave her children a lot of love and attention, but she really didn't discipline them. She left the disciplining to Carlos. In contrast to Tara, Carlos was more of an authoritarian parent. He was strict and expected his rules to be followed without question. Though Carlos clearly loved his children, he did not show them much affection.

Neither of the parents ever developed the other parent's strengths in their own parenting repertoire. Carlos left most of the loving up to Tara, and Tara left most of the disciplining for Carlos.

These specialized parenting roles worked well enough not only for Carlos and Tara, but also for Carlos Junior and Isabella when their parents lived together. Although neither parent individually practiced authoritative parenting, together Mom's love and Dad's authority attained some balance that "averaged out" in an essentially authoritative parenting style. When their parents split up, that balance was lost, and Carlos Junior and Isabella were left with being raised under one extreme style or the other.

Tara's and Carlos's struggles in parenting alone began right after they separated, but in the heat of their battles and the general chaos of separation, neither Tara nor Carlos paid much attention to the new challenges they faced. Once things settled down as their relationship grew appropriately more distant, Carlos and Tara raised various parenting concerns in our mediation sessions—first about what they saw to be each other's deficiencies and eventually about their own struggles and uncertainties.

A conflict over Carlos Junior's dropping grades was a turning point for his parents. Always a straight-A student, Carlos Junior brought home several Bs in the two marking periods immediately following his parents' separation. Tara attributed his slipping grades to her son's anger at his father and his general distress over the divorce, and she advocated doing nothing about the decline. After all, she reasoned, Carlos Junior had always been a good boy; he was entitled to be upset and distracted.

Initially, Carlos followed Tara's lead in parenting, as he had done when they were together. He felt that she was the expert when it came to the children's emotional lives. However, his cooperation ended abruptly when Carlos Junior got a C in algebra and a C+ in history on his next report card. Without consulting Tara, he grounded Carlos Junior indefinitely on the weekends, including those the boy spent with his mother. Carlos also told his son that he would not be allowed to apply for his driver's license (which he soon would be eligible to do) until he once again had straight As.

When he returned home from his weekend with his father and appealed his case to his mother, Carlos Junior found a sympathetic ear. Tara told him that she would talk with his father, and she said that Carlos Junior would *not* be grounded at her house. When she telephoned Carlos to chastise him for his lack of understanding and tell him about her position on the grounding, Carlos got furious. "Why are you undermining me?" he demanded. "I listened to you, and I did it your way, and what happened? Carlos's grades did not improve—they got worse."

"But can't you see how upset he is about the divorce?" Tara pleaded. "That's what this is all about." Tara paused and continued in an accusatory tone, "And grades aren't everything. You know, everyone doesn't have to be a 'big success' like you to be happy."

An angry argument ensued, but fortunately Tara followed a rule we had set in mediation in order to keep their relationship more businesslike. When they couldn't come to some understanding after talking for five minutes and the discussion continued to be heated, Tara said she was going to end the conversation. She told Carlos, "We're getting nowhere, and I'm going to do what Dr. Emery said to do. I'm going to hang up now and call him for an appointment."

When I met with them a few days later, the discussion began with a lot of anger. Completely losing his temper for perhaps the first time in mediation, Carlos shouted at Tara, "You are undermining my fatherly duty and doing harm to a boy who can easily earn As!"

Tara was obviously angry, too, but Carlos's loss of control gave her the upper hand for a change. She replied, "I believe that I am Carlos Junior's parent, too, and I will not support your harsh punishment when the boy is so clearly upset by our divorce. Can't you see how upset he is? Can't you understand that there are things more important than grades?"

A heated but ultimately productive discussion followed this initial outburst. (Managed conflict that occurs out of earshot of your children *can* be constructive.) During this time, it became obvious that not only were Carlos and Tara struggling with their own parenting shortcomings, but they also were attempting to compensate for the failings they perceived in each other. After Carlos half yelled, "I have to discipline him because you won't," and Tara shot back, "And I have to sympathize with him because you can't," I jumped in and confronted them about their attempts to compensate for what they saw as each other's weakness as a parent. I was relieved when they both readily agreed—somewhat self-righteously—that they each were trying to compensate for the other's failings.

"You each have your own strengths and weaknesses in relating to your children," I said. "But you seem to have gone too far in trying to balance each other out. You remind me of two children who keep moving farther and farther toward the end of a seesaw in order to keep things balanced. Eventually, someone's bound to fall off and get hurt. There is a much better way for you to keep things in balance. What would happen if you both moved a little bit toward the middle instead of further toward the edge?"

The image seemed to work for Tara and Carlos. After a few minutes of much cooler conversation, Tara actually admitted that she did need to learn to discipline not only Carlos Junior but Isabella, too. Lately, she admitted, Isabella had been ignoring her household chores and talking back to her in a very disrespectful tone.

Tara's admission freed up Carlos to acknowledge his own problems. He confessed that he sometimes had a hard time relating to the children; he was at a loss about what to do with them. Tara took advantage of the opening and jumped in with several suggestions, "How about letting the kids have friends over to your house? They'd be happier, and that way you would get to know their friends—and see how the kids acted around them."

When Carlos nodded in agreement, Tara added, "And why don't you try eating more meals at home with the kids, even if you have pizza, instead of always having 'dates' with them at fancy restaurants?" Tara paused to see how Carlos would react to this, and when he nodded again, she said, "And, Carlos, the most important thing you can do is just listen to the kids. They want to know you're *there* with them."

This last remark provoked Carlos, who started to get defensive again, but I interrupted him before he could really get started and said, "Tara is suggesting that you listen more, and I think she really is trying to help you. Maybe now is a good time to show her that you can take her advice. Try to just listen to what she has to say."

I held my breath while Carlos struggled with his emotions with a pained look on his face. I breathed a sigh when he said, "Okay."

And Tara took the cue perfectly. She said, "I need to listen, too. And maybe you're right. Carlos Junior does need to do better in school. What can we do?" Carlos then outlined some suggestions that were stricter than what Tara might have been inclined to do. For example, Carlos believed they should insist that he devote a set number of hours to study each night and that he attend the special help tutoring sessions after school. Tara objected that this was too much; Carlos Junior would rebel. She admitted that she had been allowing Carlos to study in front of the television. How about if she made him study in his room—and no television until he was done? Carlos agreed to give this a try and to implement the same rules at his house. And, no, they agreed, no driver's license until the grades improved.

Finally, Carlos agreed that he would talk to Carlos Junior about his son's feelings about the divorce. Tara suggested several strategies to Carlos to help him manage this difficult discussion: "Why don't you go for a drive so neither of you will be distracted by Isabella, the telephone, or anything else? I think it's all right if you share some of your own feelings with Carlos Junior He wants to know how you feel and that might help him to open up. Just listen to Carlos Junior. Don't try to tell him how he should feel."

For the first time in a long time, Carlos and Tara really discussed their concerns about their children in some depth, like parents do. Eventually, they agreed that Dad would talk with Isabella about allowing her to have friends over to his house and also letting her go to the mall with friends on occasion. He also offered to talk to Isabella about her disobeying and talking back to her mother. Carlos said he would tell Isabella that he expected her to follow Mom's rules and that Mom was going to let him know if things did not improve.

During our next mediation appointment, Carlos began by thanking Tara for her suggestions. He also told her, proudly, how Carlos Junior finally did open up to him a little. For her part, Tara smiled at Carlos and thanked him for talking to Isabella. The back talk had decreased substantially.

Parenting apart, Tara and Carlos could no longer easily compensate for each other like they did when they were married, but they did learn to stop trying to overcompensate. And they admitted—to themselves and to each other—their need to learn new parenting skills. Because of their admissions, they were able to give each other some really useful tips on parenting, and as best they could, they started to support each other as parents. Carlos still was more authoritarian and Tara still was more indulgent, but they really did move toward the middle on their parenting seesaw.

New Parenting Roles

Tara and Carlos faced problems that many people encounter in learn-ing to parent and coparent for resilience after divorce. Any load is heavier to carry by yourself. Even if your ex was not a very involved parent, now you probably appreciate some things you once took for granted. Little things like being able to run to the store without pack-ing your two-year-old into the car, having someone to consult when your six-year-old gets into trouble at school, or having someone who could take over the conversation when you are on the verge of losing it with your fourteen-year-old.

Besides an extra pair of hands, when you were married you and your ex probably worked together by specializing in your parenting roles, perhaps not to the degree that Tara and Carlos did, but most people develop some parenting specializations. Maybe you did this be-cause your philosophies differed, you fell into stereotyped roles, or you just were better at or simply enjoyed doing different things with the kids. Whatever the reason, you could specialize when the two of you were running this business of parenting together. Now that you are operating separate franchises, you both need to learn new facets of the business. For example:

- You need to learn new ways to discipline, especially if you are a mother who used to tell your disobedient children, "Just wait until your father gets home!"
- You need to learn new ways to show your love if you are a father who used to rely on your wife to nurture your children and per-haps nurture your relationship with them.
- You need to learn how to play both good cop and bad cop if one of you used to discipline the kids while the other supported them through their punishment.
- You may need to learn how to change a diaper, to throw a ball, to kiss a wound, to ignore a whine, to listen better, to say no.

Children still have a mother and a father even though their parents are separated. But when your children are with you, you have to be both their mother and their father. One of the biggest challenges of parenting apart is that parents can no longer be specialists in their parenting roles.

Good Parenting Is Good Therapy

Most children do not need therapy in the weeks and months after their parents' separation. Unless your conflicts or your children are out of control, a decision about getting therapy for children probably can wait for several months or longer; maybe even forever if you can find a way to establish some real stability in your children's lives. What children really need in the months after a marital separation—and for the rest of their childhood—is not so much the weekly professional therapy session as clear, consistent, loving, and authoritative parenting every single day.

What children need from their parents is not terribly complicated, but knowing what to do is not the hard part of parenting. The hard part is doing it. Being a good parent is hard enough work in a happy marriage. The challenge of parenting alone is far greater. But the best way you and your ex can help your children is to do what Tara and Carlos did: Find new ways to be good parents and coparents despite the many changes and challenges of parenting apart. You *can* coparent for resilience, and good parenting really is the best therapy for your children in the crisis of divorce.

Dealing with Children's Problems— and Problem Children

Of course, a huge part of the challenge of parenting apart is dealing with children's problems. Parents want to help their children through their worries and sadness, their anger and misbehavior. But how do they do this? How much should parents talk with their children about the separation and what should they be telling them? What should a mother do when her six-year-old son tearfully says, "I miss Daddy"? What should a father do when his twelve-year-old daughter screams, "I want to go back to Mom's!"? Should parents discipline their children for being angry with them? What if they think their anger, like Carlos Junior's, is related to their emotional struggles with the separation? Or what if, like Carlos Junior's grades, it isn't clear what is causing a child to have new difficulties? And what if parents have a child with his own difficulties—ADHD, a learning disability, a chronic physical condition, or some emotional difficulty?

What should parents do? As much as they can, they should parent the same way they did when they were together. In order to provide children with this continuity, parents have to get a grasp on their own emotions, establish better boundaries with each other, and master the challenges of parenting alone and on a schedule. Then parents have to think on their feet and find ways to respond to unexpected situations.

Challenges to Parental Authority

Residential parents often have more difficulty establishing definite boundaries of parental authority than their parental love. In contrast, nonresidential parents usually have more problems redefining the boundaries of their love than their authority. What does this mean? Discipline can be a particular problem for residential parents, because they often feel overwhelmed with the tasks of parenting alone, they no longer have someone right there to reassure them that they are doing the right thing, and because, like Tara, residential parents might not have been the primary disciplinarian in the marriage.

Eighty percent to 90 percent of divorced residential parents are mothers, and as was true for Tara, there often is a degree of truth behind the stereotype of the mother who disciplines by saying, "Just wait until you father gets home!" When Dad isn't coming home, Mom needs to learn how to discipline the children herself. Or, more accurately, children must learn that Mom's is now the final word.

Nonresidential parents—usually fathers—also can have problems disciplining children. Some of the troubles in reasserting the boundaries of parental authority are similar to those faced by residential parents, but a particular problem for nonresidential parents is they may not want to "ruin" their time with the children by disciplining them.

Every Day Cannot Be Christmas or the Fourth of July

It makes sense that divorced parents, particularly nonresidential parents, want to enjoy their limited time with their children. But every day is not Christmas. Nor should it be. Children do things wrong, and their mistakes present important learning opportunities. Parents want to teach their children that their rudeness, selfishness, laziness, or anger *is* wrong, but if they do nothing, they teach the opposite lesson. The absence of discipline teaches children that it is all right to ignore "please" and "thank you," to refuse to share with siblings, to have no responsibilities in the family, or to use threats and intimidation to get your way.

Your children particularly need your discipline if you were more of the disciplinarian when you and your ex were together. Fathers often are stricter than mothers, and if you are a nonresidential father, your kids *need* you to keep being their dad, not just their buddy. You want to have a good relationship with your kids, and the best way to do this is to have a normal, healthy, parental relationship with them. Being a parent includes fun, love, and saying no!

Discipline Strategies

Face it: Discipline is a chore. But being the boss is part of a parent's job responsibilities. Residential parents have no other choice than doing a lot of this work by themselves, and nonresidential parents also need to play a role in discipline if they want to do their job. So whatever your circumstances—residential parent, nonresidential parent, joint physical custody—here are some general rules for effective discipline:

- *Keep children busy.* Your children will be far less likely to need discipline if you keep them busy doing something fun or productive. Help them to find age-appropriate activities that involve their time, interest, and energy; for example, creative play with toys, learning the joy of reading, or taking part in extracurricular activities.
- *Focus on the positive.* Discipline involves rewarding desirable behavior, not just punishing inappropriate behavior. Invest some time in teaching your children the right way to behave and praise them for behaving well. Catch them being good. If you do, you will be a lot more effective as a parent, and you will spend a lot less time punishing your children.
- *Make the rules clear.* Children can only follow the rules that they know, understand, and are physically and developmentally capable of following. Make your expectations clear. Write things down on a star chart or work things out in a behavior contract with your older child if that helps you to be clear. Be specific about the consequences for breaking rules (for example, losing television time) and make consequences relevant to the transgression as well as age appropriate. In addition to making your expectations clear, your children will think your discipline is fairer if you set the rules and consequences beforehand, and when it comes time to play the heavy, you will feel less guilty enforcing a rule that you established previously.
- *Make rules fair.* Reasonable rules are more likely to be followed, because your kids will see them as more fair. You do not *have* to set

the same rules as your ex or as the parents of your kids' friends. Still, checking with other parents about their rules is a great place to start in setting your own.

- *Be democratic.* Particularly as your children grow older, involve them in setting the rules and the consequences for following or breaking them. Teenagers will feel more of a commitment to curfews and other rules they have helped to set. They will still break the rules on occasion (they *are* teenagers, after all), but your children will more readily accept the consequences when they helped to set them up. In addition, some democratic negotiation will teach your teenager an *appropriate* way of testing your limits. She can make her case for a later curfew by talking to you and proving that she can observe the current rules rather than just by coming in late. You also may want to involve your school-age children in some rule making. "What do *you* think is a fair punishment?" often is a good question to ask your school-age child. He may surprise you with a thoughtful reply and a suggestion for a pretty tough consequence for his misbehavior.

- *Enforce rules consistently.* Rules become rules when they are enforced, not when they are written down. When you set new rules, you need to follow through with them consistently and repeatedly or you will end up weakening your parental authority rather than strengthening it.

- *Offer children choices.* Rather than saying, "Do this!" give your children a choice whenever either option is acceptable to you. Choices can range from giving preschoolers options about whether to wear the blue or the green shirt; giving school-age children the choice of going to bed now or having no television tomorrow; or teenagers the choice between cleaning their room or missing the dance on Friday night.

- *Give children a warning.* When you see your children violating a rule, warn them of the consequences. "I'll give you until the count of three . . ." followed by a slow, firm countdown can work well with children from preschool through school age. You may rarely get to three, and by avoiding the punishment, you and your child will have a lot fewer unpleasant interactions. Teenagers also respect warnings and appreciate being given one more chance.

- *Use quick punishments.* Because kids cannot connect events too far apart in time, punishment will be more effective if it takes place soon after a transgression, particularly with younger children or children with behavior problems. Swift justice also works better for older children, but for toddlers swift is a minute and for teenagers it can be a day or even a week.

- *Use the minimal effective punishment.* At every age, use the minimal effective punishment. Paradoxically, mild punishment often is *more* effective than harsh punishment because the threat of punishment often is more frightening than the reality. And you do want the power of illusion (and the illusion of power) on your side! Harsh punishment also can undermine the closeness a child feels toward a parent. Your actions may convey less about rules of conduct and more about the narrow boundaries of your love if you dole out excessive punishments, discipline out of anger, or physically punish a child in a way that is excessive or not appropriate for his age. Finally, using the minimal effective punishment leaves you with more alternatives for making the punishment more severe if needed.

- *Time out.* Placing your child in a quiet setting as a punishment is a great technique to use with children from the time they are toddlers until early school age. A good rule for the length of a time-out is one minute for every year of your child's age. Three minutes of time-out works better than thirty minutes, because your preschooler will lose track of time—and why he is being punished—after much more than a few minutes. Is there a time-out for teens? Time-out can develop into being sent to your room or getting grounded once children reach preadolescence or adolescence.

- *Control your anger.* You want to control your anger for many reasons, including preserving the positive side of your relationship with your children. When you get really mad, your children can hear only the music—your angry emotions, and not the lyrics—the message you are trying to impart with your reprimand.

- *Work together with your coparent.* You need to learn to discipline your children on your own, but you will be a lot more effective if you and your ex work together in setting and enforcing the rules. The rules do not have to be identical from house to house, but they should reflect a similar sensibility and set of values. You can support each other, ignore each other, or subvert each other. The best choice for your children—and for the two of you—is obvious.

Pushing Guilt Buttons

Of course, we all want to be the best, most attentive parents we can be. We want to be sure that we can distinguish between behavior that is simply bad behavior and behavior that is a masked cry for help, attention, support, or love. How do you know when to take misbehavior at face value and respond to a child's troublesome behavior with discipline? How do you know when to view misbehavior as possibly something else, withhold discipline, and instead be patient and understanding?

The short answer to this question is that parents should maintain the same standards of conduct for the children now as they held when they were married. If you sent your seven-year-old son to time-out for talking back to you when you were together, why should you tolerate that behavior now? Sure, it's harder to enforce rules now. You have less time, you don't have a backup, and your children may well be more difficult to manage since the divorce. But if you don't enforce your rules today, you're going to be in deeper trouble tomorrow.

Maybe an even bigger problem with enforcing the old rules is that you have something now that you didn't have then: *guilt*. Is your son talking back because he's being obnoxious? Or is he angry with you over your decision to leave? Or could he be angry with his father for not seeing him more? Is your four-year-old daughter still throwing tantrums because she's learned how to manipulate you or because she's confused and upset over the divorce? Is your eleven-year-old son not completing his homework because he's being lazy or because he's depressed and can't concentrate? Is your sixteen-year-old daughter breaking curfew because she's sixteen or because she hates that she lives with you and not with her mother?

All of these are good questions, none of which is easy to answer objectively. Somehow, though, the guilt that many divorced parents feel tends to answer the question for them: It's my fault. Because of what they feel or have been told by friends or even experts, many divorced parents automatically assume that a child's misbehavior can be traced back to the divorce, and since they were at least partly responsible for there being a divorce, they somehow must shoulder the blame.

Even worse, *children* sometimes tell parents that it's all their fault. Your four-year-old daughter might scream, "I want Daddy," when you pick her up from her tantrum and carry her to her time-out chair. Your seven-year-old son might shout, "I never want to see you again!" when you take away television because he kept talking back. Your eleven-year-old son might whine, "I just want to be with Dad," when you make him turn off the computer game and start doing his homework. Or your sixteen-year-old daughter may shout, "I want to go live with Mom!" when you ground her for violating curfew for the third time that week.

Children have all kinds of reasons for saying these things, but the most likely is this: They're trying to push your guilt buttons. Why? Because they know, based on past experience, that if they hit the right spot, you'll give up or back down. They'll escape the consequences of their misbehavior.

Why would children do something so mean, so manipulative to get out of discipline? Is the manipulation itself a sign of deeper struggles? No, the simple answer to the searching question "Why?" is this: Children say these things because they work. There isn't a plot involving your children, your ex, and her lawyer. Your children are not suffering from some deep, dark emotional problem. What has happened is that they have found a way to influence the outcome of a situation that they don't like.

At some point, probably quite by accident, they discovered that pushing your guilt button works. It probably took only one time for the stern look and the demand to behave to melt into a hug when your daughter cried, "You don't love me," "Daddy wouldn't punish me this much," or "Why did you have to ruin my life by breaking up?" And that first time, probably no one was as surprised by your change in attitude and the speed with which the misbehavior was forgotten, the punishment set aside, as your child. Believe me, while you may have totally forgotten the exchange, it made an impression on your child she will probably never forget. Not only did your child escape the consequences that time, but she also acquired a new and highly effective tool, a strategy that plain old human nature demands she play out again and again. Remember: Kids learn by what we do, not by what we say.

What really happens in situations like this is exactly like what happens in what psychologists call coercive interactions, ordinary manipulations of parents by children. A classic coercive interaction goes something like this:

"I want an ice cream cone."
"You can't have an ice cream cone."
"I want an ice cream cone right now!"
"I said you can't have one."
"I want one! I want one! I want one!"
"Okay. Here's an ice cream. Just please be quiet."

And the child quietly eats the ice cream.

Apart from being obnoxious, the problem with coercive interactions is that they are likely to continue. Why? Because these exchanges reward *both* the obnoxious child and the obsequious parent. The child gets his ice cream, a form of positive reinforcement. The parent gets a quiet kid, a type of negative reinforcement (the definition of which is the reduction or removal of something aversive; in this case, the child's whining). When we are reinforced (be it positively or negatively) for our actions, we are more likely to repeat the same behavior.

In short, in coercive interactions children learn to be increasingly obnoxious, and parents learn to give in. When parents engage in this dance, they also teach their children that it pays to escalate, to argue, to insist, and to persist. By the time the child described above crunched the last bit of cone, she had learned an important lesson: Being loud, insistent, and bratty works. The next time she wants something from her parent, this will be her first strategy.

In separation and divorce, children often introduce a new twist on the coercive pattern:

"I want to stay up and watch one more show."
"It's time for bed."
"Why can't I just stay up for half an hour?"
"It's your bedtime."
"You'd let me stay up if Dad was here. I miss Dad."
"Oh, honey, are you feeling lonely? Come here and let's snuggle on the couch."

If nothing else, you have to hand it to this child for brilliantly combining two tried-and-true strategies: pushing the guilt button while also whining enough to make giving in worthwhile for Mom or Dad.

Why do children say such things—and much worse—to manipulate their parents? Are they truly upset? Are they trying to hurt you? Are they just all mixed up about their feelings? No. Children push parents' guilt buttons for only one reason: It's their job.

Kids have the job of getting through life in the easiest way possible. Parents have the job of making sure that the easiest way is the healthiest way for children. Parents need to learn to recognize manipulative behavior and to make sure it does not work (most of the time). When your child's attempts at manipulation succeed, you have no one to blame but yourself. In the meantime, you need to ensure that children learn other, more important parts of their job of being a kid, things like respect, responsibility, and appropriate conduct.

On the other hand, if your children come to you at a quiet time and sadly say, "I miss Dad (Mom)," then they are telling you about a problem they are having. Then this means something, and you do need to listen.

Unfortunately, divorced parents often don't have anyone right there to reassure them that they did the right thing by following through with the discipline. To get better at saying no you may have to work on your own guilt or you may need some support from your family and friends, from your ex, or perhaps from a therapist. When you learn or relearn how to be consistent with your children—when you say what you mean and mean what you say, when no means no—and when you establish the boundary of your parental authority, you will end up with a lot less conflict, a lot more fun, and a much more secure child who will be far less tempted to engage in manipulative behavior. The only way to reduce or eliminate such behavior is to make sure it does not pay off.

Confused Boundaries of Love: Caretaker Kids

Reestablishing parental authority can be a struggle in divorce and so can reaffirming boundaries of parental love. One unfortunate problem that sometimes occurs is *parentification,* a role reversal—in which needy, depressed, or overwhelmed parents become dependent upon their children for emotional support. As a result, children get put in the role of being a caretaker kid much like Susannah, the "responsible one" who learned to put her parents' emotions ahead of her own and still wasn't allowed to focus on her own needs, even as she approached graduation from college.

Emotional caretaking is very different from the common and often unavoidable circumstance where parents may have to ask children, particularly older ones, to assume more independence and responsibility after divorce. Unless they are truly burdensome, a few extra chores are unlikely to cause lasting negative psychological consequences, and a little added responsibility may help children to learn to be more responsible, caring, and appreciative.

Caring for a parent's *emotional* needs, however, is a very different matter. Children who are put in the caretaking role may look competent in the short run, but my research has shown them to be at risk for relationship struggles and depression in the years ahead. Caretaker kids not only are doomed to fail at the impossible task of making their parents happy, but they also may apply the lessons learned in this unhealthy relationship to other relationships.

A typical comment from a young woman who took the caretaker role with her parents is "It's my job to make my boyfriend happy. If he's unhappy, it's my fault." A destructive corollary of this impossible belief is that the young woman may also believe that her boyfriend is responsible for making *her* happy: "I'm not happy and it's his fault." Like the parent who saddled them with the responsibility for their adult happiness, these children approach relationships with a distorted view of who should be responsible for whose happiness. As we have seen, they may gravitate to either one of two extremes: I am responsible for someone else's happiness and/or someone else is responsible for my happiness. At bottom is a failure to understand that, ultimately, we are responsible for our own happiness.

Of course, parents do have legitimate emotional needs. *You* need someone to care for you and to support you emotionally, but your child is the wrong someone for that job. Offering your children close and secure boundaries of love means maintaining a degree of parental distance, a distance from which you communicate "My job is to take care of you. It is *not* your job to take care of me."

Lost Contact, Lost Love

Many nonresidential parents blatantly fail to reestablish clear boundaries of parental love. One of the saddest facts about divorce is how many nonresidential parents, usually fathers, drop out of their children's lives and how quickly they do it. Demographer Judith Seltzer found that in a nationally representative sample of families from the late 1980s, 13 percent of children from divorced families saw their fathers only *once a year or less* just two years after a divorce. Eleven years after divorce, fully 50 percent of children saw their divorced fathers once a year or less often. Given these facts, should we be surprised that almost a third of the resilient young adults in my studies wondered if their divorced fathers even loved them?

The problem is not so much their being fathers as it is their being the nonresidential parent. Some nonresidential parents drop out of their children's lives almost immediately, but most see their children fairly often soon after a marital separation. As time passes, however, various pressures propel nonresidential parents to see their children less and less.

One big pull apart is continued conflict between parents. Too many nonresidential parents choose to end the conflict as they would if they didn't have children. They avoid their ex and, as a result, drop out of their children's lives. (Yes, some nonresidential parents are pushed out by an angry ex, too.) If you are angry with your ex, try to find a way to work things out amicably for your children's sake. Then try again. And again. Remember: Nonresidential parents whom I assigned to mediation at the flip of a coin (instead of going on to court) were *three times more likely* to see their children at least once a week *twelve years after the mediation or legal proceedings ended*. Parents who went on to court closely tracked the national dropout rate. Because the coin came up tails, they continued down the trail of anger.

Unmanaged emotions give some nonresidential parents an excuse to drop out of their children's lives, and real practicalities can get in the way, too. Contact between children and nonresidential parents can diminish as a result of geographic distance, remarriage, children's increasing independence as they grow older, and, most sadly, parents' diminished attachment to their own children as a result of infrequent contact over time.

Children's Questions About Lost Contact

Children start to ask searching questions when nonresidential parents fail to see their children frequently, regularly, or predictably. Here are some questions that kids may ask either their residential or nonresidential parents about the lack of contact, as well as some issues to consider in answering them.

"When Will I See You?"

It's only natural for children to become sad and uncertain if they have not seen one of their parents very often since the marital separation. This happens even when that parent has made a sincere effort to be clear, consistent, and reassuring. The lost contact is painful to children, as it is to parents.

If you are in this circumstance, it is all right to share your pain with your children; giving voice to your feelings helps them to understand their own feelings. In this case, you want to tell your kids, "I miss you when I don't see you." You also want to follow up with something upbeat like, "So I am going to quiz you about everything you have done when I see you next Saturday." You want your kids to know about your sadness and their own. However, you do *not* want your children worrying about you every minute that you are apart.

The pain of separation is prolonged and intensified for children if they see their nonresidential parent inconsistently. Contrary to what you might assume, seeing your children less often but regularly is better than seeing them more often but erratically. When parent visits are erratic, children are ever hopeful, constantly disappointed, and continually in grief, never knowing when they will be reunited. The lack of structure and predictability creates a sense of uncertainty and insecurity.

If you are a nonresidential parent, you may not like the idea of seeing your children on a schedule; it may feel unnatural, and you may miss the spontaneity of just showing up and surprising your children now and then. Still, the fact is that your children *need* to see you on a schedule.

They *need* that clear boundary of your love, interest, and attention. Your children may still be sad if they see you regularly but not very often, yet they can and will adjust as long as they know when and how you will be together. When the boundaries of your relationship are certain, so is children's sense of being loved by you—even from a distance.

"Why Do You Have to Go?"

The transition from parent to parent can be difficult for many children. Children may be sad about saying good-bye, uncomfortable in the tension of the moment, or just off kilter because of the change. Troubles with transitions usually are short-lived, but they are uncomfortable for children and for parents who may wonder if their children are unhappy leaving them or unhappy coming to be with them.

Parents often wonder what they have done wrong to make exchanges difficult, but a little perspective may be an antidote for excessive guilt. Children's reactions during exchanges are not unlike what happens when kids are off at preschool for the first time—a sad/angry burst of tears, clinging, a tantrum, or sullenness. And much like that school transition, children's distress is only magnified when parents are ambivalent about leaving or fail to make a clean, straightforward exit.

So during exchanges, you and your ex want to reassure your children lovingly when you say good-bye, but you need to leave relatively quickly and without showing the ambivalence you may feel. Turning back for one too many hugs, lingering in an attempt to calm the child are the kinds of actions that signal to your child that *you* are not ready to leave.

The upset children express after one parent leaves generally is brief as long as they feel safe and secure with the parent who is taking them. Be comforting if your children are upset when they are dropped off with you, but like your departures, your reassurance also should be brief. Follow the lead of preschool teachers who quickly learn how to calm children by distracting them with engaging activities. And don't feel guilty. You will help your children by *not* dwelling too long on their distress. Also remember that once the transition occurs, you are infringing on the other parent's time. Leave gracefully.

"Why Don't You See Me More?"

How do you answer this incredibly difficult question as a nonresidential parent? The answer is especially tricky for parents who *want* to see their children more but are prevented from doing so by a legal decision, geographic distance, or some other circumstance beyond their control. If you are a parent who wants desperately to see your child more and are upset that you cannot, the question may enrage you.

As much as I have talked about expressing your own feelings as a way of helping your children get in touch with their own, there are some exceptions, and this is one. This is not the time for anger. Your child is asking for reassurance of your love, not for an explanation of the circumstances of your divorce. It may be a struggle, but all you want to do is utter a simple explanation, like "This is the schedule the court gave me" or "I had to move far away." And then say, "I wish I could be with you every minute of every day, but that cannot be right now. I love you, and your mom loves you, and let's make the most of every minute we have together."

Parents in a situation like this also find it helpful when they have ways to stay in touch with their children during their time apart. Children don't always *show* how much it means to them when they get a regular telephone call, a card in the mail, an e-mail, or they see you at their special events. But children do derive an important sense of being loved by such gestures, tender and powerful reminders that your love for them is constant, even if your presence cannot be. If you have a plan for these kinds of contacts, you need to be faithful in sticking to your promises, but you should not expect your children to be good at remembering to call or write or e-mail in return. Their forgetfulness is a sign of being a kid, not of their diminished love for you.

"Why Doesn't Dad/Mom See Me More?"

If your children see their other parent infrequently, they may not ask that parent "Why don't I see you more?" To do so would be risky, and deep inside, your children may fear that asking the question of the parent they see the least will somehow drive that parent further away.

Instead, your children may ask *you* this question as their residential parent. Your kids' tone may be neutral, sad, or angry—maybe even accusatory. Whatever your child's emotional tone, the first thing to do is take a deep breath because the question probably rings your bells. After all, you may think, I am the parent who is always here. You, too, may be unhappy with your ex's less than stellar record in maintaining his relationship with the children, and it may annoy you to be put in the position to have to tactfully explain behavior you find reprehensible.

In responding to questions like this, you do not want to express anger, nor may you be able to be reassuring. After all, there may be legitimate reasons for the lack of contact: time, distance, illness, work commitments, other family obligations, and so on. Then again, there may not be legitimate reasons, and you do not want to tell lies to your children. If this is the case, you can try to read your child's emotions and focus on reflecting *their* feelings in your response. For example, "I don't know, and it makes me kind of sad/mad for you that you do not get to see your dad/mom more often." If "mad" is the word you reflect, remember that you want to *talk* about anger rather than *be* angry.

If your child's tone is accusatory or confrontational, you may have another dilemma. Here, you may be bearing the brunt of your children's anger because they feel safe being angry with you. They know that you love them; they know they can count on you. They know that nothing they might say or do—including this—would cause you to disappear or push them aside. In this way, they may see you as the polar opposite of their other parent, whose love and presence are so inconsistent that they fear that the smallest confrontation will only drive him/her further away.

Another possibility is that your child has idealized the missing parent. Parents who are not available to the children desperate to be part of their lives become almost imaginary. They are not around enough to participate in the mundane daily exchanges and activities that render the most beloved parent human in the eyes of their kids. They are not around to insist the beds be made, to nag about getting the home-work done, to send the provocateur to his room fuming after the latest feud over who gets the Xbox.

Imaginary parents can become perfect in children's eyes, with the real and present parent dropping in their child's estimation by com-parison. In the warped logic of children in a crisis like divorce, there must be a reason why the ideal parent is staying away, and often that reason is that the other parent has somehow driven him or her away.

A third possibility is that your child has an accusatory tone because you *have* somehow gotten in the way of their relationship with their other parent. It may not be your fault, but maybe your actions con-tributed indirectly to the reduced contact. Maybe your son's time with his father has fallen off since you moved to a new place thirty miles away, refused to renegotiate your parenting plan to accommodate your ex's third new work schedule, or got remarried and found that you were no longer comfortable accommodating your ex in ways you used to do.

Or maybe you have interfered with your ex's relationship with your children more directly. Maybe you are icy during exchanges. Perhaps when your daughter talks about the fun things she does with her fa-ther, your body language tells her that you do not share her joy. Or you give your children the choice of not going on a visit—and subtly let them know that you'd rather they didn't go. Maybe you aren't aware of what you do, but your son or daughter is.

In all of these cases, you should absorb your children's reasonable anger when they express it. (I'll deal with unreasonable anger later.) Having done this, you will be in the best position to help your chil-dren to get to the next layer of their emotions: their sadness, longing, and ardent desires for real or fantasized change.

For example, imagine that your children yell at you, "I'd see Dad more if you didn't have to move so far away!" You could respond, "Don't talk to me like that!" or "Your father has a car, and he knows how to drive!" But if you did, you'd never get beyond your child's anger. But if you can control your own anger—which is hard because anger is a defensive natural reaction to being attacked—you might get to a deeper level of your children's emotions. For instance, you might get tears rather than the silent treatment from your daughter if instead of being defensive you can say something like, "I'm sorry. I know it's hard to move and it's hard not to see Dad more."

"Will You Leave Me, Too?"

Even if you are a caring residential parent, your children may doubt your love as a result of their age-appropriate fears, fantasies, and mis-understandings. Your preschool-age children especially may not understand the reasons for and meaning of your separation. As a result, your young children may openly or secretly fear that both you and your ex will abandon them. Such fears are more common among preschoolers, but research shows that a number of school-age children fear abandonment by both of their divorced parents.

Your young children's fears of abandonment may reflect frightening but developmentally normal concerns. The Brothers Grimm played on abandonment fears in crafting fairy tales that engage children emotionally. But developmentally normal fears can cause problems for divorced parents.

I recall a mediation case where a father came storming into my office complaining that his former wife was poisoning their four-year-old daughter against him. His concern? The little girl, who lived primarily with her mother, was suddenly searching for monsters and having trouble sleeping through the night at his house. Even worse, she asked for Mommy when she got scared. The father accused his ex of telling his daughter bad things about him and was enraged by the subversion. He was furious—until the mother told him that their daughter was expressing the same fears of monsters, "bad guys," and the dark at her house. This new information, and my reassurance that his daughter's fears were developmentally normal, appeased Dad's fury. And his little girl no longer cried for Mommy once Daddy responded to her irrational worries with loving reassurance rather than anger.

Another concern you can anticipate in your children is their off and on worry about intimate relationships during their adolescence and young adult life. Young people from divorced families often have concerns about intimate relationships, but they are not alone. Whether their parents divorced or have been married for thirty years, most young people today worry about forming and maintaining intimate relationships—and with good reason considering today's high rates of divorce, living together, delaying marriage, and having children outside of marriage.

You will be a better parent, and save yourself much angst, if you are able to avoid viewing everything your child does through the filter of your divorce. How can you do this? You can anticipate developmentally normal issues, talk with other parents about what is going on with their same-age children, and, most important, talk with your ex about *your* kids.

"How Come You're *Always* Busy?"

Your children also may have legitimate reasons for feeling less secure in *your* love if you are the residential parent. You may be overwhelmed with a million different concerns as the primary parent, and it can be a struggle to maintain your good humor, patience, and warmth with your children. Besides, whatever you do may not seem to be enough for children who are more demanding during these rocky times. Maybe they are demanding because they feel insecure and upset, but maybe your kids are just misbehaving. With everything else going on, how are you supposed to figure this out?

You also may legitimately have less time with the kids because you now work more or need time to pursue a new social life. Or you may just be more tired, distraught, and lonely in the middle of the devastation that once was your life. Or maybe your children know just the wrong way to push your buttons, perhaps even by doing things the same way as your ex or because of your ex. When you are the one juggling day in and day out, it is annoying to hear "Dad does it this way," "Mom isn't always so busy," or just "I miss Dad."

The solution? Hire a maid, a live-in nanny, a cook, and a companion. If that is impractical, give yourself a little time and space. You are going to be even more frustrated if you try to be perfect because you are only going to fall short. So make a little time for the kids every day and make a little time for yourself every day, too. For the rest of the day, do the best you can. And let the kids in on the deal. "After dinner is your time. After nine is my time. For the rest of the day, we're all just going to do our own parts as best we can."

"Is Love a Lie?"
From a child's perspective, it may be logical to wonder—and worry— that you might stop loving them. After all, you two stopped loving each other. Your children may wonder if, like Santa Claus, love is all a big lie. You can (and should) tell your children that you will love them forever, but they surely thought that you and your ex would love each other forever, too. So what can you tell your children to convince them that there is a difference? Here are some options.

"The Love Between Parents and the Love Between a Parent and a Child Are Very, Very Different."
"Sometimes husbands and wives stop loving each other, but parents and kids *have* to love each other forever. Whether you like it or not, you will be my kid forever. I can get mad at you and you can get mad at me, but we still have to love each other. I hoped to love Mom forever, but something changed and even I do not know exactly why. Nothing can ever change my love for you, though. Nothing ever has and nothing ever will change it. I know that with all of my heart, and I want you to know that, too."

"I Do Still Love Him—as a Parent."
"I do still love your father as a parent even though I do not love him as a husband. I am sad and sorry that our love as husband and wife did not last, and I hope more than anything that you will find a husband whom you will love for all time. But I want you to know that I

do still love Dad as a parent because he gave you to me. I *have* to love him for a gift as perfect and precious as you. We are your parents, we always will be your parents, and we both will love you forever."

"I Do Love Him/Her but . . ."

"I do still love your mother, but we just could not keep living together because [we were fighting too much; she had a bad problem with drinking; she did not love me anymore and I wanted her to be happy]. I hoped that I could make things better, but I could not. With you, how could I make you any better? You are such a wonderful kid, and I am so proud of you. And besides, parents *have* to love their kids no matter what they do. So I will love you no matter what you do wrong. But don't think that means that you won't be in big trouble if you do!"

These are some things you may want to tell your children when they have doubts about your love for them. More important, through your actions in the months and years after your separation, you will want to *show* your children that your parental love is unconditional and unending.

Two Parents Still

Even as you focus on parenting on your own, you need to remember that you really are not parenting your children alone after divorce. Like it or not, what you do affects your ex and vice versa. You can enhance, or undermine, each other's parental love and authority depending upon whether you develop a cooperative, disengaged, or angry divorce.

As I have said, you can never be completely divorced if you have children. Your children's other parent is there, and he can prop you up, pull you down, or just let you fall—and you can do the same to him. But what he does for you or fails to do, and vice versa, affects more than just the two you.

Divorce is not just the breakup of a romance. Divorce is the breakup of a family. You are former partners now, but you are still parents. So you need to find some way to work with your ex—or at least not work against her—even as you focus on the all-important task of being an authoritative parent, of parenting your children for resilience in getting through the divorce.

CHAPTER NINE

Exploring
New Relationships

A ffairs. Dating. One-night stands. Reconnecting with old loves. Searching for new loves at work, through your friends, in the grocery store, on the Internet, at PTA meetings, or in the personal ads. Getting into a new relationship, getting out of one that is going nowhere. Getting serious. Considering marriage. Moving in together. Getting remarried. Intimate relationships come in many shapes and sizes before, during, or after divorce, and all of them are complicated—a lot more complicated than they were the first time around.

A romantic relationship can be one of the most positive, fulfilling aspects of your life. It can also be one of the most difficult. Most of us find that even the "right" relationship with the partner of our dreams presents its own challenges. Still, despite the ups and downs, the broken hearts and bruised emotions, most of us continue to believe in love and its power to enhance and complete our lives.

In the heat of a divorce, or during one of those late-night talks with your best friend, you might have sworn off relationships forever, but that rarely lasts. Sooner or later, most divorced people find themselves falling into a new relationship. Of course, they hope that this one—or another one, perhaps, later on—will be what they have been looking for.

It is only natural to reach a point at which you feel ready to try again. For some, that search for a new love happened before and perhaps even precipitated the divorce. For others, it may be years before they venture forth again. For most people, however, within a year or two they are in a new relationship or at least looking, hopeful yet cautious, trying hard to be realistic and at the same time hoping for just the right person so as not to repeat the mistakes of the past.

New relationships can be complicated for parents after divorce, because you are no longer alone but part of a package deal: Your children are a part of any new relationship you pursue. You have to think of the children, not just yourself, as you negotiate the contours of your new relationships and your feelings about them. And the person you are dating has to think about your children, too. He may even have his own children as well and be part of a package deal himself.

If things get more serious, your children will have to evaluate your new relationship, too. You get to pick your partner, but whom you get involved with is an arranged marriage for your children. Your children don't get to pick your partner so you have to choose carefully for them, and your children have considerations and concerns that may be very different from your own. You may see your new love as completing your family or at least as filling a huge hole in your life. Your children may see him as an intruder, as a complication they do not want in their relationship with you, their father, or just around their house. So they will assess your new partner and how your relationship is affecting their lives, for better or worse. Children may not get a direct say in accepting or rejecting their arranged marriage, but they may actively accept or reject their new stepparent or "adult friend."

Then there is your ex to consider and maybe your new partner's ex, too. Like it or not, your exes are part of your new relationship. While she is at your house, for example, your ex might telephone or stop by to get the kids. Or your ex (or his ex) will *not* show up when he is supposed to get the kids, and there goes the time you had planned to spend alone.

Your new partner also may have feelings and opinions about how you get along with your ex, and her views can put you at ease, in the middle, or on the defensive. She may support your cooperative coparenting, or she may be jealous of your good relationship with your ex and the time you spend together. She might find that your angry divorce intrudes too much into her life. Or she might be reassured by your anger and stoke the fire as a way of soothing her own jealousy and insecurity over this new relationship.

And, of course, everyone's reactions, particularly your ex's and probably your children's, will depend upon how your new relationship got started. If it began as the affair that ended your marriage, you can expect it to take a very long time, maybe forever, before your ex and your new partner accept each other. Naturally, things will be much smoother if you waited to work on your own stuff first: your anger, sadness, and grief, your relationship with your ex. Things are likely to begin on a better foot if you spend some time establishing new boundaries around your parenting and coparenting relationships before getting involved with someone new.

You are older now and wiser, too. You almost certainly are a lot less naïve about relationships and probably a lot less trusting of members of the opposite sex, of love, commitment, and marriage, less trusting of yourself and your judgment. Your fantasies of living happily ever after, if you ever had them, might be long gone, and in some ways, that's just fine. But people can be too guarded about new relationships, too. All relationships require a leap of faith; they require trust. Love is about taking chances, and there is no guarantee that you won't get hurt again and maybe more than once.

Samuel Johnson called remarriage "the triumph of hope over experience." It's a witty, sardonic line, but maybe there's another side to it. Hope *is* a triumph. All intimate relationships are triumphs of hope, of taking chances, of trust. But how do you recover trust in relationships once your hopes have been dashed? Obviously, people do find a way. Statistically, about three out of four divorced adults will one day remarry, and even though there cannot be accurate statistics on relationships that do not end in marriage, almost every divorced adult gets involved with someone else again—sooner or maybe a lot later.

A new relationship may seem like the perfect solution to the struggles of divorce, and in many ways it can be. To some, it seems like the only solution. But new relationships mean new transitions for you, for your children, and, yes, for your ex. For all of these reasons, the most important thing to remember about new relationships—however they start, however wonderful they may be—is this: Go slowly.

Continuing an Affair

If you are involved in an affair and are desperate to be together, proceed with caution. You may not *want* to go slowly; in fact, you may feel that it's impossible, but you must. Why? For one thing, you have a lot of things to work out with your ex. Your relationship is not over just because you said you wanted a divorce, just because you said you were in love with someone else. That might have ended your marriage, but your relationship—under a new name, with new rules—goes on.

You are going to have to deal with your ex now or you surely will have to deal with your ex later, maybe in court. The affair may give your ex a focus for his rage, perhaps an accurate one, or maybe, as you might believe, his fury about your affair might be a way for him to avoid acknowledging his own failings in your marriage. Either way, your ex's emotions are real, and they affect you if for no other reason than that they affect your children.

And you do have to go slowly because of your kids. You may have fantasies of becoming the Brady Bunch, the blended family from the television show where a couple who each had children from a previous marriage lived happily ever after. But the *Brady Bunch* was fiction, and even if it had occurred in real life, the Brady parents were widowed. No divorce, no exes to consider, no divided loyalties among the kids, and no conflicts about discipline or real problems in getting along—all issues you face here on the other side of the television screen, in the real world.

If you got involved with someone as a result of an affair, you need to go slowly out of respect and consideration for your children's emotions. Children are upset and confused by divorce. In the wake of divorce, children need a period of stability before you can reasonably expect them to take on another round of change in their lives. Also bear in mind that introducing your children to a new relationship is a change that can be postponed, as necessary. It is also a change that ideally your children should be able to approach when they are at their best in terms of their general emotional state and their sense of security.

Not only is that better for your children; it is also better for whatever your relationship will evolve into over time. In national surveys of married couples in which one or both partners brought children from a previous relationship, children were listed as the number-one cause of conflict between spouses. And divorce rates are higher for second marriages than first ones—and even higher if one partner brings children to the new marriage. You want to set the scene for success and happiness for everyone.

Introducing children to a new partner or future stepparent is a *big* change for kids. Children can have a hard time getting used to any person their parents get intimately involved with after divorce. For one thing, your romantic interest in other people represents a major shift for your kids. Suddenly your children—particularly those who are preadolescent and older—are seeing you in a new role that they may not be entirely comfortable with, no matter how much they may like, or come to like, your new love interest.

Then there is the possibility that some parents cannot imagine: Your kids simply may not *like* your boyfriend, period. Your new love may be great as your confidant, your friend, and your lover, but this is irrelevant to your children. While your friends may be able to understand your attraction to this person, your children probably cannot. After all, what you like about him are things that are (and should be) beyond the realm of your children's knowledge and experience.

Rather than think about why you would like them to like him, try to see it from their point of view. How do they see him? It all depends on how you have handled your divorce, where the divorce fits into your family history, and how your children perceive the roles you and your ex played in bringing it about. Especially if your relationship started as an affair, you cannot expect your children to welcome your new friend with open arms.

You also should go slowly with an affair because you want to make sure that she really is the right one for *you*. The passion may be incredible, but that probably is not a strong basis for a long-term relationship.

The best relationships are built on friendship, too, not just passion. Unfortunately for many divorced people, passion might have been missing from their lives for months, if not years before the divorce. Sexual attraction is a powerful force, and being the object of someone's desire can magically erase the private self-doubts and insecurities of an earlier rejection.

Of course, passion is important, but your passion will have to be terribly potent to keep you together when you get bounced around by the unavoidable ups and downs of real life. Affairs are based in fantasy not reality, but if you hope to turn your affair into something different, something more, reality is about to arrive in a hurry.

Danielle's Affair

Danielle, the assertive corporate accountant you met in the introduction, barely listened to my advice when I gently suggested that she go slowly with her affair. As you will recall, Danielle had confessed her affair to Frank, who, though devastated by this news, fought through his emotions in an effort to maintain a cooperative relationship with Danielle. Frank wrestled down his pain and rage out of love for his six-year-old son, Sam, out of respect for his long and strong friendship with Danielle, and because, as he freely admitted, he still wanted her back. Frank also admitted that his past failures as a husband—his emotional unavailability, his preoccupation with work, his taking Danielle for granted—had helped to set the stage for Danielle's affair.

Danielle did not blame Frank for her affair, as some unfaithful partners try to do. She took responsibility for what she did, and she was ashamed of herself for going outside of her marriage. Danielle also recognized how her affair affected her marriage. She said, "My marriage was fifty percent ruined—maybe seventy-five percent—before I had the affair. But whatever was left of my feelings for Frank crumbled when I got involved in this relationship, when I saw what I could have and what I didn't have." Danielle admitted that her affair contributed to wrecking her marriage, but she was blind to how her marriage—and her having a son—were going to destroy the fantasy she was living in her affair.

In the months after they came to see me in crisis just before Christmas, Danielle and Frank did just about everything right when it came to Sam and working together as coparents. They each kept their focus on Sam when they were with him (but not *too* much focus), they communicated with each other as needed, and they supported each other in parenting Sam. I saw them periodically for about nine months after their separation, and they both were genuinely and deservedly proud of how they had handled parenting Sam, who was doing beautifully, despite everything. From all indications, Sam was well on his way to being a truly resilient kid.

But as I found out when Danielle asked to see me for an individual appointment, her affair with Myles (whom I never met) apparently was not going so well. Myles had never been married, and he had no children. He was a strong, passionate man, and Danielle was captivated by his emotion and energy (not to mention his British accent) during their yearlong affair. But once Danielle separated from Frank, Myles quickly became possessive. He was jealous not only of Frank but also of Sam.

Myles wanted Danielle to spend all of her time with him, and he didn't understand why Danielle refused to let him sleep over during the weeks that Sam was with her. When about a month after her separation Danielle tried to introduce Sam to Myles, things went badly. According to Danielle, Sam was a bit resistant when he met Myles— nothing unexpected or out of the ordinary, but he was just uncomfortable and distant.

In contrast, Myles was impatient, demanding, and petulant. He wanted Sam to like him, but he really didn't make much of an effort to relate to him. And during the few times that the three of them were together, Myles demanded far more attention from Danielle than Sam did while Danielle wanted to do just the opposite. She wanted to focus more on Sam during their every other week together. After all, she reasoned, Myles had her all to himself during her off week.

A few weeks after the big introduction, Myles demanded that Danielle either accept him as a part of her new life or else. This was the first time Danielle had glimpsed Myles's intense anger, which she described as an "infantile outburst." Danielle quickly decided that they should see each other only during the weeks when she didn't have Sam. Myles was not happy to hear this, but he agreed, grudgingly.

What Danielle did not say was that she was having major doubts about their relationship—and, to her surprise, about her decision to leave Frank. "Ambivalence is not a strong enough word to describe how I felt—how I still feel," she told me when I saw her alone.

Over the next few months, Myles became insanely jealous of Frank. He constantly accused Danielle of thinking of Frank, of sleeping with him, of planning to get back together with him. Danielle wondered if Myles sensed her unspoken ambivalence.

Before long, however, Danielle's getting back with Frank ceased to be an option. About six months after the separation, Frank began seeing someone else. At first, Danielle was pleased and relieved. She told me, "I was happy for him, and honestly, I was happy because his dating eased some of my own guilt. Still, part of me also was jealous, part of me still wanted him back. Of course, I didn't share my uncertainties with Frank. I didn't think that would be fair. I knew he still wanted me back then, before he started to get serious about this new relationship. But I didn't know what I really wanted, and I didn't want to put him through all of the hurt again. So I didn't say anything to him. I wanted to be one hundred percent sure. Now he's sure that he *doesn't* want me. Ironic. There's another word that isn't strong enough to describe my situation."

Danielle paused for a minute and continued, "But if you want me to be honest with you and with myself, I'm still not one hundred percent sure that I really want Frank back." Her voice trailed off and she added, "I'm not one hundred percent sure of anything."

Over time, Myles started to pull away from Danielle. At first, she thought he was just testing her, or, in Myles's words, "giving her a taste of her own medicine." But shortly before she asked to see me individually, Danielle found out the truth: Myles was involved with another woman. "I feel like such a fool," Danielle whimpered to me in tears. "I gave up my marriage, I put my son through all of this, for what? I knew I couldn't trust Myles, but what we had between us, the passion, it was like a drug. I knew he was bad for me, but I couldn't give him up. I had been deprived of passion for so long with Frank . . . even though I realize now the good parts of my relationship with him: our friendship, our love for Sam." She cried so hard that she couldn't speak while I sat there, waiting for her to go on. "And now Frank's gone, and Myles is gone, and I'm all alone and I have no idea what I'm going to do."

Some people might feel that Danielle got what she deserved. You reap what you sow. What goes around comes around. But affairs happen. And they happen for all sorts of reasons. Some affairs happen because the person who is involved in the relationship is selfish, reckless, unthinking, and cares only about her own pleasure. Other affairs happen because the person having the affair is lonely, rejected by her spouse, and desperate to connect with someone. Sometimes even the person having the affair is searching for a way to preserve her marriage by getting her needs met elsewhere. Other times affairs happen for no good reason. Maybe the person involved in the affair simply wants some affirmation that she is still young, attractive, and desirable.

Affairs happen but they rarely work out in the long run. Reality intrudes into the fantasy of an affair—reality in the form of exes, children, day-to-day life, the impossibility of maintaining passion at such a high pitch, court battles, and time. The few happy endings I have seen—affairs that turned into real and lasting relationships—have taken *a lot* of time to work out, three years, five years, even longer. I know the advice is almost impossible to hear when you are flying through the emotional high of an affair, but it *is* good advice: Slow down.

Go Slowly with Children and Romantic Relationships

Whatever the nature of their parents' new romantic relationships—from the most casual dating to remarriage—children do best if their parents go slowly. Parents need to allow time to assess how well their potential future partners get along with their children. It may seem absurd, rushed, or unnecessary, but parents have to assess their dates' interest in children soon after they start dating, and far more carefully than in the past.

When you were younger, maybe you vaguely wondered what kind of father your boyfriend might be one day. Or maybe you never paid any attention to this distant and seemingly irrelevant speculation. (Now, you probably are telling yourself, "Boy, was I naïve!") Or perhaps you didn't really evaluate your date's potential as a father when you were younger because you didn't want to scare him away. Well, you don't want to scare your dates away now (they can be hard to find), but divorced parents do have to evaluate their dates' potential not just as a future partner but also as a future stepparent.

When parents date the second time around, children are not some distant fantasy. Children are very much a reality even as people contemplate going out on a date. "Sounds like she's got everything . . . but three children? I'm not sure I want to get involved with someone with that many kids, or with any kids." "He sounds like a nice guy, but he's thirty-eight and never had children? I'd scare him away—sooner or later—and I don't want to put my children through another failed relationship." "She's divorced and has a little girl my daughter's age. That sounds great. Do you know what her custody arrangements are? How does she get along with her ex?"

And if you keep dating the same person, sooner or later your children will need to meet the man you're getting involved with. Later is better because you don't know how your children are going to react, how he is going to react, or exactly what you want out of this relationship.

Maybe you're involved in the classic rebound relationship and don't know it. He's great looking, three years younger than you, and full of energy. Well, the laughter, the late nights, and the sex might be great, and delicious food for your ego, but where is this two-month relationship going to be after six months? Maybe your kids will really like him, and he'll be gone—off with a younger woman with no children—just when your kids are getting really attached. Or maybe your kids *will* scare him away, and there goes that wonderful little fantasy. The bubble was going to burst anyway, but it might have been nice to float in it for a while longer. You probably deserved a little escape after all you've been through.

Or maybe you want your children to see you relating warmly with a man, but this is just the wrong guy. His attentiveness to you is great when you're alone, but it gets in the way around the children. You'd be better off getting together with your divorced male friend and his kids and your kids, too. There may be no spark there, but there's a great friendship and this guy *knows* about kids. Seeing you with a good male friend who loves kids is not such a bad model of relationships for your children, even if the two of you aren't in love.

What if you think your new love might be the one for you, even though it's too soon to know for sure? Still, it's just been you and the kids for nearly a year and a half. You have dated this terrific woman for a few months, and the time seems right for her to meet the kids. She's eager to meet them, and you're anxious to see how it goes. The timing may seem perfect, but the go slowly advice still holds.

Maybe she doesn't have children but loves them and wants to show you how great she is with kids. She bubbles with enthusiasm and tries to engage the children in doing things with her right away. In response, your eight-year-old son is indifferent while your ten-year-old daughter says a grudging "Hello" and then storms off to her room.

You are embarrassed by your children's rudeness, but here's what's really going on: Your son wants to play catch, not draw pictures with some strange woman, and he wishes she'd just go home so he could play with you. Your daughter's reaction is more complicated. She's thinking about her mother, about you, about the two of you. She writes in her diary, "They aren't even divorced yet, and he's *dating*. I thought they might get back together—I think that's what Mom wants. And now he's trying to get me to be nice to that *thing*. No way!"

In a circumstance like this, kids still need to get used to the reality of their parents' divorce *and* the idea of one or both parents' dating. You may see dating and seeking a new relationship as a natural next step after divorce. Your child, however, will see these as two entirely different things.

Going slowly in this case might involve talking to the kids more about the divorce, telling them about plans to start dating, and suggesting to your dates that they take it slowly when they meet your children and not to try to come on too strong. Maybe a brief, casual meeting—where a date just says hello to the children—would be a good idea at first. Your kids might have a negative reaction, but with less exposure, there is less chance of your date's inadvertently offending your children or stumbling over boundaries where she is not welcome. In other words, the less time your children spend with your new love early on, the fewer mistakes and misperceptions you will have to correct later on.

Another word of caution: Do not spend too much time or energy campaigning for your new friend. Making her sound wonderful may just give your children a bigger target for finding more shortcomings down the road. Even if your children aren't looking for reasons to reject your new friend, setting low expectations is usually a good rule. Let your children be pleasantly surprised to learn just how great she is, when they really get to know her at the right time, in their own time.

Parents who are wise enough to wait before introducing their children to their new boyfriends or girlfriends also need to remember that it took them awhile to get to where the relationship is now. Children need to "date" the new person in their life for a while, too. They need the opportunity to get to know this person on their own terms, not yours. They need to discover what their relationship to this person will be.

While having a solid romantic relationship may be terrific for you, like everything else in divorce, your children's circumstances and perspectives are different from yours. Children may resent that a new boyfriend is taking a parent's time and attention away from them. Or children may feel torn loyalties or become ensnared in direct and intentional pulls for their loyalty between your new intimate relationship and their relationship with their other parent. Your children may *like* the new man in your life, but they sense—or hear a tirade about—their father's resentment, jealousy, or worse. They like the guy you're seeing, but if it comes to a choice, they'll choose their father. And maybe your kids do feel like they have to choose.

You keep your options open if you go slowly. If you go slowly and your children warmly welcome the new man in your life, then it is easy for him to move closer to your children a little more quickly. But if your children have trouble accepting this new person—if they're confused, angry, torn, or just don't like him—then it's much harder and more confusing for everyone if you have to beat a hasty retreat.

Scott's and Cindy's New Relationships

New intimate relationships complicated things in the beginning for Scott and Cindy, the couple with the angry divorce and three children who were caught in the cross fire between their parents. More than two years after our couples' therapy ended and their venomous divorce disputes began, Scott contacted me for some individual therapy, and not long after, Cindy did, too.

As is my rule, before seeing Scott alone I checked with Cindy to make sure she was comfortable with this. I had seen each of them alone from time to time during their legal battles, but we all treated these individual appointments as an extension of our couples' therapy. I hadn't seen or spoken with either of them in almost a year, and Scott clearly asked for something different when he telephoned. Cindy's two-sentence e-mail response to my inquiry was "I don't object to your seeing Scott in therapy. He needs a lot of help." Reading this, it didn't seem like their relationship had improved much.

During our first individual appointment, Scott told me that after a year and a half of angry legal exchanges (including several court hearings), their divorce became final and so did all of the details of their settlement. Based on the recommendation of an independent psychological evaluation and the high degree of acrimony between the parents, the court awarded physical and legal custody to Cindy and set up a schedule for Angela, Joey, and Colleen to be with Scott every other weekend and every Wednesday evening for dinner.

According to Scott, Cindy apparently felt vindicated by her victory in court. She certainly acted triumphant around him. In turn, Scott felt cheated—by Cindy, by the legal system, and by his own lawyer. He told me that he was torn between initiating another suit for more time with the children and simply accepting his defeat. Scott said bitterly,

"One day the kids will be able to read the court records and learn how much I loved them and how the legal system views a man only as a paycheck, not as a father. As for their mother, well, it won't be long before they understand what kind of a woman she really is."

I worried that Scott was joining the ranks of fathers who find in their legal defeat glory—and an excuse. I have worked with a number of men who seem bent on going down in flames in a legal battle. Long before they go to court, they expect that they will lose, and at some level, maybe they even want to. But in the glory of a lost battle, these men feel vindicated in slowly—or suddenly—dropping out of their children's lives. After all, men in this position can, like Scott, claim that they fought for their children and lost. These men can say that they didn't drop out of their children's lives of their own volition. In their view, they were pushed out.

While it is true that a legal decision like the one in Scott and Cindy's case makes it more difficult for a father to maintain the level of contact with his children that he might have wished, there's something more at work. It's much harder to hang in with your kids and to realize that, for your children's sake, you need to try—sometimes again and again and again—to find a way to work with your ex.

But Scott hadn't come to see me to help him to decide what to do about the children. He came to see me because he was involved with a woman, Katrina, whom he had started dating right around the time his divorce became final. It was now eight months later, and they were getting serious about their future together.

Unfortunately, Scott's kids, particularly the girls, got along poorly with Katrina and her eleven-year-old son, Erik, who was two years older than Angela. Scott said that Erik was an only child who had been spoiled by Katrina, and he came on too strong in general—and way too strong for Angela. According to Scott, Erik was boisterous, selfish, and lazy, and Angela, who was quick witted like her mother, ripped Erik to shreds verbally. Erik often responded with physical threats, and Scott said that he and Katrina had to constantly monitor the two children when they were anywhere near each other.

Scott went on to brag about how much Angela had helped him

around the house and with Joey and Colleen. Once he got involved with Katrina, Scott expected Katrina to take over these responsibilities from Angela when the kids were with their father. Recalling my concerns about Angela's caretaking in the family and his own history of being a caretaker child, Scott was trying to do the right thing. So he was puzzled by how much Angela resisted Katrina.

As for Colleen, consistent with her style, she withdrew whenever Katrina and Erik were around, which was most of the time during the weekends that the kids were with Scott. Colleen was quiet and polite, but lately she had started asking Scott—sometimes in tears—if she could go home to Mom's house. Colleen's requests hurt Scott, and although Colleen wouldn't tell him why she wanted to go back to her mother's, Scott was pretty certain he knew why: Cindy was pulling Colleen's strings.

At least Joey was doing all right according to his dad. He liked Erik, and even though the two boys got pretty wild together, Scott was glad to see them getting along. "Joey is Daddy's boy," Scott told me. "And that's the only thing that's saving him, because their mother is undermining the kids' relationships with Katrina and Erik at every turn."

Perhaps reading my look or anticipating what I might say about the importance of cooperative coparenting, Scott continued, "But you don't have to take my word on this; have a look at these." Scott then produced several handwritten letters from Cindy. The letters were full of anger and ranged in content from attacking Katrina's morals to telling Scott how upset the children were about his new relationship. At the bottom of the pile was a typed letter from Cindy's lawyer to Scott's lawyer. In it, Cindy's lawyer stated that because Scott's new relationship constituted a change in circumstances, Cindy would be seeking to reduce Scott's visitation with the children unless he stopped exposing them to Katrina and Erik.

"And how's this for being a hypocrite, Doc?" Scott added. "I know that Cindy has been seeing someone at least for the last couple of months!"

Scott was livid, and although he had good reasons to be upset, it was clear to me that one problem—probably still the big one—was that he and Cindy had not yet emotionally disengaged from each other. What were the signs? In addition to Cindy's vitriolic letters, Scott's anger was just *too* intense at this stage of their coparenting relationship. Cindy remained the focus of Scott's emotional energy—not Angela, Joey, and Colleen, and that was a problem.

Scott had a right to be angry, but the dominant emotion I'd expect at this point would have been worry—for his children, about the potential of losing even more contact with them, and about their genuine struggles with his new relationship—not more rage against Cindy. As for Cindy, how could she have possibly known enough about Katrina to attack her moral values? Clearly, a lot of thought and anger had gone into those letters—too much.

I suggested to Scott that maybe we should try to involve Cindy in some therapy or mediation, but he refused outright. He wanted help with his children and Katrina, and that was all he was interested in. It did seem, though, that they all could use some help. Based on what Scott told me, he and Katrina had rushed things too soon with the children and were still moving too fast. After only about six weeks of dating, they had introduced their children and attempted to proceed as a blended family from there.

Even when it was obvious that neither of them was being fully accepted by the other's children and that Erik and Angela did not get along, there was no attempt to slow down. "I couldn't back down," Scott told me. "Even before the letters started, I knew that Cindy was behind the girls' resistance."

This was interesting for a couple of reasons. First, it gave Scott a reason to pin his current problems on his past with Cindy. It seemed not to have occurred to him that maybe neither his kids nor Katrina's was quite ready for this. Second, it allowed him to keep his emotional focus on Cindy, not on his own kids.

No doubt the children were trying to communicate several things to Scott about the current situation, the most obvious of all was that they did not want to share him, at least not now, and not this way. When I asked Scott if he thought the children were getting enough alone time with him now, he launched into another tirade about the legal system. When I interrupted and said, "I meant alone time without Katrina and Erik," Scott looked perplexed and replied, "We're trying to make a family. Maybe I didn't make myself clear. Katrina and I want to get *married*—soon, probably this summer."

I met with Scott, and on a few occasions, Katrina, for half a dozen sessions over the next couple of months. I urged them both to slow down with the children—not to step back, but to slow down—and to be sensitive to their children's needs.

For example, instead of spending every other weekend with all six of them together at Scott's house on Friday night, all day Saturday, and part of Sunday (sometimes with Katrina and Erik sleeping over in the guest room), I urged them to limit their "family" time to Saturday afternoon. Dinner out on Friday night or a picnic lunch on Sunday might be fine on occasion, too, but Scott's children needed some time just with him. He needed to work on rebuilding *his* relationships with the kids, particularly the girls. Katrina couldn't do that for him. In fact, as things stood right now, through no fault of her own, she was hampering that process, not helping it.

We also discussed various parenting issues, including how Scott could normalize his time with the children by doing routine things, like letting the children have friends over to his house, rather than continuing to make every weekend together an extravaganza of fun. Scott also eventually revealed to Katrina how he saw Erik as being spoiled by her, and he suggested some ways she could set limits for him.

It was difficult, but broaching this topic eventually led Scott and Katrina into an important discussion. They each had been hoping for the other to take over in areas where they lacked confidence in their parenting. Katrina had hoped Scott would help her to discipline Erik, and Scott had hoped Katrina would take over various girls' activities with his daughters. By discussing their hopes and concerns, Scott and Katrina came to realize that they each had to be parents to their own children first—to do the jobs of discipline and girls' stuff with their own children rather than delegating them to each other. They could help each other best not by taking over but by coaching each other about how to discipline, how to relate to the girls, and about what problems they could see in each other's relationships with their children from the outside looking in.

Of course, Scott and Katrina often raised the issue of Cindy. Despite my encouragement, they continued to balk at the idea of trying to involve her in therapy. I knew that it was a long shot for therapy to help, but without an improvement in Cindy and Scott's coparenting relationship, I told Scott and Katrina that I could only offer them imperfect solutions: They could not change Cindy's behavior, so they should focus on the things they could control—their relationships with the children and with each other. Even if Cindy was undermining them, they should support her with the children. In doing so, if nothing else they would have the solace of knowing they did the right thing.

As our meeting progressed, Scott and Katrina talked less about Cindy and more about their own relationships with their children. In fact, when we ended our brief course of therapy, their relationships with the children were improving notably. For one thing, less clearly was more. Everyone got along much better when they were together for briefer periods of time on Saturday, especially if the children were allowed to do "normal" things during these times instead of forcing them to use this time to get to know Katrina and Erik.

During their time together, Katrina worked on developing her relationship with the girls, but she heeded their signals for when to move forward and when to back off. She now understood Angela's caretaker role, and how even though it was a burden, being the caretaker made Angela feel important and needed. Rather than trying to usurp her position in the family, Katrina joined in helping Angela do her tasks. Katrina's goal, which she shared with Scott, was to slowly ease Angela out of the position of being a caretaker kid. When they were apart, Katrina worked on discipline with Erik, and Scott worked on spending more quality time with the girls, including letting them do their own thing, including having their friends over.

These changes were very important, but as I learned a few months later, when Cindy called me for an individual appointment, another big change had been taking place in the background. Cindy had been getting serious with someone herself. William, a divorced man ten years her senior with two grown children, connected with Cindy through their shared interest in their faith. The friendship had become personal and romantic, and they were considering marriage.

What Cindy wanted from me was guidance about how to introduce her children to William. Despite having been serious about him for more than six months, she had not brought them together, in large part because of the problems she knew they had had with their father and his new girlfriend. Wisely, Cindy didn't want to complicate the children's lives further, and she didn't want to repeat the mistakes Scott and Katrina had made.

I welcomed Cindy's genuine interest in the children and her willingness to go slowly for their sakes, but what really struck me was what was missing: the intensity of her anger toward Scott. Sure, she still disparaged Scott in various ways, but her concerns now focused on the children, not him. He was, as he should have been at this point in their coparenting relationship, an important figure in her life but someone in whom she was not terribly emotionally invested.

She had not arrived at this point alone, however. It was William who had urged Cindy to focus on her children's needs. And, based on his own experience, he was able to convince her of the importance of their relationship with their father. William also helped Cindy indirectly in a much more fundamental way. He loved her, and she loved him, and in learning to love William, Cindy finally let go of Scott and the anger that was so much a part of her grief.

Some people learn to disengage from their exes on their own after divorce. Some people are never able to disengage from their exes. For others, like Cindy, a healthy new relationship is the healing force that helps them to disengage from their past and to embrace their future. Although I was sure that my therapy with Scott and Katrina had helped them with the children, I was equally sure that Cindy's letting go of her anger—and Scott's learning to focus on things he could control—had made many of the positive changes possible. As Scott and Cindy found a way to separate emotionally, their angry divorce was actually growing into a healthier, distant divorce.

Remarriage

The same go slowly rule for new relationships after divorce also applies to children and remarriage. If anything, by the time you are considering remarriage, you should be moving even more slowly, with one foot hovering over the brake. People remarry every day, and blended and stepfamilies are so common now that some people may not give much thought to how to make these extremely complex new family units work. But making stepfamilies work requires a lot of planning before a remarriage and a lot of work afterward.

Just as our understanding of divorce has evolved over the years, so, too, has our understanding of remarriage and its impact on all family members. Some experts used to think of remarriage as the reconstitution of the two-parent family. According to this view, remarriage put all the parts of a family together again: mom, dad, and children. What this view of the remarried family failed to recognize, though, is that Mom and Dad are not replaceable parts in a family. Children whose parents divorce and remarry *already have* a mom and a dad.

For a parent, remarriage may be the ultimate solution for the struggles of divorce: You once again have a mate, a lover, and a partner—emotionally, practically, and financially. You no longer are a single person living in a couples' world. Although remarriage may seem the opposite of divorce for a family, for children the two have a lot in common. Remarriage represents another transition for children—often a difficult one.

We can only begin to consider the many potential touchstone issues and complications involved in remarriage—and it is hoped that remarriage is something divorced parents *are* only beginning to consider in the first couple of years after a separation. But to gain a little appreciation of the many challenges, think about all the things that are typically fun and relatively simple the first time around: how long you two date before getting engaged, the proposal, your wedding day, your honeymoon, and where you will live after you're married.

Now pause to consider some questions that may arise about these same issues for a second marriage. Maybe you should date longer to give the children time to adjust, but what if you're older or maybe want to have another child together and you hear your clock ticking? And once you have said yes to getting remarried, when do you tell your children—and your ex—and how? Is your wedding going to be a big event or do you want something smaller and more private this time around? What if this time is the first time for your new bride, and she has always dreamed of that special ceremony? What role will your children play in the wedding, and how comfortable will they feel being a part of, or being left out of, the event? Will your ex watch the children while you're on your honeymoon? And depending on what kind of divorce you have had, will he help the children—or fan the flames—if they feel left out, torn, or even scornful while you are gone? When you return from a fantastic honeymoon, how are the two of you going to manage the realities of moving in together, potentially moving your children from their home with you, and, most critically, managing your new partner's relationship with the children and your life together as a stepfamily?

Let's consider your new spouse's relationship with your children in a little more detail because it is so crucial and it illustrates the layers of complications within the complications. Especially if your children are older and their other parent is involved in their lives, it is wise for stepparents to see their new role as initially being an adult friend to their stepchildren rather than as another, or substitute, parent. If the children are young—and if their other parent is a small part of their lives—a stepparent may be able to move into a true parenting role sooner and with a warm reception from children. But remember: It is much easier for stepparents to move closer if they have gone too slowly at first than it is to move back if they have gone too fast.

How children address their stepparent is a symbolic touchstone issue for beginning to think about a stepparent's role as an adult friend. Forcing children to call someone "Dad" or "Mom" can convey the wrong message about a stepparent's role in the children's lives and about your expectations of the degree of affection, trust, and respect they should be feeling and expressing. No one can be told whom to love, least of all children.

Older children who regularly see their mom or live with her most of the time already have a mother, and they are not likely to want or need a new one. Rather than calling a stepmother "Mom," older children from divorced families usually are more comfortable calling stepparents by their first names, as they might be allowed to do with only a few other close adult friends of their parents. Forcing children to share a term of endearment reserved for someone so unique and special in their lives with someone of your choosing is unfair and insensitive. When it comes to calling a stepparent Mom or Dad, your child should be the one to decide when—and if—she will.

There is another complication within this complication: The children's real mom is not likely to be pleased when she hears her children complaining that their father is forcing them to call his new wife "Mom." Once again, we're back to the critical role of your relationship with your coparent—and your children's mother or father, not your new spouse, *is* your coparent.

While it carries great symbolic significance, what your children call your new spouse should be pretty low on the list of priorities for laying the groundwork for a successful family and marriage (and when it comes to stepfamilies, the two are very much interrelated). On the bright side, there is a lot to be said for the good that a successful blended family can achieve for all of its members: new parenting supports for children, an additional and positive adult in children's lives, improved finances, healthy relationships between stepparents and the other parent, a positive model of marriage, remarried parents who are less angry and far happier, and perhaps new siblings.

Still, we cannot overlook the hurdles that even the healthiest stepfamilies often must clear on their way: struggles with stepparenting, angry and rejecting children, jealousy and renewed conflict between former partners, changes in the parenting plan, and difficult relocations, perhaps far away from the children. A remarriage is more likely to be successful and a smoother transition for children if parents go slowly and lay the groundwork from the beginning, so here are some points to keep in mind:

- Parents should talk with children repeatedly, as needed, about divorce and its finality so that the children don't see the beginning of new relationships as symbolizing—or causing—the end of their parents' marriage. To the extent possible, it is important to separate your new love interest from the divorce, although this may be impossible to do if your affair with this person was—or was perceived by your children as—the reason you got divorced.

- Parents should tell children about the fact that they are dating without going into a lot of details and without introducing children to every date. Talking about dating also includes telling your ex that you are beginning to see other people, so your children won't be in the middle and have to keep a secret or break the news to your ex.

- A divorced family is still a family. Like it or not, children and exes are a part of any new relationships that parents develop after divorce. Recognizing and tending to these unavoidable facts will help everyone to adjust, including new partners and perhaps their own children.

- Divorced parents need to look at each date—other than those carefree rebound relationships—as a potential stepparent as well as a potential partner. Parenting is always challenging, and stepparenting is more, not less, of a challenge. So divorced parents are wise to look for mates whose interest in children is as deep and genuine as theirs.

- Parents do best to introduce children to only the people they are seeing regularly and starting to get serious with. Children can get attached to new adults in their lives, especially if their other parent has essentially disappeared from their lives and they wish for a new dad or new mom to make them feel more like the other kids. In order to avoid additional losses for children, parents want to make sure that there is a reasonable chance that the relationship will continue before encouraging their children to get close to their new boyfriends or girlfriends.

- Divorced parents—and the people with whom they are involved—need to anticipate that children may have a hard time accepting a new adult friend in their lives. Children may resent the intrusion into their relationship with their dating parent, or feel torn loyalties between one parent's new partner and their other parent's hurt, jealousy, or loneliness. Other times children may not click right away with someone you are dating, for whatever reason, or they may be reluctant to get close to someone when this person may be gone from their lives in a short time. Being aware of the children's perspective can help new adult friends not to rush their relationship with children but instead follow the children's lead.

- Boyfriends or girlfriends—or new stepparents—should not expect to jump into a parental role right away but work to become children's adult friends first and perhaps finally. A parental role is an honor only your child can bestow on them.

- Being an adult friend means trying to build a warm relationship with children first and assuming a role as a disciplinarian only later, if at all. Biological parents build their attachments with their children before introducing discipline into the relationship, and stepparents should follow this same developmental sequence.

- Parents and stepparents must recognize that there is not a one size fits all solution for anyone or anything in divorce or in remarriage. Young children are likely to more readily accept a new adult figure in their life, particularly if one of their parents is not very involved with them. Older children are likely to be more reticent about dating and remarriage, especially if they have a good relationship with both of their parents.

- Parents need to remember that remarriage is not the re-creation of the two-parent family for their children. For children, remarriage is another major transition in their lives.

Go Slowly for Yourself

Let's not forget that you have your *own* reasons for taking things one step at a time. Or you should. You may feel like a new relationship is healing, and it can be. But hurried relationships can heal in the same way that a few drinks heal a hangover. It's a quick cure but one destined to also quickly create the same problems for you. You need to get over your relationship hangover if you hope to avoid making the same mistakes you made in the past.

How do you know when you are ready to date? You're ready to date when you're ready to tell other people—including your ex and your children—that you're dating. It's too soon if your friends raise an eyebrow about you dating, if you just know your ex is going to freak because it's so soon, or if your children are so caught up in the emotions of divorce that you just can't lay this on them, too. In this case, chances are it isn't just too soon for them, but it's probably too soon for you as well. You need to take care of your stuff first, and your family relationships are both a part of your stuff and a barometer on how far you have progressed in taking care of your own emotions. Beginning to date after divorce is kind of like unprotected sex: You shouldn't start doing it unless you're prepared to deal with the consequences.

Of course, as a member of the human race, people are allowed to make mistakes once they do start dating. You can't expect to find the right person for you and your children on your first date. So you want to allow yourself the time, the space, and the distance (from your children) to have a rebound relationship or two or three. Like Cindy, you may have feelings that you can expect to be working out as a part of your new relationships, and as a result, when you first start dating you may be angrier, more cautious, or more dependent than is healthy for you.

The same rules apply to the person you may be dating. You want to go slowly if you are dating someone who has recently been separated. Like you, that person needs to do some experimenting and make some mistakes before she is ready for a real relationship herself. The first question divorced parents ask about a potential fixup with another divorced adult is, "Does he have children?" The second question is, "How long has he been separated?" Like other parents, you should be cautious about dating someone who hasn't been separated for at least a year, maybe two—and if it hasn't been at least a year that you have been separated, you should be cautious about yourself, too.

New relationships are complicated in divorce, and chances are, the last thing you need is *more* complications. So before jumping into the dating pool—or at least the deep end—try wading in the shallows. If you want to swim deeper, do not venture too far from the side.

Most important, though, be sure that you are working on your relationships with your children, with your ex, and with yourself, too. Your next relationship—no matter how great it seems to you in the vacuum of the time you two spend alone—depends very much on the larger emotional environment in which it must fit and grow once outside the hothouse of pure romance. Like plants that must adjust from the perfect world of a greenhouse to the more hostile and unpredictable terrain of a real garden, your relationship needs to acclimate slowly. If you want to ease that transition, tend carefully the garden of relationships you have now so that there will be room and welcome when the right person for you comes along.

CHAPTER TEN

Putting the Lessons into Practice

As parents negotiate the sometimes treacherous roads of divorce, they discover that dealing with its multiple tasks can challenge their emotions, time, patience, and energy. Still, most families find a manageable route through the complex course of divorce.

For some people, though, the journey through divorce is marked by wrong turns and dead ends, which are often the result of trying relationships or very complicated family circumstances. There are all kinds of potential obstacles that might require expert assistance from a mental health professional or a lawyer—or a concerted effort on your part—to get around or through. Some parents get lost in their anger; others are unable to find their grief. Some parents struggle to redefine the boundaries of their new relationships; others cannot find a way to coparent together. And sometimes the problem is not one that can be controlled by either parent. One parent might get transferred to a new job, perhaps far away, for example. This chapter addresses many of these common concerns, roadblocks that many but not all divorced parents encounter on their journey to a new life.

When to Consider Therapy

One important question people often ask during their uncertain journey through divorce is: When are things bad enough that parents should consider getting therapy for themselves, for their children, or perhaps together as a family? You should consider therapy if you, your ex, or your children are stuck or lost in a bad place and just cannot get started moving in the right direction within a reasonable period. How long is "reasonable"? It depends but, generally speaking, you should give yourself a couple of months to try to solve things on your own.

After this time, how do you know if you are still stuck or just stalled or idling? When you have tried sincerely to change your feelings, your children, or your relationship with your ex, and you are out of patience, out of ideas, and you are losing hope fast. You know you are stuck when your problems are so big that you cannot function. You cannot sleep. You cannot relax. You cannot stop thinking. You cannot concentrate. You cannot work. You cannot control your tears. You cannot control your anger. You cannot control your kids.

The most common problems to look for in your children (and yourself) as a result of divorce are depression and acting-out problems—things like anger, aggression, chronic rule breaking, and unsuitable risk taking. But other problems like anxiety, substance abuse, or even eating disorders might be exacerbated or revealed in divorce. Even if divorce has not caused these problems—and most emotional disorders have multiple and complex causes—the added stress or lost support due to divorce can make it far more difficult to cope with a serious psychological problem.

The line dividing what is normal from what is abnormal can be very narrow, particularly in the middle of a crisis like divorce. But if you find yourself or your children or your relationship with your ex to be full of anger or anguish, you should at least try therapy. You have little to lose and much to gain. Even if you are a therapy skeptic, there is something of indisputable value therapy can offer: a fresh and unbiased perspective. Good therapy offers much more than this, but even if all therapy will buy you is a new way to consider looking at things, it's worth the time and the money.

You may want to consider therapy before you get so stuck or lost. Some people are smart enough to ask for help when they are uncertain where to go instead of assuming they will find a way themselves.

These people may look at problems from a more proactive perspective or they may feel that the divorce puts enough on their plate as it is.

There are others who view therapy as a preventive measure. Given everything else that is going on in a divorce, they feel more comfortable having access to the outlet and the fresh perspective good therapy can provide before they make mistakes or reach the point at which they feel that they really, really need help. Therapy may not be necessary if you or your children are in pain but coping adequately, but therapy still can offer you both some perspective and some support in helping you to cope.

If you are looking for perspective and support more than help with specific problems or feelings, you probably should be thinking about therapy for yourself rather than for your children. Your children will benefit from therapy if they *want* to talk with a neutral and expert adult, but your children are not going to get much from therapy if they aren't interested in it. Sure, some reluctant children learn a lot from therapy and come to value it. Other children would benefit from therapy, but they simply don't know enough to ask for someone to talk to, or they want to ask but don't know how.

Still, you need to remember that you—and your ex—are your children's best therapists, at least potentially. If you can negotiate your own emotional stuff, you should be in a good position to help your children through these troubled times. Three exceptions are if you and your ex cannot deal with your own emotions and the children are caught in the middle, if your children are having serious problems with their behavior or feelings, or if your children's school or some local agency runs a group specifically for children of divorce.

This last option—groups run by schools or community agencies—is a special and potentially valuable opportunity. Even if your children are not having problems, research shows that they may well benefit from talking to kids in similar circumstances to theirs. Children can offer one another perspective and support in a way that no adult—not a parent, not a professional therapist—can. Because they lack maturity and life experience, most children come to divorce truly believing that no one else in the world could ever imagine how they feel. If you and your ex are having a less than cooperative divorce, your children may feel that they cannot talk to you or that doing so automatically puts them where no child ever wants to be: in the middle. Learning that other kids face similar situations may not solve your children's dilemma, but it should help them to feel less alone in trying to cope.

People make very personal and highly individualized decisions about whether to get therapy, when to start, and whether they are benefiting from treatment. For these reasons, let's consider several new but brief case histories to illustrate some common problems that often bring people into therapy in divorce and some of the ways that therapy is unique to every individual and every family. These case histories demonstrate many of the lessons of divorce we have discussed and may help you to put them into practice before things get really, really bad for you, too.

Stuck with an Angry Ex

Kate returned to individual therapy about two years after she separated from her husband, Mike. Kate had sought counseling with me a few years earlier because she was unhappy in her marriage but torn about leaving. Her marriage to Mike had been cold and distant. They rarely talked, never laughed together, and sex was infrequent and mechanical. They shared no real emotion in any part of their relationship, even raising their two children, eleven-year-old Crystal and ten-year-old Willis. Kate revealed in tears, "Even on my wedding day, I knew I was marrying the wrong man, but I didn't have the courage to say 'I don't.'" So Kate married Mike and stayed with him for thirteen years.

Besides the emotional distance, Mike's anger and sarcasm hurt Kate terribly. In tears during our first session years ago, she blurted out, "I've been emotionally abused. Mike is handsome and a terrific athlete, and he turns on the charm in social situations. But he's always so mad at me whether we're alone or with other people."

Kate started crying harder. "I'm a kindergarten teacher and proud of it, but do you know what he calls me? 'Kindergarten Kate'—as if I'm a kindergartener, not a teacher! He'll dismiss me at home by saying, 'Okay, Kindergarten Kate.' And he'll even do it around other people. Like he'll tell a stupid joke at a party, and if I don't laugh, he'll say, 'I guess that was over Kindergarten Kate's head.' I could kill him! But I just sit there and take it like an idiot because I don't want to cause a scene."

Kate had agonized about what to do. She wanted to leave Mike, but she was frozen by her guilt. "I don't love him—and he can't love me. But leaving would still feel like I was abandoning Mike. He depends on me in ways he doesn't realize—relating to the kids, making friends, managing everything. And what would I tell the kids, and my friends and my family? I couldn't stand it if everyone blamed me for breaking up our family. I feel enough like a failure as it is."

On several occasions Kate resolved that she was going to leave Mike, but she never could muster the courage to tell him that. Then one day after another put-down, Kate screamed at Mike, "Get out! I want a divorce!" Mike didn't argue. He left the house and never came back. Nor did he ever talk to Kate about what went wrong or about trying to save the marriage, despite her desire to do both.

Now two years later, Kate said that in many ways she was relieved to be divorced. But in other ways, she wondered if she really was better off. Mike was as angry and difficult as always. True, his anger no longer was a constant in her life, but because of the kids, she still needed to deal with him, his hostility, and his obstinacy.

Kate complained that she had a lot less control over many things since her separation. She especially worried about losing control over the children. Kate had been in charge of the children when she and Mike were together. Now she said, "I feel like I have to take care of the kids in *two* households! And whenever I make a suggestion about the kids, Mike either refuses to discuss it or we get into a huge argument! So what am I supposed to do? Fight over every little thing or let him do it his way—and let the children suffer?"

Kate particularly worried about Willis's anger at his father. Willis didn't talk about being angry, but Kate found him more difficult to control since the separation and was sure she knew why. And Crystal seemed to be growing more distant from Kate. Kate wondered if Mike was putting Crystal down—or maybe putting down Crystal's close relationship with her mother.

Kate tried to get Mike and Crystal and Willis to talk with her about her concerns, but when she did, Mike got angry, Crystal clammed up, and Willis acted flip and uninterested. Exchanges of the children during their every other weekend overnights and Tuesday dinners with their father had become increasingly tense, and Kate wondered if she should take Mike to court to try to limit the children's exposure to him. (They negotiated a settlement through their lawyers when they separated.)

She also wondered repeatedly if she had made a mistake in leaving Mike. At least when they were together, she could protect her children from him. Now, she just did not know what was happening at his house.

I offered to try to work with her and Mike together, but Kate told me, "Mike would never agree to come here, and besides, I couldn't bear to sit in the same room with him if he did. I just want you to help me figure out what to do about Mike, his temper, and the kids."

I agreed to try to help her, and for several sessions Kate talked at length about Mike. I sympathized with Kate. It wasn't easy dealing with an angry ex who also was a distant father. But it became increasingly clear that Kate needed to redirect her energy and focus inward. Her wishing and hoping and trying were not going to change Mike. It did not work during thirteen years of marriage, when, at least for some of the time, Mike cared about her. At this point, why Mike would not or could not change was a question that Kate had to let go of. This was a question she had to let Mike answer for himself.

His anger hurt her, and that was terrible and unfair, but Kate needed to shift her focus from Mike, whom she could not control, onto something she *could* control—her reactions to him. I wondered out loud what would happen if Kate stepped back and stopped trying to manage Mike's relationship with the children. Could she let what happened happen between him and the kids? It's really sad that the children don't have a more loving father, but like it or not, Mike is their father, right? Stepping back might not make a difference, but doesn't it seem like an experiment worth trying? Maybe Kate needed to discover the Zen of divorce: You can gain control by giving up trying to control others.

It was not easy for Kate to step back. The big reason, of course, was that Mike's anger and his lack of attention to parenting *were* real problems for Kate and for the kids. But some other things really were Kate's problems. She was tormented by her own guilt, self-doubt, and longing for something more. She could live with the guilt if her decision to leave Mike made things better, but right now everything seemed even worse—for her and for the children. Had she failed as a mother as well as a wife? She felt like she *had* to work on Mike's parenting because she always had, because she believed that was her job. Deep down, Kate believed that her decision to divorce might be better justified if she could improve the children's relationship with Mike.

Among other things, Kate's guilt clouded her thinking about who was responsible for the end of her marriage. True, she had uttered the word "divorce" first, but Mike wasted no time in walking out the door she briefly opened. And whether she wanted to or not, she *had* to let go of Mike and of managing his relationship with the children. Losing control over your ex and your children's relationship with him is one of the inevitabilities of divorce.

As she slowly recognized and accepted these realities, Kate confessed not only to worrying about the children but also to being incredibly lonely living alone. She was jealous of the women Mike dated and more so of the fact that he was dating and she was not. She resented the fun the children sometimes had with their father, and constantly wondered—and sometimes asked the children—if they were doing things together with one of Mike's girlfriends.

As Kate's guilt eased and she accepted (with repeated reminders) that she really could not change Mike, she did step back and let his relationship with the children be whatever it was going to be. To her great surprise, the experiment worked. Once she stepped back, her relationship with Mike started to improve. He did not become the world's greatest father, but he and Kate fought less, Kate worried less, and to her disbelief, Mike even asked Kate's advice about a couple of problems with the children.

Before long, the kids started talking more to Kate about what they did with their father—now that they sensed that their mother was more relaxed and ready to hear about it. Kate still worried about Mike's parenting, and her children sometimes complained to her about their dad. But she put herself in a better position to help and in a much better position emotionally when she stopped trying to control something she could not.

Kate's inner changes helped her, and so did starting to date, a move I encouraged. Dating alleviated many of Kate's fears of being alone and much of her jealousy. Dating also gave her a new focus for her considerable emotional energy. The parting goal of therapy for Kate was to put the lessons learned about Mike into practice with her children and in her new relationship. Her children were young adolescents now, and Kate was realizing that she had to give up some control over them. She also realized how she tried to make every intimate relationship work, because she believed that was her job. She was recognizing that she needed to give her new boyfriend—and herself—the space to explore their relationship without forcing it.

Kate had learned the Zen of divorce. Now she needed to master the Zen of parenting and the Zen of new relationships.

Kate was a dedicated and loving mother and a warm and giving woman. If she had married someone else, her "problems" might not have been problems but strengths. But Kate did not marry someone else who could offer her that option. She married an angry man who constantly denigrated her. Family therapy might have helped Mike to change, but Kate's life with him was too full of what might have been. Individual treatment taught Kate that she—like all of us—played a role in shaping her relationships.

From Mike's perspective, Kate's constant effort to help probably seemed like micromanaging and an intrusion on his relationships with his children. Maybe he was not a very good father because he had never had to learn to be a dad. After all, Kate was in charge.

I would never want to blame Kate for Mike's problems, but she did have to learn to take responsibility for herself. She needed to overcome her excessive guilt, to get out of the quagmire of blaming everything on Mike, and, therefore, of being unable to change herself. Kate needed to learn how to step back to let some things happen in her close relationships rather than trying to make them happen.

Children Making Parental Decisions

Alicia and David had been separated for about a year and a half when they came to see me for family therapy and possibly mediation. They had two sons. Tommy was eight years old, and Henry was six. Alicia was concerned about David's parenting, and she also worried about the boys' adjustment to the separation and soon-to-be-final divorce. Her worries about the boys weren't specific—they were good kids, they just seemed kind of unhappy and tense. David also was concerned about the boys. In addition, he was upset with various changes in the schedule that he said were cutting more and more into his already limited time with his sons.

David and Alicia's separation agreement, which they had worked out partly on their own and partly with their lawyers, indicated that the children would "reside primarily with their mother and spend every Friday overnight and perhaps some additional time with their father, to be decided according to the children's best interests." The parents apparently reached the agreement in good faith, but over time, they came to interpret it differently. David had assumed that the boys would be spending a lot more than every Friday night with him; he saw that once-weekly visit as just the minimum, a starting point.

For her part, Alicia thought that extra visits might take place occasionally. In her mind, the Friday overnights that David saw as a definite may not even occur if that was contrary to the boys' best interests. Surprisingly, the differing interpretations did not cause a lot of conflict because David almost always accepted Alicia's decisions about the schedule, albeit grudgingly.

And Alicia found frequent reasons to change the schedule. She strongly believed that the boys should have a voice in what *they* wanted to do, where they wanted to spend time. Because of her belief—or perhaps for more subtle and selfish reasons—Alicia asked the boys before almost every scheduled visit if they wanted to go see their dad.

The boys were uncomfortable in their father's cramped apartment in a new neighborhood, and they frequently responded that Dad's place was boring and that they would rather stay home with Mom and play with their friends. (Alicia had stayed in the marital home in a neighborhood where the boys had several friends.) If they said something like this, Alicia called David and told him that the boys didn't want to visit him. Hurt and dejected, David usually acquiesced to Alicia's judgment about the boys' wishes.

While relating this information, Alicia glanced at David and said to me, "Another reason why they don't want to go is that David doesn't do anything with the boys himself. He's a fine sports dad, but that's about it. The boys aren't comfortable at his apartment. They're bored and"—she turned, looked at David again, and then said what was really on her mind—"I'm really worried about their exposure to secondhand smoke."

At this point David shot back, "I *never* smoke around the boys, and you know that!"

Alicia snapped, "Then why do their clothes always smell like smoke?"

I asked the parents if we could talk about secondhand smoke another time and focus on the schedule for the time being. All of the changes in the schedule meant that David and Alicia were constantly negotiating about when and whether to exchange the boys. Rather than working out the conflicts between themselves, both of them asked the boys what they wanted to do. They thought that asking the boys not only was reasonable, but that it also was a way of being sensitive to the boys' needs. And Alicia was as pleased that the boys needed her as David was dejected that they didn't need him.

As I listened to the parents talking, I doubted that the boys felt empowered by being asked what they wanted to do. I certainly did not feel empowered being in the middle of David and Alicia. I felt tense just being in the same room with the two of them, although I could not point to anything blatant as the source of my discomfort. They did not fight openly, but the tension and unstated competition between them was palpable.

Alicia dominated the discussions. She was smart, articulate, and tuned in to the boys. Surprisingly, though, she was blind to how she was putting them in the middle. Unlike Alicia, David was not terribly quick on his feet. He would try to explain what he wanted and why, but his arguments generally were ineffective. When he failed at persuasion, he became passive aggressive: sullen, stubborn, uncommunicative.

If I had been seeing them for marital therapy, I would have focused on Alicia's and David's communication styles, but changing a longstanding pattern like that usually is not the goal of family therapy in divorce. Usually, former partners have tried and failed to change their way of relating; that's often one reason why they get divorced. So, family therapy in divorce tends to be more practical. I wanted Alicia and David to develop a clear schedule, stick with it consistently, and stop turning to the children to resolve their disagreements. Unfortunately, several weeks of therapy got us nowhere in working toward these goals. Then six-year-old Henry solved a big part of the problem.

David and Alicia came for a therapy appointment, but Alicia brought Henry with her because he was home from school with a cold. During the appointment, the parents told me about an incident that had happened with Henry the past weekend. Henry had broken his arm during a soccer match on Saturday. Fortunately, it was just a simple fracture, and, fortunately, both parents were at the game. Dad was coaching, and Mom had brought Henry and two teammates in a car pool.

Henry took a terrible fall and lay moaning on the ground. Clearly, he needed to go the emergency room. Someone had to take him, but who? Alicia and David started to argue—they each wanted to take him—but needed the other to take over the car pool or the coaching.

They solved the problem as they usually did. Mom asked Henry, "Who do you want to take you to the hospital?" Lying on the ground in tears, Henry replied, "Both." So David forfeited the game, and he, Alicia, Henry, and his two friends tore off to the hospital together.

As they related the story, David clearly felt proud that he was there for Henry when he got hurt and glad that Henry wanted him to go to the hospital, too. Mom was unimpressed. But my thoughts were on Henry. I asked Mom and Dad if it was all right for him to join us. They agreed and when the four of us sat down together, I told Henry we had been discussing how he got his cast. His father then asked Henry, "Weren't you glad that Dad was there to take you to the hospital with Mom?"

David clearly thought he had won some points in his unspoken contest with Alicia, and he wanted Henry to tally them for him. But before he could answer, Alicia gave Henry a look that even I could read. It said, "Watch out! This is a trap."

Much to his credit, Henry did not take the safe route of either clamming up or siding with one of his parents. Instead, he let loose. He yelled at his parents, "I'm *not* glad that you both took me to the hospital! I'm mad at *both* of you. Why did you have to ask *me* who should take me? I was hurt. *I had a broken arm!* Why couldn't *you* decide what to do? Why do you always put *me* in the middle?"

The truth of Henry's outburst hit Alicia and David like a shot. They were stunned, but to their credit, they both took his words to heart. At last, they saw how they put the boys in the middle, and this opened them up to change. Within a few weeks, they worked out a new, clearer schedule, and they stuck to it religiously. Alicia no longer asked the boys if they wanted to go to Dad's. Instead, she gave David advice on how to improve his now-regular Friday-night visits, including not smoking in his apartment when the boys were *not* there. They had complained to her bitterly about how Dad's place stank. David also stopped asking what the boys wanted, and he gratefully accepted Alicia's advice. Instead of competing with each other, David and Alicia got back on the same team as parents.

•   •   •

Henry's thirty-second tirade cut to the heart of a mistake made by many well-meaning parents and well-meaning professionals. The mistake is not just putting kids like Henry and his big brother Tommy in the middle. The more specific mistake is putting kids in the middle by asking them what *they* want to do.

Like Alicia and David, parents end up doing this to children because in some ways it makes sense. Parents want to do what's best for children, and what better way is there to figure out what a child wants than to ask him? Sadly, professionals—judges, lawyers, guardians *ad litem*, mediators, psychologists—also sometimes inappropriately ask children what they want to do about a parenting plan. In ways that may be subtle or not so subtle, parents and professionals ask children, "Who do you want to live with: Mom or Dad?"

A child's immediate answer to this question might be a plaintive "Both." But as Henry said, what children from divorced families really want to say in response to big and small questions like this is "Don't ask me! This is for grown-ups to decide!" Part of accepting and embracing parental responsibility is trusting your own common sense. How many children would be truant if parents asked them every morning if they wanted to go to school—and actually let the children decide? In divorce, a bigger issue is parents avoiding conflict—and responsibility—by turning to their children and asking them to make adult decisions for them.

Learning to Grieve

After talking with him for five minutes, it was clear that Chuck's typical day would probably never include seeing a therapist. But his wife of twenty-seven years, Nancy, told him that he needed to talk to someone, so here he was. Fifty-one years old, Chuck had retired from the army three years earlier after putting in twenty-five years as an enlisted man. Chuck did things by the book in the service, in his new career as a computer technician, and, he thought, in his marriage. His life seemed well ordered and predictable until about six weeks earlier, when Nancy told Chuck she wanted a divorce.

Chuck was blindsided by Nancy's announcement. During our first appointment, Chuck asked if the real problem might be Nancy's menopause, what he called her change of life. He heard that women sometimes acted strangely during this change, and Nancy's actions certainly were strange. I told him that I seriously doubted that menopause was the explanation, but my response did not seem to answer Chuck's question or end his search for the one simple problem that he could fix to save his marriage.

Chuck never thought his marriage was particularly troubled or, he supposed, particularly happy. He just never thought about his marriage much at all. He said, "I know things haven't been perfect in our marriage, but we've *never* had serious troubles. Sure, we have different interests—I like to work with my hands and she's more interested in the finer things in life—but it's all right with me if she's interested in different things."

Chuck hesitated, then blurted out, "Okay, I might as well tell you that our sex life has pretty much died." He paused, smiled at me, and said, "But I always figured that was more of a problem for the man than the woman, right?" He added, "Over the years, I've gotten used to having sex only on rare occasions, or special ones."

About the only thing that Chuck could remember arguing about with Nancy was Melinda, their eleven-year-old daughter. Melinda was a surprise who trailed long behind Chuck and Nancy's twenty-six-year-old daughter and twenty-four-year-old-son. Chuck loved his baby girl and showered her with affection. Nancy, though, had taken a much less active role with Melinda than she had with the older children. According to Chuck, when Nancy learned that she was pregnant she told him, "This was *your* accident. I've raised two children by myself. Now it's your turn." They never discussed her comment, but for eleven years, Chuck took Nancy's proclamation to heart. He took the lead in raising Melinda.

Nancy refused to come to therapy with Chuck. She had her own therapist, and in any case, she was not interested in working on her marriage. Nancy told Chuck that she cared about him and wanted him to get some help, but she did not want to be married to him anymore. Even when he related stories like this, Chuck remained stoic. Freely but without much emotion, Chuck discussed the events of his life, including some terrible details about his childhood. Chuck revealed that his father abandoned his mother when he was a very young child. She remarried when Chuck was seven years old, but his stepfather abused him physically and emotionally until he left home at the age of eighteen.

The stories of rejection, denigration, and abuse that Chuck told about his childhood made me sad and angry. When I told him this, Chuck denied ever having had similar feelings himself. He said he knew his stepfather was an unkind man, but both he and his mother had been dead for ten years. The most emotion I got out of Chuck was when he grudgingly acknowledged, in an even tone of voice, that he was a little upset and pretty angry with Nancy. He could not describe his emotions with any intensity or much more detail.

Reality began to hit Chuck a few weeks later, when Nancy told him that she was in love with someone else. Nancy confessed she had left Chuck for her high school sweetheart, a man with whom she had reconnected thirteen years earlier at her twentieth high school reunion. Nancy told Chuck that she felt terrible, but, yes, they had had an affair off and on for thirteen years. No, she had no doubt who was Melinda's father. Chuck was Melinda's father. In fact, Nancy was prepared to let Chuck have primary physical custody of Melinda and stay in the house with her. All Nancy wanted was for Chuck to agree to let Melinda spend summers with her. Nancy was going to move to Maine to be with her recently divorced boyfriend.

Chuck did not rage at Nancy or beg her to stay. In therapy, he still seemed disbelieving, although he understood what was happening. Chuck also was clearly depressed. He had now lost fifteen pounds and woke up in the middle of most nights unable to get back to sleep. He felt tired all the time and had trouble concentrating on his work. The only symptom of depression that Chuck lacked was a sad or irritable mood. At one point, I even read him all of the symptoms of depression from *The Diagnostic and Statistical Manual of Mental Disorders,* the official manual for diagnosing mental disorders. Chuck agreed that the symptoms described him, except, no, he did not feel depressed.

Finally, I decided to take a different approach to try to help Chuck to get in touch with his feelings—his sadness, anger, hurt, and grief. After greeting him, I sat back in my chair and avoided eye contact by staring at the ceiling. I started talking about how I might feel if I was in Chuck's shoes. Devastated. Numb. Furious. Cheated. Hurt. Lost about what to do. Worried about Melinda. Mad at Nancy, the guy she was involved with, and at life for doing me wrong. Hopeless.

Soon Chuck was mirroring my body posture, and before long he was reflecting my words as well. Yes, he did feel mad. This whole thing was not fair. He had not done anything wrong. And hurt. He hurt a lot. His pain felt more physical than emotional, like someone had just punched him in the chest. Yes, he was sad, too—sad about so many things for so many years. Chuck continued like this for the entire therapy hour. In fact, when I left to go home after another appointment, Chuck was still sitting in his Explorer in the parking lot and staring, unseeing, out of the window. His emotional dam had broken.

Chuck kept talking for months in therapy. He talked about his feelings about Nancy, Melinda, his older children, his mother, and his stepfather. He tied his different feelings together. Chuck recognized how, as a child, he had learned to shut out his emotions in order to protect himself from feeling pain. He realized that he needed to grieve, and he did grieve—for Nancy, for Melinda, for the loss of his marriage, for the childhood he had never had.

Chuck felt the hurt and anger, but, no, he did not want to stop Nancy or to hurt her back. Yes, he *felt* like hurting her back. He felt like driving up to Maine, telling her off, and punching this guy in the nose. But he knew that would not do any good. Chuck said that what he felt mostly was sad. He missed Nancy, but he knew he was going to have to let her go.

Over the next year and a half, Chuck did let Nancy go. He took care of Melinda with all the love he had always felt for her. He worked out a fair and amicable divorce settlement. He let go of Nancy, not by denying his emotions or by giving in to anger but by really feeling his feelings. For the first time in his life, he grieved.

For fifty-one years, Chuck had closed off his feelings. During our last appointment, he told me, "I suppose that one good thing came out of Nancy's leaving. I learned how to feel. And I still got to be Melinda's father. I couldn't have stood it if I had lost her, too." Chuck continued, "Of course, that doesn't make Nancy's leaving right. Still, I guess that something positive comes out of everything you go through, even divorce."

At first blush, Chuck seemed so wrong for therapy, but he got a lot out of treatment—and I got a lot out of working with him. For fifty years, all of his feelings had been lost behind the walls he had built around his emotions as a child, walls that were reinforced by the experience of being a man in a world that discourages men from expressing feelings. With a little help and guidance, Chuck not only scaled his walls, but he also searched beyond the easily found anger and discovered a more painful but much richer set of feelings: hurt, sadness, longing, and grief.

Some people are never able to grieve for their divorce, and at the beginning of therapy, I would have bet that Chuck would be one of them. At the end of treatment, I instead found myself admiring his newfound insight.

Another thing I admired about Chuck was his straightforward sense of justice. Nancy was wrong to leave him and to do what she did to Melinda. But two wrongs did not make a right in Chuck's view. He was as hurt as any man whose wife leaves him for someone else, but Chuck thought about it and consciously chose not to act on his feelings. He decided to do what he knew in his heart was the right thing. He decided to love Melinda instead of hating Nancy.

Is Court the Answer?

Many parents call a therapist when things break down. Other parents call a lawyer, because tricky legal issues can create a major roadblock for postdivorce family relationships. As I have noted repeatedly and as you will see again here, emotional issues often cause or complicate legal conflicts. If parents can address their emotional concerns, solving the legal issues becomes a much less difficult task—perhaps even an unnecessary one.

Becoming Parents Again

Rod and Frances had been divorced for two years when they came for mediation and family therapy. In a recent custody hearing, a judge had ordered them to seek treatment because they had a long history of custody battles and the judge thought it was time to try a different approach. Their lawyers each submitted a list of three names of counselors whom their client was willing to see, and my name was on both lists so they agreed that I was to be the family's therapist.

Rod and Frances had three children. Eight-year-old Ian was an energetic and bright boy who was often out of control with his parents, especially his mother, misbehaved in school, and did not perform up to his academic ability. Christine, who was twelve years old, was a quiet and well-behaved preadolescent who was the worrier and the peacemaker in the family. Fifteen-year-old Jen was charming, histrionic, rebellious, and, according to her mother, only concerned with looking hot, flirting, and manipulating boys and men, including her father.

In the four years since their parents' separation, the three children had lived with the two parents in almost every conceivable constellation. Initially, the three children lived primarily with their mother, but Frances had such a hard time with Ian that during one of their custody fights, she let him move in with his father.

Jen followed Ian several months later, but Jen changed her primary residence frequently over the years. Whenever Jen had a major fight with the parent she was living with, she insisted that she wanted to go live with the other. Whoever it was, Mom or Dad, welcomed her back, more as a way of getting back at the other parent than of helping Jen.

Christine had stayed with her mother for a long time, but she moved in with her father after he successfully sued for custody of all of the children. Yet all three later moved back with their mother when Rod was sent out of the country on business for six months. His return prompted yet another custody battle that was resolved by putting the girls with their mother and Ian with his father. Currently, though, Jen was living with her father, Ian, and her stepmother. (Rod remarried shortly after the divorce.) Christine was living with her mother and Frances's longstanding boyfriend.

I saw Rod, Frances, and the children together and separately for a few months. All of these meetings only revealed more details about family problems—the basic problems were obvious from the outset. Rod and Frances not only failed to support each other in parenting, but they often deliberately undermined each other, too. They were so preoccupied with their own disputes and so eager to have the children on their side that they disciplined their kids rarely and inconsistently. The children clearly suffered as a result, yet the parents were blind to what they were doing. Frances and Rod constantly fought with each other and increasingly with the children, but their arguments kept going around and around in a circle, like a cat chasing its tail. They never solved any problems, and neither of them took charge with the children.

I could see these problems, and so could twelve-year-old Christine. She spent a lot of her time mediating back and forth between her parents or trying to get one or the other to calm down. Christine also did her best to mother Ian, both by giving him special attention and by reprimanding him as well as she could. She and Ian had a good relationship, although Ian did say that he was tired of Christine's being a little mother.

Jen also ridiculed Christine's attempts to be a little mother, and told Christine that she needed to loosen up. But Jen gave the impression that she was not as emotionally loose as she pretended to be. Her frantic efforts with boys seemed to reflect a carefully hidden but desperate search for affection and stability in her life. Christine might have been more uptight—she was overly responsible and an anxious caretaker kid. Yet, in fact, Christine was in better touch with her feelings than Jen.

I shared my observations with Frances and Rod, but to little avail.

They agreed that their fighting created problems for the children and for their own parenting, and they also agreed that they needed to work together better. They also said that they liked coming for therapy and thought treatment was helpful. However, when it came time to make a real change and move forward, Frances blamed Rod and Rod blamed Frances.

Despite their frequent fights, the arguments between Rod and Frances did not have a vicious edge, and we developed a somewhat playful rapport that allowed me to confront them without my becoming the target of their anger. During our fifth or sixth session, as they were going around again, ignoring my efforts to help, I remarked in a somewhat flip tone, "Well, I'm glad the two of *you* are enjoying yourselves."

They stopped arguing. First Rod and then Frances broke into a sly smile. Yes, they admitted, arguing with each other *was* fun—just like it was when they were married. They liked the debate. It was challenging, and it was energizing. They liked that they could still get a rise out of each other. After all, Frances laughed, if Rod really did not care about her opinion, why did he get *so* angry when he disagreed with her? Rod grinned as Frances said this, and the atmosphere in the room changed like a cool front moving in after a thunderstorm.

Once they directly acknowledged their feelings, Rod and Frances no longer needed to test each other indirectly by fighting to see if they could get a rise out of each other. They spent several more sessions discussing their feelings about their marriage, their divorce, and their children. They talked about being hurt. They apologized for all the things they had done wrong. They reminisced about the good times, especially with their children. They confessed that they had struggled, and were still struggling, with parenting the kids. They reflected a little on what they had lost. They even admitted that they still had feelings for each other. Yet for the first time, they acknowledged that they had to say good-bye to their marriage.

Frances and Rod wanted to try to be friends, but they were unsure whether they could handle being friends emotionally—or whether their new partners would accept their friendship. Whatever was going to happen in their relationship, they resolved to be better parents to the children. They agreed that they needed to focus on giving the children what they needed, including their love, attention, and some firm discipline.

I offered to continue to work with Frances and Rod to help them make the changes they wanted to make. But they said that they only needed one more session. They wanted to bring their three kids in for a final appointment, apologize to them, tell them that they both loved them, and warn them that the two of them would be working together in the future. No more playing Mom and Dad off against each other.

It was one of my happiest—and easiest—family therapy sessions. I sat back and just watched. Frances and Rod told the children everything they wanted in a tone that was loving, at times contrite, and thoroughly authoritative. Better than any words could convey the message, their tone made it clear that they were the parents in this family and they were going to start doing their job as parents.

While Rod and Frances were talking, Ian sat up and paid attention. Jen rolled her eyes and looked skeptical. Christine looked relieved and smiled what certainly looked like a happy little smile.

Conflict and anger often are not about what they seem to be about on the surface. Longing, hurt, grief, and fear often fuel the conflict and anger. Therapy helped Rod and Frances to see feelings they were blind to or too proud or too anxious to acknowledge. Counseling gave them a forum for dealing with unresolved feelings that they could not address elsewhere.

Rod and Frances eventually did what parents need to do in divorce: They established a more businesslike relationship with clearer boundaries around their relationships with each other and with their children. Rod's and Frances's anger fooled them into thinking they were far apart in their divorce, but their conflict really kept them together. Like many parents, Rod and Frances took a long time to learn this seemingly simple but emotionally complex lesson of divorce.

Creating Options When There Seem to Be None

Melvin and Felicia had been separated for two years when they came for mediation. They had two young children, five-year-old Anthony and three-year-old Collette. At the time, Melvin and Felicia were caring for their children according to a complicated schedule. They each did exactly half of the child care, just as they had shared their parenting duties before they separated.

Felicia and Melvin worked out their schedule for the children completely on their own. They each saw therapists individually, but they did not consult a family therapist about the children or talk with a mediator. Each met with a lawyer on their own before they separated, but after a single consultation, neither of them went back except to file the final divorce papers. They decided they wanted to work things out in their own way. With the help of a few books on children and divorce, they did.

By all appearances, Melvin and Felicia did a remarkably good job of putting their children first. Felicia moved out of the family home, but she returned several times a week to watch the kids if that worked better for them. Melvin also watched the kids at Felicia's apartment when that was best, and they both juggled their work schedules to accommodate the children and each other.

Although they both worked full time, Melvin and Felicia were lucky because their flexible schedules allowed them to limit their hours at the office and do a lot of work at home. Melvin ran a small technology start-up company, and as long as they got the job done, he allowed his employees to be flexible with their work schedules. Felicia worked as a special consultant to the information technology department at the local university. Most of the time, she was bored; she knew she could do so much more. On the bright side, though, barring a major disaster there, like a computer crashing, she came and went as she pleased and did most everything from home.

In mediation, Felicia and Melvin talked frankly but sensitively to each other about their feelings, their ambivalence about their divorce, and their desires for a new life. Their lives were still deeply intertwined even two years after they separated, but they chose to do things this way.

So what brought these good parents and good people into mediation? Felicia wanted to move from Virginia to the West Coast, and she had good reasons for making this big change. She had a terrific job offer in Silicon Valley, where she and Melvin had lived before, and she thought she deserved the chance to take it. She wanted to be back in the hub of the high-tech revolution.

In fact, when they moved to Virginia five years earlier so that Melvin could follow his dream job, he had promised Felicia that they would be back in California within five years. Melvin had insisted that Felicia was going to get her chance to pursue her dreams in return for being so good about letting him pursue his. For five years, Felicia had been marking the calendar, and Melvin's time was up.

After a couple of meetings, it was clear that Felicia's and Melvin's problems really were practical, not emotional. We started to brainstorm some possible solutions. When they came to me, Melvin and Felicia thought they had two options: Felicia could either move or she could stay. Brainstorming is a technique that helps people to recognize and create far more options.

In brainstorming, you begin by listing as many new or old solutions to a problem as you can. You want to come up with all sorts of ideas, even crazy ones, as a way of opening up the mind and encouraging creative thinking. You are not allowed to evaluate possible solutions until later. First, you have to come up with a long list of possibilities and give yourself time to mull over the options.

In mediation, brainstorming has several advantages for getting around some of the emotional dynamics of divorce. Anything goes during brainstorming, and many parents use this freedom to float trial balloons they have been wanting to voice but could not. For example, one partner might suggest, "Well, we could get back together"—a real offer that can be dismissed as mere creative thinking if the other partner shows no interest.

In fact, I have seen a number of parents do exactly this, including Felicia, who said, "We could buy a nice house in California and all live together." She paused, looking at Melvin out of the corner of her eye, and added, "We could live in separate wings."

When one partner voices an option that her ex does not like, he is not allowed to get angry or offer a rebuttal. Instead, both parents must take some time—often days or weeks—to consider *all* the suggestions, even the truly crazy ones. This prevents people from responding reflexively, getting angry, and shutting down the negotiation. The delay also can help people to see the nugget of a good idea in a plan that at first seemed absurdly bad. And brainstorming really does encourage creative thinking.

Felicia and Melvin succeeded in brainstorming and coming up with a number of new options: Melvin could move to California with Felicia. She could delay her move for another year until Melvin's business was better established. Or Felicia could move to Silicon Valley, and Melvin and the kids could join her in six months. Or the children could move with Felicia, and Melvin could make the move in six months. Melvin could hire Felicia. Felicia could hire Melvin. All of them could move to someplace new and start fresh in neutral territory. Or maybe Felicia could move and Melvin could stay, but they could exchange the children during the school years and summers, or even more regularly if the children attended a private school that had branches on each coast, so that their education would not be disrupted.

When their creative thinking began to run dry, I threw out a couple more options: They could each take one child. They could send the children to live with their grandparents in Florida. They could fly the children back and forth every two weeks. In making these kinds of outlandish suggestions, I was trying to open the door for more creativity, but I also was sending Felicia and Melvin a message: Your options are far from perfect, but there are *worse* alternatives.

While I was working with Felicia and Melvin, I gave a guest lecture on mediation to law students in a class on divorce law. I thought that Felicia and Melvin, their concern for their children, and their creative brainstorming offered a nice illustration of mediation and how it contrasted with adversary legal negotiations. I disguised the case thoroughly (as I have for all of the cases throughout this book) and presented it to the class. I engaged them in the process of brainstorming options for Felicia and Melvin, too. I hoped that one of these extremely bright, young law students might come up with a creative option that had eluded Melvin, Felicia, and me.

The students did come up with a number of clever ideas. One student suggested that Felicia move to California but fly back every week to have custody of the children on the weekends. Another student suggested Melvin move to California, but only for five years. Then it would be Melvin's turn to pick again.

But an outstanding trial lawyer who was coteaching the class offered the most revealing alternative. She suggested that the class consider a different approach to Felicia and Melvin's problem. If she was representing Felicia, she might offer her this advice: Quit her job or, even better, get laid off. Felicia hated her consulting position, and not working had other advantages. Felicia would be free to take care of her young children most of the time, and Melvin would have to pay her child support and maybe alimony, too. If Felicia stayed out of work and took care of the children for a year or so, she would be in an excellent position to sue for sole custody later. Once she had sole custody, Felicia could move anywhere she wanted—with or without Melvin's consent.

I thought this advice was brilliant—from the perspective of a vigorous advocate for Felicia. Of course, the brilliant tactics disturbed me greatly considering the potential impact on Felicia and Melvin's relationship, Melvin's fathering, and the children. In fact, the tactics disturbed me so much that I started feeling a whole lot better about the imperfect options we had come up with in mediation. Yet I had to admit that the lawyer raised many real concerns about a cooperative approach. For example, if Felicia moved to California ahead of Melvin and the children, what would keep Melvin from refusing to join her and suing for sole custody himself? What if Melvin met someone? It hadn't happened yet, but who knew? You cannot avoid uncertainty and risk.

Melvin and Felicia eventually decided to delay the move for another year while Melvin ramped up his business and planned to relocate his operations to California. Felicia felt confident that a good job would still be there for her in twelve months, and in the meantime, Melvin hired her as an independent consultant for his company. Part of her job involved traveling around the country, including to California, and Melvin agreed that the children could accompany her on some of these trips.

Relocation is one of the most difficult issues parents can face after divorce and one of the most contentious and inconsistent areas in the law. Some states allow parents with sole custody to move anywhere they choose as long as they have a good reason. Other states allow parents to move wherever they like but insist that children stay where they are. They order a change in custody if the move occurs. Still other states allow parents to move a great distance within the state, but prohibit them from moving to another state. For example, a parent might be allowed to move from Manhattan to Buffalo, six hours away, but not across the George Washington Bridge into New Jersey.

Relocation *is* a difficult problem. You may feel your anxiety rising even as you consider the prospect. But as Felicia and Melvin showed, it is possible to come up with creative options to the most difficult, anxiety-producing problems. So unless a move is imminent, you do not want to try to figure out *what* you will do if someone moves. Instead, you want to decide *how* you will decide what changes you will make in the children's schedule as a result. You might, for instance, agree to give each other at least six months' notice and try to resolve differences in mediation before initiating any legal action.

Lessons Learned

All of the people we visited in this chapter had unique problems, and all had to learn the lessons of divorce in their own way. For most of them, the learning was, at least in part, emotional. They needed not only to understand what they were doing wrong but to *feel* that it was wrong—and to see the positive results of doing things differently, of acting on their new feelings instead of their old ones.

In order to feel what is right and to do the right thing, parents have to understand what is wrong about so many of the thoughts, feelings, and actions that *seem* so right, or at least so understandable, in divorce. The feelings themselves usually are not wrong. Parents' fear, despondency, hurt, and rage are natural reactions to loss, rejection, and pain. What is wrong is how these feelings, and the conflict that stems from them, affect children.

In fact, the lesson for parents who want to have a successful divorce for their children is learning to do something *un*natural. Divorced parents need to find ways to address their own intense feelings, yet they also need to learn to control their feelings around the children—and find a way of developing a new, productive, working relationship with the source of their pain, their ex. There is only one reason why anyone would do something so emotionally unnatural: Your ex is your children's other parent. As Chuck said, divorced parents need to love their kids more than they hate their ex.

CHAPTER ELEVEN

Letting Go and Moving On

As hard as it might be to imagine today, eventually, you and your children will move on to the challenges and opportunities of your new life after divorce. You will move on or life will push you on—even if you do not feel ready to look ahead yet. You may still be nursing your wounds, but you may see your ex moving on with his life, your children ready to get past the divorce, or perhaps someone who wants to see you socially now. You may not feel fully prepared, but sooner or later you must take the plunge into a future that is not exactly what you planned or foresaw just a few years before. For better or worse—and I do believe that it can be better—this is a new world for you and your family.

When is it time to turn from the past and fully face the future? It is not always easy to say. Former partners can be *too* eager to get on with a new life and perhaps with new relationships. In their hurry, they may not tend to the essential emotional business of divorce. You don't want to be stuck forever in an emotional quagmire, but the path out of the quicksand of divorce leads directly through your emotions. You need to face and embrace your feelings and renegotiate your family relationships if you hope to keep your past from forever coloring your future.

Like so much else in divorce, your emotions can provide the best gauge to when might be the right time to move on. But your chaotic emotions can make it difficult to know how you really feel. You may *think* you're doing great now, and then three months from now you look back and realize "Boy, was I a mess!"

If you're waiting for your pain to go away completely, it's going to be a long wait. Your grief, your seemingly contradictory feelings of love, anger, and sadness—about your ex, your marriage, and your family life as you once believed they would or should be—will lessen greatly over time. But your divorce can't help but mark you in some way, not for years, but forever.

Because of the jumble of emotions and the uncertain course of sorting out those powerful feelings, it helps to have some time markers to help you to decide when you should be putting the intense focus on divorce behind you. When a loved one dies, a common expectation is that the bereaved need about a year before they can begin to really let go and move forward with their lives. In divorce, grieving and renegotiating family relationships usually take longer. So if you have been separated for less than a year, it is almost certainly too soon to hope to move on to a new life. But if you have been separated for more than two years, you should have sorted out most of the tasks of divorce and be looking toward your own and your children's future.

Of course, in order to move on to the future, you have to begin to let go of your past. To let go of the past does not mean to forget or to pretend that your marriage never happened. It means that you have to let go of your hurt and anger. You have to let go of your guilt and shame. You have to let go of the idea of being a family together with that spouse. And that means you have to let go of your ex and let go of your grief.

It is important to understand that letting go is not the same as getting over your emotions. Letting go does not mean that your troubled feelings are gone or forgotten. Instead, letting go means starting to live day to day without constantly hoping, wanting to hurt back, or being lost in your grief. Letting go means finding a place in your heart where you can store your pain so that it does not spill over and taint everything that is or could be positive. Letting go means finding a place where you can comfortably shelve your feelings, but also a place where, from time to time, you can take your feelings off the shelf, look them over, try them on, then put them back where they belong, turn out the light, and close the door.

In order to move on, you have to let go, but you also have to face and embrace new challenges. You must face your fears of being alone. You have to learn how to manage your children, work a job, run your house, do the finances, and juggle everyone's schedules. You may also have to learn to ask for and accept the help of others, like the co-worker who covers for you so that you can take your child to the doctor, the neighbor who lets in the repairman because you can't get away from work, or the friend who offers to take your son to Little League so you can get your daughter to soccer practice. Moving on also means facing the excitement, and the dread, of being single again, dating, learning to trust romantic partners, and learning to trust yourself in love.

Who Am I—Now?

"Divorced" can be an uncomfortable adjective, one you probably never wanted to attach to yourself. But moving on means accepting that "divorced" is a label that applies to you while understanding that the label is *not* who you are.

You are no longer a wife or husband. You are a divorced (or soon-to-be-divorced) woman or man. You are still a mother or father, but you may feel less secure and confident in who you are as a parent. And if you identified yourself primarily as a wife and mother, a husband and father, you may be struggling as you try to answer the question "Who am I—now?" You might have lost the roles that were central to defining who you are, and as a result, you also might have lost a big part of your sense of self. You may even feel like who you are now is . . . nobody. You may be in the middle of an identity crisis.

The famous psychologist Erik Erikson pointed to an identity crisis as integral to the process of coming of age in our culture. Erikson argued that adolescents must grapple with the question "Who am I?" and eventually find their own answers. Young people try on different answers to this question by experimenting with different goals, interests, values, relationships, and social roles. In fact, Erikson argued that it is healthy and necessary for young people to give themselves a moratorium, a time of uncertainty, confusion, and exploration, before expecting to resolve their identity crisis and move on to assume a lifelong adult identity.

As you certainly understand now, people's identities are not fixed throughout adult life. "Who am I—now?" is a question that, as a result of divorce, many people must grapple with again. And it is a question that you need to start to answer as you begin to move on with your life.

A Divorce Moratorium

If you are lost about who you are, you might feel disoriented, confused, frightened, and even desperate. You may be eager—too eager—to grab on to some new identity or some new relationship that will give you a new sense of self and a new sense of security. If this sounds like you, try not to jump too quickly into the new role or the new relationship, at least not with both feet. Follow Erikson's advice. Give yourself a moratorium. Give yourself some time, not to be a hermit but to experiment with new interests, new roles, and new relationships.

I know it may sound trite, but as you struggle through the crisis of separation and divorce, you *can* turn your upheaval into an opportunity to grow. You can use this time of uncertainty and self-doubt to figure out some of the things that *you* did wrong, some things that you want to do differently in the future. You can use your divorce moratorium to evaluate and set new goals for your new life and to make resolutions about how you want to do things differently the next time around.

As you start to set a new course for your life, as you decide on the changes you want to make and the mistakes you vow never to repeat, try giving yourself a little more time and a bit more room for imperfection. Like adolescents who become ardent rebels before concluding that their parents' lessons were not *all* wrong, divorced adults often overshoot the mark in the beginning. You may want to rebel, too; you may want to turn your life around 180 degrees, but you certainly were not all wrong in how you acted before. Not all of the choices you made were mistakes. The solution for your future probably is not to do the opposite of what you did in the past, but instead simply to do some things differently. Growing through your divorce demands that you learn from your past, not just reject it.

Expanding Roles and Identities

One healthy goal for most adults during a divorce moratorium is to go beyond redefining old roles and to expand upon their identity, to discover new interests and roles. True enough, most divorced adults want to become a wife or husband again someday or at least a significant other in an intimate relationship. And divorced parents *are* still Mom or Dad even if they do not feel terrific about themselves in that role. You can use your time of uncertainty not only to find ways to set new goals for your familiar roles, but also as a time to grow—a time to expand your identity as a friend, daughter, brother, teacher, athlete, musician, or simply as a caring, moral, or religious person.

How can you expand the range of your roles? There are two steps. First, you need to give yourself permission to be in crisis or at least to be confused. Second, you need to expand your roles and identities. Your identity is grounded in your actions. The best way to try on a new identity is to act the part. If you want to feel better about yourself as a parent, carve out more time for the children. Start saying no more often or more consistently. Find ways to keep in better contact with your kids. Tell your children how much you love them and how much their other parent loves them, too.

If you want to feel more confident about your value in the workplace, get a job—any job. Work a little harder. Set your sights on moving up to the next rung on the ladder. Redo your résumé and test the waters of the job market. Or go back to school to pursue that degree or that other career you always wanted.

If you are lonely, isolated, or bored, try out new activities. Ask a friend to do something with you. Pick up the telephone and call that interesting guy you just met. Join a book club. Take up a new sport. Read in cafés where you might meet people. Go to office parties and don't hide in the corner. Sign up for a group hike. Talk more, and talk more openly, to other parents when you are together watching your children's activities, at the PTA meeting, or at a sports event.

If you want to be more assertive, take a stand—with a cashier, with someone who cuts ahead of you in line, with your boss, with your ex. If you are tired of being superresponsible, leave the dishes in the sink, take a mental health day off from work, let someone else solve a problem, say yes to that blind date.

The Point Is to Try

What you do may not work. It almost certainly won't the first time, but that is not the point. The point is to try. Your moratorium is about experimenting, not about achieving instant success. It's about flexing a muscle, not pressing five hundred pounds. Your moratorium is about trying on a lot of different clothes to see what fits, not about buying the first outfit you put on, refurbishing an entire wardrobe, or giving up because you no longer are a size 6 or 8 or 10.

You can expect to feel lousy when new roles and new relationships do not fit you. You can expect to wish that you could go back to being who you once were. Yet after you have once again decided who you are, you almost certainly will look back on this time of confusion and uncertainty as a turning point. It may seem hard to imagine now, but in the future, you may remember your divorce identity crisis with feelings that are bittersweet. No doubt the pain will still be bitter, but when you look back on your struggle to find yourself, you may well find some sweetness in that time of uncertainty—sweetness in the hope for change, the potential of the future, and your strength in charting a new course for your life.

Sharing Grief

Moving on also means beginning to get past your grief, but how do people do this in divorce? First, they have to grieve. You need to let yourself feel the anger, the sadness, and the yearning. But feeling your feelings is not the same as expressing them. You may *feel* like Jekyll and Hyde, but you do not want to act that way.

You do not want to act on many of your feelings, but your feelings still do need some outlet. Part of grieving has to be shared. The rituals for grieving death are painful *and* comforting because through them, we share our loss with other people.

Unfortunately, many adults end up mostly grieving divorce alone. Unlike so many major losses, like a death, people fully share the loss of a marriage with only one other person and that's their ex. But as we discussed, you cannot grieve with your ex because the two of you have been, and are almost certainly still are, in very different places in your grief, in your separate cycles of love, anger, and sadness. Finding a way to get along with your ex is likely to be hard enough. Trying to find a way to grieve together is probably impossible.

Even just getting along with your ex complicates your grief. By finding a way to get along, you give up much of the healing power of anger. You open yourself to the vulnerability of hope. All of this is probably enough emotional work—and more than enough emotional complication—for you to face with your ex.

You can share some of your grief with your children, but you should not count on your children for much support. Your job is to comfort and support your children, to share the painful feelings of grief, but also to be strong and positive in doing so. Your job is to support your children, but their job is *not* to support you. You can share your grief with your children, but most of the sharing should be controlled and purposeful. You cannot, or should not, express too much of your private grief with your children. If you do, you risk turning them into caretaker kids.

You can grieve some with your friends and family. Family and friends can support your grief and share it to some degree, yet your feelings obviously will be more intense and more enduring than theirs. Sooner or later, family and friends become exhausted by the intensity of even a loved one's feelings about divorce. For the divorced adult, this can feel like their supporters no longer get it about how she feels. This, too, is a common and lonely part of grief in divorce. You can expect your family and friends to be ready to move on long before you are, and you should also be prepared for them to expect or encourage you to let go before you are ready.

If you feel alone or stuck in your grief, therapy may be the best option. Why? Because you don't need to worry about your therapist's feelings or your therapist's objectivity, and you don't need to worry about wearing out your therapist's tolerance.

A therapist can help you through your grief, yet the thought of using therapy to grieve may make you feel alone. Unfortunately, there is no salve for the loneliness of grieving divorce. It is a sad and lonely but unavoidable fact that most people have no choice: Most people grieve the end of a marriage alone because they are grieving a unique relationship that they shared with only one other person in the world, a person who is now, most likely, emotionally unavailable to them. That is the nature of divorce.

Letting Go and Forgiveness

What can help you let go of your grief and move on to your future? Emotionally, you need to ride the roller coaster of your feelings. Intellectually, you can smooth out the ride if you can let go and, and ultimately, if you can forgive.

Letting go means giving up hope, not giving up feelings. You must tell yourself it is over—again and again until you believe it, and finally begin to accept that your marriage is dead. Letting go gives you a point of departure in your grief, so you are not sucked back into the vortex of your emotions every time your ex is kind or your kids are tormented.

Forgiveness is an old-fashioned idea, a virtue that seems out of style in an in-your-face world. Today, the idea of forgiveness can seem naïve, even laughable, particularly in the midst of the turmoil, anger, hurt, and pain of divorce. Forgiveness seems quaint in the contemporary context of getting even, of getting what is rightly yours, of getting all you can.

Yet if you can forgive, you can and will move on. If you find it in your heart to forgive, you may be naïve or old-fashioned but you will have accomplished something beyond mere emotional wisdom. If you can forgive, you will indeed have achieved something virtuous.

The only way to forgive is to choose to do so. Grief is basic to human nature, a process and experience that even many animals endure following loss. Forgiveness is something different, something more, and something uniquely human.

People forgive by deciding they will no longer try to hurt back, hold a grudge, be consumed with getting even, or expect to be constantly compensated for what they have endured. Why would anyone do this? People forgive to be moral or kind, to put their emotions and themselves second to their children or second to their values. But these are the sorts of high reasons to forgive that people need to find within themselves or through their moral or religious beliefs. Psychologically, the motivation is more basic. The reasons why you want to forgive are to help you find a way to get along with your ex and to free yourself of the burden of the feelings you are likely to harbor if you do *not* forgive. Emotionally, the reason to forgive is that forgiveness helps you to let go, especially to let go of your anger.

Finding a Place for Your Grief

One day after spending a year or two being tossed about by waves of love, anger, and sadness, you will find yourself drifting in calmer waters. Around this time you might realize that you no longer ride just one wave of emotion at a time, but can feel some love, anger, and sadness about your divorce, about your ex, all at once. In one single moment you can simultaneously remember the good times, get angry about all the hurt, and feel sad about all you have lost, about all that might have been. When you feel this way, you will know you are getting very close to moving past your grief.

What will you do with your grief then? There is no right way to grieve and no right way to resolve grief. Grieving is a very personal process. Whatever your personal journey, wherever you end up, one thing is clear: Getting past your grief is not the same as getting over it.

You will never get over your grief, and you would not want to. To get over your grief would mean abandoning your history, your love, your life. To get over your grief would mean losing the emotions that created your children as well as the feelings that ended your marriage. You do not want to get over your grief. Instead, you want your love, anger, and sadness to grow small enough to fit into a drawer in your heart, a place where you can put away your feelings instead of throwing them out.

Children Moving On

Children also need to move on and find a place to put their feelings about their parents' separation and divorce. Children will move on, but only as long as their parents do. Remember the example of the parent on the airplane putting the oxygen mask over his face before putting the child's on hers. As parents progress beyond the pain and crisis of divorce, they free their children to come to terms with the upheaval in their family and to get back to the business of being a kid. If parents do not move on, they implicitly withhold permission for children to move forward themselves. And if parents do not move on, they deprive their children of a model of how to cope with grief.

If you and your ex do not move on, your divorce might end up *being* your children's childhood. If you remain stuck in your grief and anger, your child's life will become one of conflict, tension, and sadness. You cannot deny the pain and upheaval of divorce for your children, but you and your ex need to move on when the time is right in order to help give your children the childhood that all children deserve. If this was the only reason to move on, I believe it would be reason enough. We worry about our children's education, their teeth, their general health, and millions of other things because of what we fear they will mean for their future. I know from experience, and the research backs me up: The enduring effects of divorce on children do not result from the fact of divorce itself as much as from how parents handle it.

Even when parents succeed in doing their job of being parents and letting their kids be kids, children are not done dealing with divorce. As children grow and mature, as they encounter new circumstances and challenges in their lives, they revisit their parents' divorce, including the circumstances that led to the divorce, the way the divorce took place, their current relationships with both of their parents, and the meaning of it all. If you are accepting and your children are open, they can share some of these new struggles with you. Still, children must resolve many of their challenges on their own. Your job as a parent is to do your work on the divorce so that they will be better able to do theirs. There are countless ways you might help your children through this crisis. However, you cannot bring them to terms with your divorce or point out to them where it all fits within the context of their lives. That's work only your children can do for themselves.

New Understandings of Families and Divorce

As children grow older and revisit their parents' divorce, parents can help to guide them to a new level of understanding. Infants and toddlers need divorce explained to them when they become preschoolers. Your preschooler will start to notice that other children have two parents living in the same house, and they will want to know why they do not. But as with other "why" questions, your preschooler needs only a simple explanation and some emotional reassurance. Listen to Barney the dinosaur's song about families, and you'll hear what your preschooler needs: "A family is people, and a family is love. That's a family." You could do worse than begin your explanation about divorce to your preschooler with "It's like Barney says . . ." and explain how families really do come in all different sizes and kinds—and especially that your family is just right for you.

Early and late school-age children also often ask new questions about divorce. Your nine-year-old son's renewed questions are likely to be motivated partly out of curiosity and partly out of a search for emotional reassurance. So when he asks why you got divorced, he is not looking for a confession or a trial, but maybe for a little better understanding for himself, a reason why his father sees him infrequently or an explanation he can give to friends who ask.

As children move through adolescence, they may ask more questions, perhaps pointed ones, but this *still* is not the time to give them all of the gory details. Unless there was some clear reason for the divorce that your children could not understand at a younger age—one parent's serious emotional problems, for example—the time probably will never come when children need to know all of the details.

Holding your tongue is about respecting boundaries—boundaries around your relationship with your ex, because your views may still be polarized—but especially boundaries between you and your children. Remember our facts of life analogy. Children do not need to or want to know details about their parents' sexual past or present, and like sex, the ins and outs of your divorce probably are just too personal to share with your children.

You can answer your adolescent's questions honestly but briefly, making the concepts and language older but without a lot of background information. "We fell out of love" might be the essence of one, more abstract explanation you can give to a teenager that you couldn't tell her when she was younger because she wouldn't have understood. Or, like anticipated questions about sex, your teenager may *not* ask you about your divorce. Even so, you still can broach the topic from time to time and, in doing so, be prepared to underscore the one message you most want to get across.

Personally, I found it easiest to talk to my daughter, Maggie, while driving in the car because she was captive yet there were distractions to help us through awkward moments. My message was "I am sorry that you have had to live with divorce, and I'm ready to listen if you want to talk. But I hope you know that Mom and I always loved you so much and always will." The message I've heard back from Maggie most often is that the divorce was hard, but she also believes it made her both stronger and more sensitive than peers who grew up without hardship. For my part, I think she's right.

Your Children's Identity Crisis

As your twentysomething son moves through his expected identity crisis and rewrites his autobiography, his life story to date, your divorce may play a central role in the drama. The transition to adult life is a time of reflection, questioning, uncertainty, and exploration for most young people, and their parents and families often are a focus of their doubt, even their scorn. Many young people challenge and perhaps reject the interests, relationships, and values of their families, at least temporarily. Your divorce may not become a central part of your children's identity crisis, but if it does, how can you best help them through their questioning and sorting?

You can listen to and support your adolescent and young adult children emotionally, suggest alternative possibilities now and again, and mostly try to be patient while they work out all of the questions and answers for themselves. Some of their turmoil surely is due to the divorce; other aspects involve normal, exaggerated rebellion. As you search for your patience, you might find solace in the phrase attributed to Mark Twain, "When I was a boy of fourteen, my father was so ignorant I could hardly stand to have the old man around. But when I got to be twenty-one, I was astonished at how much the old man had learned in seven years."

Of course, some of the questions and accusations that you hear from your courageous twenty-one-year-old daughter may be right on the mark. If your young adult child comes to talk with you about your divorce, you need to listen more than you need to explain. This also may be a time when you need to apologize. And this may be a time when, at last, you should start to do things differently. Maybe your daughter is now finally able to tell you the things she withheld out of fear, a child's lack of perspective, or her desire to protect you. Maybe you are hearing the truth—her truth—for the first time.

So listen, take it in, and, after you do, try to do things differently. It's not too late, even now, but it may be your last chance. If you don't change, your young adult child has options now that she did not have when she was younger. She can distance herself from you, turn to her other parent, or maybe try to replace you both with her boyfriend's family—a family that may seem like the one she always wanted.

Finding Meaning in Your Pain

In the end, whether you are a parent or a child, the only way you can come to terms with all you have been through is to find meaning in your experiences. This is not some cliché exercise, where in the end you conclude "Everything happens for the best." A long search is the only way to truly find meaning in great pain, and it's a search you cannot begin—or end—looking for an answer. You cannot sit down one day and decide what it all means. Meaning making is a discovery not an invention.

What might you discover at the end of your long and arduous journey through divorce? You cannot know. You might discover that you are stronger than you realized. You might reevaluate your goals and priorities and learn to better appreciate your children, your friends, or your emotions. You might discover the value of becoming more sensitive and appreciative of other people's struggles. You might discover the limits of your own control and decide that your only choice is to trust in a higher power. You might discover that, to your surprise, you really *can* trust in yourself. Two, ten, twenty years hence, you may see it all in an entirely different light.

I cannot tell you what lesson you should take away from your pain, but I can share my own. I have been humbled by my personal shortcomings, a hard but important lesson for someone as proud as I am. There is no escaping the fact that my choices caused pain for others, including Daddy's little girl, Maggie. I also have been humbled by recognizing how many things I cannot control, despite my determination or good intentions, and by having to admit that I may want to do the right thing but I do not always succeed in doing it.

Recognizing my own failures, I try to be more patient with the failures of others. I think I now better appreciate the intensity of the loss, the struggles, the pain, the fear, and the searching set off by separation and divorce. I certainly better appreciate how hard it is to do the right thing in the emotional storm of divorce.

And yet I still do not accept failure easily. I would find the greatest meaning in my personal struggles and personal failings if you are able to use the research, clinical work, advice, and personal experience in this book to do a little better with your ex and with your children.

Notes

INTRODUCTION—**Putting Children First When a Marriage Comes Apart**

Page

   2 **In the United States today over one million children every year:** Statistics on the number of children affected by divorce and predictions for future divorce rates can be found in the U.S. Bureau of the Census, "Marriage, Divorce, and Remarriage in the 1990's." *Current Population Reports* (P23–180) (Washington, D.C.: U.S. Government Printing Office, 1992).

CHAPTER ONE—**Divorcing Emotions: Riding Alone on the Emotional Roller Coaster of Grief**

   20 **In her influential 1972 book:** Jesse Bernard's book on "his" and "her" marriage is: J. Bernard. *The Future of Marriage* (New York: World, 1972).

   21 **It is hard to overstate:** The separate worlds and the lack of communication of "his" divorce and "her" divorce can be startling. In one of my studies, *both* the wife *and* the husband agreed that "I am only going ahead with the divorce because that was what my husband/wife wants" among about 15 percent of couples. See R. E. Emery. *Renegotiating Family Relationships: Divorce, Child Custody, and Mediation* (New York: Guilford Press, 1994), 9.

   27 **To more clearly explain this:** I first described my theory of grief in *Renegotiating Family Relationships*.

   28 **Recently one of my graduate students:** The first paper from the "beeper" diary study of grieving among college student couples is: D. A. Sbarra and R. E. Emery (in press), "The Emotional Sequelae of Nonmarital Relationship Dissolution: Descriptive Evidence from a 28-Day Prospective Study," *Personal Relationships*.

   32 **Anger helps us to deal:** Psychologist Len Berkowitz demonstrated how pain provokes anger, a response he referred to as "aversively stimulated aggression."

For example, see L. Berkowitz, "Aversively Stimulated Aggression: Some Parallels and Differences in Research with Animals and Humans," *American Psychologist, 38* (1983), 1135–44.

32 **Threatening situations trigger:** The famous stress researcher Walter Cannon is generally credited with calling attention to the fight-or-flight response, which is now discussed routinely in introductory psychology textbooks.

33 **Dr. John Bowlby:** John Bowlby's work on attachment strongly influenced my thinking on grief, particularly his three-volume series *Attachment* (New York: Basic, 1969), *Separation: Anxiety and Anger* (New York: Basic, 1973), and *Loss: Sadness and Depression* (New York: Basic, 1980).

36 **If support is so hard to find:** I have discussed the issue of the leaver and the left in several papers and in *Renegotiating Family Relationships*. It is surprising how infrequently psychologists have considered this important and commonsense distinction in relationship dissolution.

37 **about 60 percent of all U.S. divorces:** For a summary of evidence and a discussion about why women may be more likely than men to initiate divorce, see L. Buckle, G. G. Gallup, Jr., and R. A. Zachary, "Marriage as a Reproductive Contract: Patterns of Marriage, Divorce, and Remarriage," *Ethology and Sociobiology, 17* (1996), 363–77.

CHAPTER TWO—**Separate Spheres: How to Keep Your Emotions from Running Your Divorce**

48 **We establish interpersonal boundaries:** I credit family systems theory, particularly the insightful observations of Salvador Minuchin, for shaping much of my thinking about boundaries in close relationships. See S. Minuchin, *Families and Family Therapy* (Cambridge, MA: Harvard University Press, 1974).

53 **just two things: love or power:** I elaborate on love and power as the basic dimensions of relationships as well as on the confusion of intimacy conflicts and power conflicts in R. E. Emery, "Family Conflict and Its Developmental Implications: A Conceptual Analysis of Deep Meanings and Systemic Processes," in C. U. Shantz and W. W. Hartup, eds., *Conflict in Child and Adolescent Development* (London: Cambridge University Press, 1992).

CHAPTER THREE—**Children's Realities: The Truth About Kids and Divorce**

62 **The truth is much more complex:** Social scientists have engaged in a longstanding debate about the consequences of divorce for children. One extreme suggests that serious consequences are underestimated, often undetected, and certainly underappreciated. The other extreme suggests not only that chil-

dren are resilient but that they also can benefit from divorce—children will be happier if their parents are happier. I review the controversy and the truths and the errors at both extremes and in the middle in R. E. Emery, *Marriage, Divorce, and Children's Adjustment*, 2d ed. (Thousand Oaks, CA: Sage Publications, 1999) and in a recent article coauthored with divorce researcher Joan Kelly (2003), "Children's Adjustment Following Divorce: Risk and Resilience Perspectives," *Family Relations, 52,* 352–62.

64 **children from divorced families:** I review these and other statistics on the risk divorce poses for psychological problems among children in *Marriage, Divorce, and Children's Adjustment*. Sociologist Paul Amato has statistically compiled evidence on the risks for children associated with divorce across different studies in P. R. Amato and B. Keith, "Parental Divorce and the Well-being of Children: A Meta-analysis," *Psychological Bulletin, 110* (1991), 26–46, and P. R. Amato, "Children of Divorce in the 1990s: An Update of the Amato and Keith Meta-analysis," *Journal of Family Psychology, 15* (2001), 355–70.

65 **one major national study, conducted by Nick Zill:** Data on the percentage of children from married and divorced families who see a mental health professional come from N. Zill, D. R. Morrison, and M. J. Coiro, "Long-term Effects of Parental Divorce on Parent-Child Relationships, Adjustment, and Achievement in Young Adulthood," *Journal of Family Psychology, 7* (1993), 91–103.

67 **Indeed, scientists have determined that:** One of the earliest and most important prospective studies to conclude that many problems found among children after divorce actually predate the marital separation is A. J. Cherlin, F. F. Furstenberg, P. L. Chase-Lansdale, K. E. Kiernan, P. K. Robins, D. R. Morrison, and L. O. Teitler (1991). "Longitudinal Studies of Effects of Divorce on Children in Great Britain and the United States," *Science, 252* (1991), 1386–89.

68 **how children and families function:** My research showing that many parenting problems found after divorce actually predate the marital separation appears in D. S. Shaw, R. E. Emery, and M. D. Tuer, "Parental Functioning and Children's Adjustment in Families of Divorce: A Prospective Study," *Journal of Abnormal Child Psychology, 21* (1993), 119–34.

68 **The truth is that:** I first called attention to the key role of conflict in causing children's emotional problems in divorced *and* married families in a widely cited paper: R. E. Emery, "Interparental Conflict and the Children of Discord and Divorce," *Psychological Bulletin, 92* (1982), 310–30.

68 **Continued problems in parent-child relationships:** My long-term colleague at the University of Virginia, E. Mavis Hetherington, conducted extensive research on the role of parenting in contributing to children's psychological problems after divorce; see E. M. Hetherington and J. Kelly, *For Better or for Worse: Divorce Reconsidered* (New York: Norton, 2002).

72 **Children in the caretaker role:** My former graduate student Michelle Tuer Martin conducted one of the best studies of parentification (a role reversal in which the child takes care of the parent's needs, in particular his emotional needs) in divorce. Unfortunately, her work is available only as an unpublished dissertation: M. Tuer Martin, "Mother-Daughter Relations in Divorced Families: Parentification and Internalizing and Relationship Problems," unpublished doctoral dissertation (Charlottesville, VA: University of Virginia, 1995).

73 **Resilience is very different:** I have written several academic papers about resilience among children from divorced families; for example, R. E. Emery and R. Forehand, "Parental Divorce and Children's Well-being: A Focus on Resilience," in R. J. Haggerty, L. Sherrod, N. Garmezy, and M. Rutter, eds., *Risk and Resilience in Children* (London: Cambridge University Press, 1994), 64–99.

80 **even the most resilient students:** My work with Lisa Laumann-Billings on the pain found among even resilient children from divorced families can be found in L. Laumann-Billings, and R. E. Emery, "Distress Among Young Adults from Divorced Families," *Journal of Family Psychology, 14* (2000), 671–87.

81 **the difference between resilience and pain:** Psychologist Judith Wallerstein, whose popular books suggest that divorce almost invariably has serious and lasting effects on children, agrees that our distinction between pain and pathology resolves the great debate about the consequences of divorce for children. Wallerstein recently wrote, "Some researchers claim that while these differences [between children from divorced and married families] are significant, they are not a cause for serious worry. Others find them very troublesome and see them as a wake-up call for new interventions and policies. . . . Drawing on several samples of young adults from different social classes Laumann-Billings and Emery find strong evidence for both sets of findings," in J. S. Wallerstein, "Children of Divorce: A Society in Search of Policy," page 73 in M. A. Mason, A. Skolnick, and S. D. Sugarman, eds., *All Our Families: New Policies for a New Century* (New York: Oxford University Press, 2003), 66–95.

CHAPTER FOUR—Seasons of Change: The Tasks of Divorce

92 **Twelve years later:** I have published the results of my studies of couples randomly assigned to mediate or litigate child custody in a series of papers beginning in 1987; see R. E. Emery, and M. M. Wyer, "Child Custody Mediation and Litigation: An Experimental Evaluation of the Experience of Parents," *Journal of Consulting and Clinical Psychology, 55* (1987), 179–86. The most recently published report from the twelve-year follow-up study is R. E. Emery, L. Laumann-Billings, M. Waldron, D. A. Sbarra, and P. Dillon. "Twelve-Year Follow-up of Mediated and Litigated Child Custody Disputes," *Journal of Consulting and Clinical Psychology, 69* (2001), 323–32.

CHAPTER FIVE—Talking to Children About Separation

101 **children fare *better:*** As noted, I reviewed much of the evidence on the de-structive effects of parental conflict on children in an early paper, Emery (1982), op. cit. Other comprehensive reviews reach similar conclusions; for example, E. M. Cummings and P. Davies, *Children and Marital Conflict* (New York: Guilford, 1994), and J. H. Grych and F. D. Fincham, "Marital Conflict and Children's Adjustment: A Cognitive-Contextual Framework," *Psychological Bulletin, 108* (1990), 267–90.

102 **children have *more* problems:** The first report that children from *low* conflict marriages suffered *more* problems following divorce (while children from high conflict marriages improved) was P. R. Amato, L. W. Loomis, and A. Booth, "Parental Divorce, Marital Conflict, and Offspring Well-being During Early Adulthood," *Social Forces, 73* (1995), 895–915.

111 **Exactly what you:** Rich descriptions of the reactions of children of different ages to parental divorce are found in J. S. Wallerstein and J. B. Kelly, *Surviving the Breakup: How Children Actually Cope with Divorce* (New York: Basic, 1980).

CHAPTER SIX—Keeping Emotions Out of Legal Negotiations

135 **In the 1980s:** See R. E. Emery and M. M. Wyer, op. cit.

136 **repeated, objective evaluations:** See R. E. Emery et al. (2001), op. cit.

152 **Most parents who mediated:** ibid.

CHAPTER SEVEN—Parenting Plans

163 **a modest increase in children's well-being:** A recent statistical summary of findings across studies found a reliable benefit associated with joint custody for children's psychological well-being and family relationships; see R. Bauserman, "Child Adjustment in Joint-Custody Versus Sole-Custody Arrangements: A Meta-analytic Review," *Journal of Family Psychology, 16* (2002), 91–102.

163 **the best *and* the worst arrangement:** Although research is somewhat inconsistent, a number of studies have found that when parental conflict is high, children in joint physical custody have *more* psychological problems than children in sole custody; for example, J. R. Johnston, "Children's Adjustment in Sole Custody Compared to Joint Custody Families and Principles for Custody Decision Making," *Family and Conciliation Courts Review, 33* (1995), 415–25. I have found the same pattern in my own unpublished data.

176 **In comparison with parents:** Bauserman, op. cit.

176 **Only a minority:** I discuss the data on which I base my estimates of joint

physical custody in *Marriage, Divorce, and Children's Adjustment* (2nd ed.). For example, one study of a California sample (where joint physical custody often is assumed to be common) found that only about 10 percent of families maintained the arrangement, and the frequency of maintaining joint physical custody tended to decline over time. See E. E. Maccoby and R. H. Mnookin, *Dividing the Child: Social and Legal Dilemmas of Custody* (Cambridge, MA: Harvard University Press, 1992), and C. M. Buchanan, E. E. Maccoby, and S. M. Dornbusch, *Adolescents After Divorce* (Cambridge, MA: Harvard University Press, 1996).

177 **different parenting plans can work well:** I credit the model schedules developed by a committee of attorneys, mental health professionals, and judges in Maricopa County, Arizona, for inspiring the idea of considering different schedules for parents with different divorce styles.

179 **a stable *attachment relationship:*** A perspective suggesting that separations from an attachment figure (including overnight visits) is harmful to young children is J. Soloman and C. George, "The Effects on Attachment of Overnight Visitation on Divorced and Separated Families," in J. Soloman and C. George, eds., *Attachment Disorganization* (New York: Guilford, 1999), 243–64. A counterpoint suggesting that young children are more able to adapt (including to overnight visits) and pointing to the importance of multiple attachments is J. B. Kelly and M. E. Lamb, "Using Child Development Research to Make Appropriate Custody and Access Decisions," *Family and Conciliation Courts Review, 38* (2000), 297–311.

CHAPTER EIGHT—Coparenting for Resilience

208 **parents in one of four categories:** The work of Diana Baumrind is the research foundation that forms the original basis for these parenting styles; for example, D. Baumrind, "Current Patterns of Parental Authority," *Developmental Psychology Monograph, 4* (1971), (1, Pt. 2). The four styles of parenting described here, however, are based directly on the conceptualization articulated in E. E. Maccoby and J. A. Martin, "Socialization in the Context of the Family: Parent-Child Interaction," in E. M. Hetherington, ed., *Handbook of Child Psychology*, 4th ed., vol. 4 (New York: Wiley, 1983), 1–102.

224 **What really happens:** Psychologist Gerald Patterson has described and studied coercive interactions at length; for example, G. R. Patterson, *Coercive Family Processes* (Eugene, OR: Castilia, 1982).

228 **Demographer Judith Seltzer:** J. A. Seltzer, "Relationships Between Fathers and Children Who Live Apart: The Father's Role After Separation," *Journal of Marriage and the Family, 53* (1991), 79–101.

228 ***three times more likely:*** Emery et al. (2001), op. cit.

CHAPTER NINE—Exploring New Relationships

258 **Remarriage represents another:** E. Mavis Hetheringon and Glenn Clingempeel conducted some of the first research demonstrating that remarriage is another, often difficult transition for children; for example, E. M. Hetherington and W. G. Clingempeel, "Coping with Marital Transitions: A Family Systems Perspective," *Monographs for the Society for Research in Child Development, 57* (1992).

CHAPTER TEN—Putting the Lessons into Practice

267 **This last option:** JoAnne Pedro-Carroll has developed numerous school-based programs for children from divorced families and systematically tested their effectiveness; for example, J. Pedro-Carroll, L. Alpert-Gillis, and E. Cowen, "An Evaluation of the Efficacy of a Preventive Intervention for 4th–6th Grade Urban Children of Divorce," *Journal of Primary Prevention, 13* (1992), 115–30.

CHAPTER ELEVEN—Letting Go and Moving On

294 **The famous psychologist Erik Erikson:** See E. H. Erikson, *Identity and the Life Cycle* (New York: Norton, 1959, 1980).

Index

Raynham Public Library
760 S. Main St.
Raynham, MA 02767